Gurpreet Kaur Bhatti

Gurpreet Kaur Bhatti writes for stage, screen and radio.
Her first play *Behsharam* broke box office records at Soho Theatre/
Birmingham Rep. Her second play *Behzti* was sensationally closed after
protests at the Birmingham Rep and sparked an international debate
about freedom of expression. *Behzti* won the Susan Smith Blackburn
Prize. Other credits include *Choir*, Chichester Festival Theatre; *Marriage
Material*, Lyric Hammersmith/Birmingham Rep; *Scenes From Lost
Mothers*, Clean Break; *A Kind of People,* Royal Court Downstairs;
Khandan, Royal Court Upstairs/Birmingham Rep; *Behud*, Soho Theatre/
Coventry Belgrade; *Silence*, Donmar Warehouse; *846*, Stratford East;
Elephant, Birmingham Rep; *Dishoom*, Rifco/Watford Palace Theatre;
Fourteen, Watford Palace Theatre; the feature film *Everywhere And
Nowhere*; *DCI Stone*, Radio 4; *Londonee*, Rich Mix; *Dead Meat,*
Channel 4 and *An Enemy Of The People*, BBC. She was a core writer on
The Archers, part of the team who created the ground-breaking Helen
and Rob domestic violence story and has written for *EastEnders* and
Hollyoaks.
She is developing various projects for stage and screen including original
series *Masala* for Hometeam/Universal, as well as *Brando's Bride* by
Sarah Broughton as a feature for Ffilm Cymru and writing her hit show
Scenes From Lost Mothers as a film. *Baby*, a new play for
Clean Break, will be produced at Brixton House in 2026.
She is a member of BAFTA, a trustee of the Peggy Ramsay
Foundation, an ambassador for Birth Companions, a charity that works
to improve the lives of women and babies who experience inequality
and disadvantage and a Fellow of the Royal Society of Literature.

Gurpreet Kaur Bhatti

Plays 2

Elephant
A Kind of People
Scenes from Lost Mothers
Marriage Material
Choir

With an introduction by the author

methuen | drama

LONDON · NEW YORK · OXFORD · NEW DELHI · SYDNEY

METHUEN DRAMA
Bloomsbury Publishing Plc, 50 Bedford Square, London, WC1B 3DP, UK
Bloomsbury Publishing Inc, 1359 Broadway, New York, NY 10018, USA
Bloomsbury Publishing Ireland, 29 Earlsfort Terrace, Dublin 2, D02 AY28, Ireland

BLOOMSBURY, METHUEN DRAMA and the Methuen Drama logo are trademarks of
Bloomsbury Publishing Plc

First published in Great Britain 2026

A catalogue record for this book is available from the British Library.

A catalog record for this book is available from the Library of Congress.

ISBN: PB: 978-1-3505-9565-1
ePDF: 978-1-3505-9566-8
eBook: 978-1-3505-9567-5

Series: Contemporary Dramatists

Typeset by RefineCatch Limited, Bungay, Suffolk
Printed and bound in Great Britain

For product safety related questions contact productsafety@bloomsbury.com.

To find out more about our authors and books visit www.bloomsbury.com
and sign up for our newsletters.

Contents

Introduction

I was supposed to be a chemist, initially studying chemistry at university. But that didn't quite work out. My interest in the narratives of science and logic, was overwhelmed by an almost physical draw to make sense of the world through stories. I had always been fascinated by the cause and effect of human actions and events, partly because of the dramas that surrounded me from as far back as I can remember. Someone once told me that your first play seeps out of your first wound. And the works in my first collection, *Plays One*, are certainly informed by some early experiences – a family spread across three continents, the wins and losses that accompany diaspora, extremes and darkness behind closed doors and so many complicated souls, broken, ambitious, beautiful and ugly, all of them desperately flawed and doing their best to meet life.

For me, there is nothing more intoxicating than telling a story in a live setting to a group of people. Constructing an adventure for an audience, then seeing how what is happening on stage affects them and feeling their often palpable reactions is an intense and powerful thing. As a playwright, creating that ride is a fine balance between provocation, confrontation, emotional impact and entertainment, while allowing the imagination the freedom to invent and run riot.

That same spirit is contained in this second volume of five very different plays. Each one has its own distinct inception and evolution, and each arena has offered me an opportunity to expand my scope as a writer and delve deep into my heart and mind.

Elephant was commissioned by the Birmingham Rep after my play *Khandan*, a classic family saga, had resonated strongly with Rep audiences – the theatre had actually put on extra shows as demand for tickets was so high. Set amid a modern British Sikh family, *Elephant* is a much darker and disturbing tale, literally a different beast. The protagonist, Vira, a woman who hasn't seen her sister for years, returns to the family home and is led to disclose a history of abuse. Her revelations trigger a terrible set of events. It's a deeply personal play, written at a tender time. There is a continuation of themes from earlier works like *Behzti* and *Fourteen*, but in *Elephant*, Vira risks her much longed for connection with family by becoming the truth-teller. She breaks through the façade of blood ties and sheds a skin, enabling her to eventually live with renewed vitality. This was the first time I worked with Lucy Morrison, then associate director at the Royal Court. Her forensic approach as dramaturg and director brought about its own revolutionary moments for me as a writer. She interrogated every single word and I loved the rough and tumble of this approach. The process unlocked something and the learning I gained about form and craft has been applied to everything I've written since.

A Kind of People started life at the National Theatre. However, after reading an early draft, the theatre decided not to proceed. That's fine, it happens. But I remember leaving the NT Studio after our final meeting and walking up The Cut feeling deflated and lost. My play was dead. Three years later, the same play opened at the Royal Court Downstairs and my name was lit up over Sloane Square amid the Christmas lights. This story about race, class, inequality, a community under pressure, ignited huge debate and the conversations around it continued long after the theatre bar was shut. It was one of those productions where the alchemy of cast, text, director and design aligned beautifully and it was a truly happy time. This experience also highlighted that once work is created, something is released and whether that work is produced or not, a cage has been rattled. The artist's energy must land somewhere, be it in another fashion or shape and you never ever know how things will unfold.

I was writing a new play for Clean Break, when Anna Herrmann, Artistic Director of that wonderful company, approached me about Lost Mothers. This was a research project, led by Dr Laura Abbott, examining the effects of separation of babies from women in the criminal justice system. I was presented with a huge file of findings and spent time speaking to the lived experience team from the charity Birth Companions. It was a real gift to be trusted with this sensitive work, and my goal was to create a thirty minute campaigning piece, amplifying the stories of those most affected by separation. Thus, *Scenes from Lost Mothers* was born. Three actors play a multitude of characters, A, B and C, to explore the machinations and often devastating consequences of a broken system. Performed by members of Clean Break, the play toured universities, prisons and professional settings. The show was supposed to finish in March 2025 but gained so much momentum that it continued until July. We were then invited to perform at the House of Commons, and I was also asked to adapt the play as a film. The whole process from beginning to end, was one of the most special and important of my career.

I met Sathnam Sanghera a few years ago to discuss adapting his novel, *Marriage Material*. He was incredibly generous in handing over his work, giving me virtual free rein. I became completely absorbed in the story, recognising immediately the heartbreaking and hilarious first-generation world he had written so insightfully. The novel cuts between the past and the present but my instincts wanted an audience to get lost in the 1969 section and then be faced abruptly with the aftermath and outcomes of the characters' lives. I established a new structure which I felt honoured both the past and the contemporary alongside the epic and the intimate.

Sometimes a play has a higher purpose and the play connected profoundly with audiences who attended in their droves. It smashed its target at the magnificent Lyric Hammersmith and then transferred to the Birmingham Rep (my fifth show at that theatre). Some of the reactions, particularly from South Asian women, were both moving and humbling. I recall one woman saying after the show that she'd always been a Kamaljit, but in her soul, she was a Surinder and had never been able to live as her authentic self. Kiran Landa, who played Kamaljit, created an education pack for the play ((with her sister, Priyenka Kaur and mother, Pritpal Kaur, who are both English teachers), so *Marriage Material* will hopefully be taught in schools in the Midlands.

Choir emerged from my own experiences of singing with a local choir, so I was familiar with the healing and delight that comes from a kind of collective effervescence. I had also wanted to write a comedy for a long time. Key figures in my life had faced the most harrowing moments with dark humour, and comedy has often been a feature of my storytelling. *Choir* had its own twisty route to the stage. It was initially conceived as a potential Christmas show for Hampstead Theatre. That didn't happen but then the play landed on Justin Audibert's desk at Chichester Festival Theatre and suddenly it was happening. The show was viewed by some as a departure from my previous work yet its themes of community, endurance, survival and the power of art to change lives are ones that I've always held dear in my writing and my life. I worked with director Hannah Joss whose bright spirit made for a brilliant collaboration. You can never predict how a new play will be received so it was great to get a message from Justin on the day tickets went on sale and learn that *Choir* had outsold *Hamlet*. The show is full of gorgeous music and turned out to be a real crowd-pleaser. Chichester said they hadn't seen an audience reaction like it and the sense of communal exuberance was infectious.

It has been the joy and privilege of my life to make a living by writing drama, to challenge, provoke and entertain audiences. This has only been made possible because of successive Artistic Directors who have believed in the work, fostered what may be perceived as radical or rebellious and approached commissioning and programming with courage and imagination. For this collection, that includes Vicky Featherstone, Anna Herrmann, Rachel O'Riordan and Justin Audibert. My love and thanks to them all and especially to Roxana Silbert who originally commissioned *Elephant, Marriage Material* and *Choir*.

Writing is largely a solitary pursuit, but a dramatist is not a novelist, and the art will always be shaped by the casts and creatives involved. Every one of these plays exists in their current form because of the rigorous work I did with dramaturgs like Jane Fallowfield and Nicholai La Barrie and particularly with directors Lucy Morrison, Michael Buffong, Anna Herrmann, Iqbal Khan and Hannah Joss. They all pushed me to make each play the most like itself and do the best I could. They are all fabulous artists in their own right and I'm lucky to have received their wise input and incisive questioning.

What a thing this is we do, making stories for an audience. I have loved working with each of these companies and crews – the warmth and laughs alongside the discomfort, agonies and breakthroughs that occur in every rehearsal room. We do it because we know there is nothing to match that feeling when the audience enters and the moment they start watching. Hopefully the play stimulates and surprises, and the human connectivity that follows always makes my heart soar.

Finally, I am both grateful and honoured that this second volume of plays has been published. The blank page is where it all starts and from *Elephant* to *Choir* that page has been the source of both excitement and terror. My mother always told me to be brave. For myself as an artist, this has been the greatest instruction.

Gurpreet Kaur Bhatti

Elephant

Elephant premiered at The DOOR, Birmingham Repertory Theatre on 15 February 2018

Cast

Barry	**Ezra Faroque Khan**
Vira	**Sukh Ojla**
Bill	**Farshid Rokey**
Amy	**Raagni Sharma**
Deesh	**Yasmin Wilde**

Creatives

Writer	Gurpreet Kaur Bhatti
Director	Lucy Morrison
Assistant Director	Madeline Kludje
Designer	Camilla Clarke
Sound Designer	Clive Meldrum
Lighting Designer	Zoe Spurr
Casting Director	Lotte Hines
Fight Director	Alison De Burgh

Stage Manager on the Book	Amber Curtis
Assistant Stage Manager	James Woods

Characters

Mum/Deesh	*late 40s*
Dad/Barry	*early 50s*
Daughter/Amy	*mid 20s*
Son/Bill	*early 20s*
Vira	*late 30s, Deesh's sister*

Location

A suburb.

Scene One

Friday early evening. Odd bits of furniture, a sparse look. **Bill**, *gentle, troubled, sits, filling out a large diary.* **Deesh**, *unkempt and restless, wearing cheap jeans and a holey jumper, brings on a tired mattress, pillows, covers etc. Starts putting a sheet on.* **Amy**, *groomed, assertive, paints her nails, watches.*

Amy   What are you doing?

Deesh   She has to sleep somewhere.

Amy   Stick her in the spare room.

Deesh   It's pristine in there! The duvet cover's brand new and I don't want it disturbed. No, she'll be alright down here. I'll keep her company.

Amy   You?

Deesh   Best to keep an eye on her.

Amy   Is she a thief?

Deesh   Shut up, idiot!

She hits a pillow with unusual force.

Give these a decent whack and they come right back to life.

Amy   Tell me you bought a new shalwar kameez.

Deesh   I found one on a sale rack up the Broadway.

Amy   Why not just go to Oxfam and ruin my life?

Deesh   It's not like you're getting married. If you were getting married I'd buy five new suits and a couple of saris, change my earrings every hour and get my face contoured.

Amy   You'd better sort that hair. And your moustache.

Deesh   We'll put on a good show like always.

Amy   Mum, it has to be better than good!

Deesh   Have me and your dad ever let you down?

Amy   Why do you have to keep an eye on her?

Deesh   She doesn't know her way around the house.

Amy   Don't you trust her?

Deesh   Course I trust her. She's my flesh and blood.

Amy   Right, I'm locking my room.

Deesh   Stop being an idiot! Vira's not an ogre. (*To* **Bill**.) What are you doing babes?

Bill   Putting Dad's jobs in the diary.

Amy   Use the calendar on his phone.

Bill   I told him but he says he wants them written down.

Amy   Nobody writes things down any more. What is wrong with this family?

Deesh   You be quiet, if that's how he wants it, leave him! (*Peers over* **Bill**.) Ah, what a lovely picture.

Bill   Just a stupid doodle Mum.

Deesh   Looks like the painting in the Chinese takeaway.

Bill   It's a famous image, everyone knows it.

Deesh   Well your one's really really good.

Bill *moves it away from her.*

Deesh (*checks watch*)   Not long now. She won't be late. Her head's sensitive to others. Same as yours, Bill.

Amy   Did you ask her to bring a shalwar kameez?

Deesh   She won't turn up naked. I'm sure she won't. She can always borrow one of mine.

Amy   Is she fatter than you?

Deesh   I dunno.

Amy   If she's fatter than you, your ones won't fit.

Deesh   She can breathe in.

Amy   Let's hope she's not as embarrassing as you.

Deesh   Shut up! Vira is the sweetest thing. When she was born our mum let me push her around in my Tiny Tears' pram. My first baby, before you lot. I was eleven years old when I held her in my arms. My little elephant. And now, she's coming home to me. You remember her, Amy.

Amy   Vaguely. She used to bring cuddly toys and Haribos.

Deesh   Not just Haribos, boxes of chocolates, family size biscuit tins. She arrived at that door, laden!

Amy   I think she made faces, made me laugh.

Deesh   And she made a commitment to you lot. From when you were tiny.

Amy (*sardonic*)   Five pounds a month?

Deesh   Don't you dare laugh! That's years of effort for some. Vira's . . . very nice.

Bill   If she's so nice why did Nani call her filth?

Deesh   I can't remember that . . .

Bill   She said she was a *kuthi, haramjadee* [bitch, bastard].

Deesh   Did she?

Amy   You know she did.

Bill   Mum, she told us that Auntie Vira was cursed, not to let her in if she knocked on the door.

Deesh   Your Nani was quite hard on people and Vira . . . always had spirit.

Amy   Good for her.

Bill   At least she sounds interesting.

Deesh   That . . . now that . . . is exactly the word. She loved her books. Enid Blyton, William Shakespeare.

Amy   Yeah we know, top dog in English, you told us.

Deesh   A vivid imagination the teachers said. Always making up stories. You couldn't trust a word that came out of her mouth. Make sure you don't ask her too many questions.

Bill   Why?

Deesh   She's had some bad luck. Don't ask me what, because I haven't a clue, it's only what I've heard.

Amy   What have you heard?

Deesh   I don't know.

Amy   From who then?

Deesh   I'm not sure, people . . .

Bill   Just tell us!

Deesh   I can't tell you stuff I don't know.

Amy   Has she got a job?

Deesh   She didn't mention an office.

Amy   Oh God, she's not depressed is she?

Deesh   We'll see.

Amy   I don't want a depressed person at my party, polluting the atmosphere!

Deesh   Give her a chance. She deserves a chance. We'll make her feel wanted.

Amy   It's supposed to be my day!

Deesh   Sunday. Your birthday's on Sunday.

Amy   Please get it into your head mother, this is not a birthday party!

Deesh   Well your birthday is on Sunday.

Amy   I know but you are not to refer to it as a birthday party. It's my going away party, understood?

Deesh   You might not go.

Amy   I've got the job, I've booked my flight . . .

Deesh   You haven't even started packing.

Amy   I'm leaving!

Deesh   We'll see . . .

Amy   Do you actually want me to murder you?

Deesh   I mentioned to Vira you were thinking of becoming an immigrant. There's a lucky girl, she said. Oh, and I told her we're all going to the Gurdwara on Sunday to mark your birthday.

Amy   I'm not sure I'm going.

Deesh   We only agreed to do this stupid leaving party if you promised to come to the Gurdwara the next day! Dad's already paid for the *langar* [lunch]. Five hundred quid. Everyone'll be expecting you.

Amy   I'll see.

Deesh   You're going.

Finishes doing the bedding.

Now let my little elephant have her moment.

Bill   Why hasn't she come before?

Deesh   I have asked her . . . Vira's . . . she's a funny one.

Barry (*offstage*)   Give me a hand, boy!

Bill *heads out.* **Barry***, genial and buoyant, brings in boxes of beers. He has the immense strength of a labourer/manual worker.*

Deesh   Where's the Bacardi?

Barry   I took the spirits to the Church hall.

Deesh   What if the Christians drink it?

Bill   They like wine Mum.

Barry   I locked the boxes in a cupboard, this young girl gave me the key.

Deesh   What girl?

Barry   I don't know her name.

Deesh   You sure there's enough?

Barry   Four hundred litres.

Bill   That's ridiculous.

Deesh   We don't want to run out babes. Imagine if someone says they went home thirsty.

Amy   Save what's left and have a do on New Year's Eve.

Bill *brings more boxes in.* **Barry** *sits on a box, opens a can of beer.*

Deesh   We're spending enough on this party! I'm not entertaining any more idiots on New Year's Eve. They end up standing in front of the telly, dropping crisps on the carpet and crisps get all embedded in the fluff . . . (*Notices* **Barry** *drinking.*) What are you doing?

Barry   Only a sip.

Deesh   You're staying over the Gurdwara tonight! What if they smell it?

Barry   I'll use Colgate!

Deesh   This is exactly the sort of thing they spread on WhatsApp!

Barry   Nobody cares. As long as I turn up . . .

Deesh (*unhappy*)   You said you'd have a couple at the party, you never said anything about today.

Barry *continues to drink. Signals* to **Bill**.

Barry   A drink, boy!

Bill   I don't really like the taste, Dad, I told you before.

Barry *opens a can. Hands one to* **Bill** *who sips it reluctantly.* **Barry** *takes out a small cuddly toy rabbit from a box, presents it to* **Deesh**.

Barry   Got you this.

Deesh   A rabbit?

Barry   For my one and only.

Amy   Dad, that is sweet.

Deesh   Idiot! Wasting your money.

Barry (*to* **Deesh**)   Take it! Who else am I gonna give it to?

Deesh (*takes it*)   Where am I supposed to put it?

Barry   Wherever you like.

Displeased **Deesh** *puts it down.*

Amy   There's a reason why people never do anything nice for you.

Barry   Leave your mum alone.

Deesh   I don't like money being spent without my knowledge.

Barry   It came free with the Bacardi.

Deesh   Good.

Bill *puts his can down.*

Barry   Have the rest, boy!

Bill   No thanks.

Barry   What you gonna do when you have to handle a woman?

Deesh   Don't scare him, Barry!

Barry *puts his arms round his son, hugs him hard.*

Barry   My special boy. These are your years. Live them. Enjoy your freedom. Right now, nobody's bending your ear, ordering you to get married . . .

Bill (*embarrased*)   Stop it. (**Barry** *lets go.*)

Deesh   You will get married one day babes.

Barry   I used to have a satin shirt and a pair of leather trousers. Really, really tight ones. Wore them to a few discos, drank a bucket of Cinzano Bianco . . . but then they introduced me to your mother. Soon, you'll have to start preparing to lead this family. This life me and your mother have created, it's all gonna be yours. Hear that, Bill, this family's down to you!

Amy   Did you ever have a girlfriend, Dad?

Barry   Course not, sweetheart. Your mum was my first true love. I knew from the first moment.

Bill   How?

Barry   Kismet. Isn't it, Deesh?

Deesh   Parents decided back then.

Bill   Would you have chosen each other?

Barry   In a flash.

Deesh   Shut up with these silly questions! (*Diary.*) Look, Bill's filled all your jobs in.

Barry (*has a look*)   Good work, son.

Deesh   And he's drawn some flowers in a vase.

Barry   Right.

Bill   I was only messing about.

Deesh   He's very skilled with that pencil. Deft.

Bill   Stop talking rubbish . . .

Deesh   I'm paying you a compliment!

Bill (*getting angry*)   . . . what do you always have to talk rubbish for?

Barry   Calm down, Bill.

Deesh   Leave him, Barry.

Bill   It's just a scribble okay, it's nothing.

Deesh   Okay, yeah. Nothing.

Amy *finishes her nails, flaunts them.*

Barry   Pretty colour.

Amy   Blood red.

Barry   Beautiful on my princess! I'm going to miss you.

Amy   I'll miss you too. When you visit, we can go to Central Park.

Deesh   I'm not flying seven hours to get mugged.

Amy   Who invited you?

Barry *and* **Amy** *giggle.* **Deesh** *freezes.*

Deesh   I forgot the cake!

Amy   It's being delivered to the hall.

Deesh   No, for Vira. I was planning to make a Victoria sponge. Oh, she'll be here in a minute.

Amy   Give her one of your biscuits.

Deesh   Vira likes cake.

Amy   I don't understand why you're so bothered.

Deesh   Do you realise everything she's done for you?

Amy   I appreciate the money, but I didn't ask for it.

Deesh   Not just the money. All those My Little Ponies and the Matchbox cars for Bill. Birthday cards, massive ones. And they always arrive on the day, never late or early.

Amy   Only weird people send cards.

Deesh   I wish that posh school had taught you kindness, Amy.

Amy   Mum, why don't you go and have a bath?

Deesh   I'm having one tomorrow.

Amy   You're starting to smell.

Barry   Your mum said she'll have one before the party, won't you, Deesh?

Deesh (*checks watch*)   She'll be here in a minute. All this'll be over on Sunday, thank God.

Amy (*getting angry*)   That's right, wish my party away! You can't be happy for me, ever.

Deesh   I've invited half of Facebook, haven't I?

Amy   Why can't you enjoy anything?

Deesh   I enjoy loads of stuff.

Amy   Like what?

Deesh *thinks, she can't answer.*

Amy   See! You only do things because you're supposed to do them. You don't have any human connection to a single aspect of your life!

Deesh   I am a human being. I am! Tell her, Barry!

Barry   Listen to me, right, all you lot. No point being angry. You get old and all that being angry don't work. You have to forget, move on.

Amy   I just want her to have a bath. (*A beat.*) Have you tried on your suit Bill?

Bill   No, it's hanging up.

Barry   Proper big man suit that is. Cut sharp. And I got him a shirt. Armani.

Amy   Come on, let's go and have a look.

Amy *and* **Bill** *head out. Agitated* **Deesh** *stares at the mattress. Tries to line it up so it's perfectly straight.*

Barry   Ignore Amy. She's nervous.

Deesh   We're all nervous. I'm up half the night scouring the internet for heart shaped bunting and she complains about my BO.

Barry *puts his can down. Hovers around* **Deesh**.

Barry   Chas says he'll add seekh kebabs to the starters. For free.

Deesh   As well as the paneer tikka?

Barry   That's what he said. And the cameraman's gonna hand out DVDs of the whole night before everyone leaves.

Deesh   Can he have them ready that quick?

Barry   Yeah! Harj'll play the dhol as the guests come in. They walk past the DJ, round the chocolate fountain, towards the life size ice sculpture of a polar bear. We'll knock them for six Deesh, like we always do.

Deesh   We should be saving this money for her wedding. I mean we paid for her school fees, then that stupid media studies course. Where's it got her? Nowhere.

Barry   She's got choices, we never knew what those were.

Deesh   People are whispering behind our backs, I know they are. Saying she's going off gallivanting, asking why she isn't settling down.

Barry   You wait, it'll be worth it. They'll be talking about this party for months. Watching the polar bear melt on the DVD.

Deesh   We've spoilt that girl. Made her believe the world'll wait for her. It won't.

Barry   She's confident, that's all. Let her go and explore.

Deesh   What's the point of that?

Barry   She wants to find herself.

Deesh   She wants to find a proper job. (*A beat.*) When Bill comes back say something to him.

Barry   What?

Deesh   Something hopeful.

Barry   Why? You keep telling him he's a gift from God.

Deesh   Be nice to hear a few kind words from you. Just say something.

Barry (*uneasy*)   Okay. (*A beat.*) So . . . do you think she'll really come?

Deesh   You saw her letter.

Barry   She might have changed her mind.

Deesh   Told you I rang her. I said she didn't have to actually turn up, but she insisted.

Barry   What did she say exactly?

Deesh   Same as what she wrote. I told you.

Barry   You're sure she didn't say nothing else?

Deesh   No! I was worried at first, but now there's something strong that's pulling me to her. I want to see her face.

Barry   That's natural, after all this time. Why come now, I mean why not before, when your mum died?

Deesh   Said she wants to see Amy before she leaves. Vira's matured, I heard it in her voice.

Barry   People don't change easily Deesh. We've had to adapt, because we've brought up kids. Life's landed at our front door, day after day. We've paid a mortgage, put in skylights, got decking. What's changed for her?

Deesh   Something. I reckon she's turning up here with a happy heart.

Barry   I don't want trouble.

Deesh   There won't be any.

Barry (*loaded but light*)   So it's your responsibility.

Deesh (*a beat*)   Yeah, alright.

Barry   She'd better not upset the kids.

Deesh   She won't. (*A beat.*) If you prefer, I'll tell her not to come.

Barry   No, don't tell her that.

Deesh   She can get off at the traffic lights, I'll go and meet her at the bus stop/

Barry   /It's fine. As long as you're sure.

Deesh   I wouldn't let her come otherwise. She's ashamed of herself, of all of it, I can tell. Just think how lonely she's been. Now, I can share the kids with her. I'm looking forward, Barry.

Barry   That's the only way.

Deesh   She was pleasant on the phone. Sounded like . . . she's gone Buddhist. Maybe she's met a nice stranger on the internet.

Barry   I can't imagine it.

Deesh   And you don't say anything. Let her talk.

Barry *nods half-heartedly.* **Deesh** *tentatively picks up the can he was drinking.*

Deesh   Have you finished?

Barry   Yeah.

Suddenly **Bill** *and* **Amy** *lead* **Vira** *in.* **Vira** *looks older than she is. Clean but unhealthy looking, she walks slowly, wears an old football shirt and baggy jogging bottoms, holds a large plastic bag and has a certain swagger.*

Vira   These two saw the smoke rising from my last B and H.

Deesh   Did the neighbours notice?

Amy   Who cares about the neighbours?

Vira   Don't you worry, I was brought up discreet.

Bill   She smokes. She actually smokes cigarettes.

Vira   Reminds me I have breath.

Deesh   You can't do that round here.

Vira   Ah, look at my cherubs. Come here both of you.

They hug her. She breathes deeply.

Vira   Hmm. This is what I've been craving, my blood, the heartbeat of the young. The scent of innocent flesh. Nothing alive in my flat, only the flies that get swatted by the carer.

Deesh   Why do you have a carer?

Vira   I need help.

Bill   What's wrong with you?

Vira   Plenty. Where's your toilet?

Amy   We've got three.

Deesh   Downstairs one is by the front door. You walked past it.

Bill   I'll show you.

Vira   Not yet, just so I know. In case I'm desperate. Hello, Barry.

Barry   Hello.

Vira   You're older. Uglier. Deep lines in your face.

Silence. **Barry** *indicates her shirt.*

Barry   I see you're still into your football. You can watch it on the telly tomorrow if you want. Live. Choose any game.

Vira   I only like the Championship play-offs. The rest of it's gone shit.

Barry   Me and Bill can't wait for the World Cup.

Bill   I'm not bothered.

Barry   Come on, you have to watch the World Cup.

Vira   Braindead billionaires having a kickabout. Little twats think they're masters of the universe.

Bill   Yeah, they do.

Vira (*glee*)   See Bill knows. He understands.

Deesh   Amy, stick the kettle on.

Barry   I'll do it.

Deesh   That's a good idea, Barry. Yeah, that makes sense.

Vira   Can he work a kettle?

Barry   Course I can.

Vira   He never used to go in the kitchen.

Deesh   Barry's . . . evolved. Haven't you?

Barry   Yeah. (*Goes.*)

Deesh   And open a packet of digestives. You sit down, Vira.

Vira *sits on a chair. Silence.*

Vira   Have you got them pink sandwich wafers? The ones in that teatime selection box we used to get from the Co-op.

Deesh   No.

Vira   I like licking them, till they go soggy.

Bill   Mum said you like cake.

Vira   Angel's my weakness.

Deesh   Barry'll nip to the shop.

They sit around on the beer boxes. Awkward silence.

Deesh   You look well.

Vira   I look like shit.

Deesh   Don't be so hard on yourself.

Vira   You're double the size you used to be.

Amy   How long have you smoked?

Vira   Started when I was thirteen, isn't it, Deesh?

Deesh   Don't ask me, I can't remember that far back. (*A beat.*) So, tell us your news then.

Vira   I had a catheter taken out. On Tuesday.

Deesh   Oh dear.

Vira   Fibroids. One was the size of a Galia melon. I'm fine but it's left my system sluggish. When I left hospital I had to stick my finger up there, give my plop plop a helping hand. I still can't feel much down below. It's a strange feeling, not feeling, do you know what I mean?

Bill   Er . . . do you feel better now?

Vira   I'm perfect. Oh, come here! My blood, my biology . . .

Holds out her hands. **Amy** *and* **Bill** *take a hand each.* **Vira** *squeezes tightly.*

Deesh (*indicates mattress*) There's your bed.

Vira   I don't sleep much.

Deesh   We've got a jar of Ovaltine somewhere.

Amy   Mum, that's from before Nani died.

Deesh   Ovaltine doesn't go off.

Vira   Don't fret. I've brought tablets. (*Observes children.*) Ah look at these two, this boy's soul . . . it's luminous!

Bill   Is it?

Vira   These faces are like the golden angels hanging off the ceiling at church. (*Sings.*) An angel from on high. The long long silence broke . . .

Amy   Are you a Christian?

Vira   Occasionally on a Sunday. When I don't fancy the pub.

Deesh   Can't imagine you paying attention to a vicar.

Vira   Two old ladies rang my bell. They drive me up there, sit me in a pew and once I've had a singalong and a slice of fruitcake, they drop me back.

Deesh   You never used to eat sultanas.

Vira   They have great songs. And they say there's no sin that Jesus won't forgive.

Deesh   Very good.

Vira   Presents!

Vira *reaches into bag. Passes presents to* **Amy** *and to* **Bill** *who open them.*

Deesh   There was no need.

Vira   You shut your mouth.

Amy   Thank you.

Deesh   What is it?

Amy   Cream. Body cream.

Vira   Organic. Made of ground up eggshells and crocodile plasma or some shit. Keeps you young till you die.

Amy   This is expensive.

Vira   I've been saving my pennies.

Amy   It's so thoughtful of you.

Vira   Who else have I got to have thoughts about?

Barry *brings in a plate of biscuits.*

Barry   Kettle's boiled.

Deesh   What did you get, Bill?

Bill   Socks.

Deesh   You need socks babes.

Bill   And a shirt. (*Shirt stays in bag.*)

Vira   Wear it tomorrow. If you like it.

Bill   I love it.

Vira   I didn't bother with you and Barry.

Deesh   Oh we don't matter.

Vira   Thought you'd have everything.

Barry   Nobody's got everything.

Vira   What are you missing?

Deesh   There's nothing, is there, Barry?

Barry   How do you like your tea?

Vira   I don't like tea.

Barry   Juice then? Or squash? There's that cloudy lemonade.

Bill   And Coca cola.

Vira   No.

Barry   How about them herbal teas, the ones you drink without milk . . .

Deesh   Leave her alone, Barry.

Deesh *passes round the biscuits. They each take one and eat in uncomfortable silence.*

Deesh (*to* **Barry**)   You'll have to pop out later. Angel cake and sandwich wafers. Pink ones.

Barry   Happy to.

Silence. **Vira** *beholds* **Amy**.

Vira   I've got puff in my lungs if you need balloons blowing.

Amy   The decorators do all that.

Vira   Very *Downton Abbey*. What's this job you got?

Amy   I'm doing an internship at a new website.

Vira   New York, New York eh? They do massive hotdogs. Everything out there's massive. You can eat till you're sick.

Amy   Have you been?

Vira   Seen it on the telly. (*To* **Deesh**.) She might meet the girl from that show you used to like, that . . . Phoebe. (*Sings 'Smelly Cat'*.)

Deesh   Stop it Vira.

Amy   I can't wait to go.

Deesh   She had a decent job here, in a clothes shop in town.

Amy   I gave my notice in. I hated the place. They kept trying to promote me to deputy manager.

Vira   I had a job once. Hospital laundry. Stank of stale blood.

Deesh   I told her retail's a brilliant career. But she wants to try this nonsense.

Amy   I'll end up earning more in a month than you earn in one year.

Vira   You follow your dreams mate. People who work have shit lives. And they moan, all the time.

Barry   Work's important, everyone needs a reason to get up in the morning, otherwise you have no self-respect.

Vira   Respect's overrated.

Amy   That is so true.

Vira   What about our Bill?

Bill   I give Dad a hand.

Deesh   Bill's had a few . . . false starts.

Barry   He's a good lad, quick with the paperwork. And he helps me out on the odd extension.

Vira (*to* **Bill**)   Never mind his shitting dead ends. You strike me as a creative individual. One of them mental ones who dress up as Little Bo Peep.

Bill   I've never met anyone like you

Amy   Do you work?

Vira   No way. I watch my programmes. Carers twice a week. Pub once a fortnight. Church when they turn up for me.

Barry   So you get everything paid for?

Vira   Yeah.

Barry   You look alright to me.

Deesh   She might have all sorts, hidden inside.

Vira   I get pains. And I can't walk too far.

Deesh   See.

Vira (*to kids*)   I'll take pictures tomorrow when you're all dressed up. Stick them on the fridge.

Amy   There'll be a photo booth at the party!

Vira   Used to be one of them in Woolworths, isn't it, Deesh?

Deesh   Woolworths?

Amy   And pick and mix. Oh and guests get a mojito on arrival.

Vira   Sounds like the shitting Pride of Britain awards!

She and **Amy** *laugh.*

Vira   What a beauty you've turned into Amy. Ah, the old masters'd be all over you, they'd hang you up in a museum.

Amy (*amused*)   I'd love that!

Deesh   Have another biscuit, Vira.

Vira (*not listening*)   I knew you'd turn into one of them It girls. I remember your potential.

Amy   From when?

Deesh   We've always written letters.

Vira   Oh yes, I heard all about you being the Innkeeper in the Nativity.

Bill   Was I?

Vira   You fluffed your lines! Called Joseph Jeremy. Weed yourself when you took your bow.

Bill   Me?

Deesh   Nobody noticed babes.

Vira   I remember every line you ever wrote about these two. I remember when you brought this baby boy home from the hospital/

Barry   /That was a long time ago.

Vira   I was a little girl then, Barry.

Deesh   Not that little. You left home when you were sixteen.

Vira   Fourteen.

Deesh   Even when you were small, you always had spirit.

Vira (*to* **Amy**)   Bet you're dressing to kill tomorrow?

Amy   I'm wearing two outfits – a fitted dress and a lehenga, Mum gets all my stuff made by a tailor in Delhi. Oh and Bill's got a gorgeous suit.

Vira   I want a fashion show. Right now!

Amy   Sure.

Vira   I'll stick my sari on. This Bangladeshi woman came round, sewed it up. I can step into it like a onesie. What shoes you got, Bill?

Bill   Just plain black . . . shiny ones.

Amy   Paul Smith!

Vira   Wear your new socks underneath.

Bill   It's good to meet you Auntie.

Vira   And you, Bill. Now I've got you, my blood's starting to flow like it was always meant to.

Amy   You should have visited before.

Vira   First time I've been invited.

Bill and **Amy** *exit.* **Vira** *takes a can of cider out of her bag. Silence.*

Barry   You still on the cheap stuff?

Vira (*drinks*)   It's what I'm used to.

Barry   Shall I get a glass?

Vira   Why? Do you want some?

Barry   No.

Deesh   Barry doesn't drink any more.

Silence. **Vira** *drinks from the can.*

Barry   Things are different.

Vira   Really?

Deesh   So you're okay then?

Vira   Yeah.

Barry   You don't look it.

Vira   Can't help how I look.

Deesh   If she says she's okay, she is.

Barry   She doesn't seem . . . happy.

Deesh   Course she does. I thought you might have turned Buddhist.

Vira   I haven't.

Barry   Feels like I should say something.

Deesh   We're not talking about that are we?

Barry   Vira, I don't want you to feel . . . uncomfortable . . .

Deesh   We are not on that subject Barry!

Barry   I'm trying to sort this out!

Deesh   There's nothing to sort. (*A beat.*) Barry knows he made a mistake. But it was a long time ago, wasn't it Vira?

Vira   Yeah.

Deesh (*to* **Vira**)   And he doesn't drink anymore. He doesn't touch the stuff.

Barry   No.

Vira   Right.

Deesh   You said yourself it was only a kiss and a cuddle. Barry knows he made a mistake.

Vira   I went to Spain in the summer. Three-star paradise. Rows and rows of loungers soaking up the sun. That is one hot sun. It was heating me up real strong. Melts your hate if you stay in it long enough.

Barry   Good . . . it's good not to hate.

Deesh   See, I told you she's alright. (*To* **Vira**.) You tell him Vira.

Vira   I'm here aren't I?

Barry   We don't want the kids upset.

Vira   You think I'd damage those two sweet souls?

Deesh   Course she wouldn't! We'll make sure they have a lovely weekend. Agreed? Vira?

Vira   Yeah.

Deesh   See Barry.

Barry   Right.

Deesh   Why don't you go the shop?

Vira *watches him leave.*

Vira   He never used to listen to you. Nobody listened to you. Mum and Dad's golden boy.

Deesh   Course he wasn't.

Vira   She loved having his male flesh in the house. Feeding him pakoreh and jalebi, ironing his overalls. You and me were nothing.

Deesh   Don't exaggerate.

Vira   He had free rein, could have strangled Mrs O'Neill next door and got away with it. You've taught him well.

Deesh   It's all down to Barry.

Vira   You still in that office . . . admin whatsit?

Deesh   Assistant. Admin assistant.

Vira   You been there a long time isn't it?

Deesh   Since Bill started school.

Vira   That was the last time I saw you.

Deesh *gets upset.*

Vira   Stop it you twat.

Deesh (*composing herself*)   I know you had your problems.

Vira   Problems?

Deesh   We all have them.

Vira   Suppose I must have.

Deesh   Let's not give it another thought, we're starting over.

Vira   That's what the ladies told me at church. You reach out they said, write a letter. Go and be part of your family.

Deesh   That vicar must be proud.

Vira   He doesn't know my name.

Deesh   I'm glad it's forgotten.

Vira   Not forgotten.

Deesh *retreats.*

Deesh   Why are you here?

Vira   They made me fill out a form at the hospital. I got to the next of kin box and I had nothing to write.

Deesh   I know, don't think it doesn't hurt me.

Vira   Look at the state of me. You lot are all there is . . . And now I've held the two little ones in my arms, seen how fantastic they are, I'm gonna try and keep them close.

Deesh   The kids are half Barry.

Vira   I know.

Deesh   Good. Very Good. We'll kick off tomorrow, set this party on fire. Show those idiots this family means something. Make them realise we're as good as any of them. Better.

Vira   Yeah.

Deesh   Me and Barry and Amy and Bill are a team. From now you're on our side.

Vira   I'm gonna watch those two blossom. You and me never blossomed.

Deesh   You're gonna do that. And more. You're relaunching your brand Vira.

Vira   I keep breathing in and out so I must want to live. I must be on this earth for a reason.

Deesh   Could be . . . coming here today.

Vira   Does feel like . . . this is where I belong.

Deesh   Oh you do belong my little elephant. You do.

Vira   Shut up now. Let me have this in peace.

Vira *drinks.*

Deesh   You mustn't say anything silly at the party. Not to anybody. You know that, don't you?

Vira *starts to sing 'Abide with Me'.* **Deesh** *hums along.*

Scene Two

The next day. Saturday early evening. **Amy** *wears a onesie and is doing her make-up.* **Bill** *is in smart trousers and a stylish pink shirt, he's doodling on a cardboard box.*

Amy   She's hilarious. Bet she bunked off school and went to acid house raves. One hundred per cent, she was a raver.

Bill   Mum and Dad act strange around her. Like they're nervous.

Amy   They probably think she's going to sneak us an ecstasy tablet. I wish she would.

Bill   I reckon they're scared she's going to tell us something. What if it's to do with Nani?

Amy   Nani was lovely and I'm really sad she's gone. But she was a bitch.

Bill   Remember when she spread those rumours about Bindu's wedding jewellery being gold-plated?

Amy   Ah, I do miss her.

Bill   I never know what's going to come out of Auntie Vira's mouth.

Amy   She's got a soft spot for you.

Bill   She hasn't.

Amy   It's obvious. You should ask what her story is.

Bill   You ask.

Amy   She'll tell you. I'm sure she'll tell you the truth.

Bill   Why do you care anyway? You're leaving.

Amy (*a beat*)   Bill, I know that after I go, you're going to be just fine.

Bill   Course. You'll be back soon anyway.

Amy   Not . . . immediately.

Vira *enters wearing her sari.*

Amy   Hello Auntie. You look . . . different.

Vira   I should hope so. I've had a shit and I've shaved my legs. (*A beat.*) Are we sitting next to each other?

Amy   Where?

Vira   At the top table?

Amy   No . . . er . . . I'll be with my friends. Mum'll put you somewhere.

Vira   Great. (*Stares at* **Amy**.)

Amy (*slightly disturbed*)   I need to do my mascara. So can I have a bit of space please?

Vira   Yeah. (*Turns to stare at* **Bill**.)

Amy   Why do you keep staring at us?

Vira   You're both so . . . perfect.

Bill   You said it was the first time you'd been invited but Mum said she asked you before.

Vira   I forget things.

Bill   Why does she call you her elephant?

Vira   I was a big baby. Enormous. Too heavy for my mum, that's why she never picked me up.

Amy   Didn't you want to come when Nani was ill?

Vira   We never got on. She didn't like me doing certain things.

Amy   For example?

Vira   Walking. I liked walking in the graveyard. It was a good place to listen.

Amy   To what?

Vira   The dead are quiet.

Bill (*blurts out*)   What's the secret?

Vira   Secret?

Amy   It's obvious there's something. Did you run away with your boyfriend?

Vira   I didn't know any boys.

Amy   Are you a lesbian?

Vira   I'm not anything.

Bill   Why did you leave home then?

Vira (*a beat*)   Hate. I hated everyone.

Amy   That's how I feel.

Vira   No. It isn't.

Amy   Do you take drugs?

Vira   Not for years.

Amy   You were a wild child I bet. That's me. The parents haven't a clue. They're so drab. I'm another breed. Like my blood isn't their blood.

Vira   Your parents have done okay.

Amy   So they've done the decent thing all their lives, and where's it got them? Mum's a joke, always going on and on about nothing. The other ladies make fun of her at the Gurdwara. And poor Dad, he's stuck with her.

Vira   Deesh tries her best.

Amy   Dad was really cute when he was young. You must remember.

Vira   What?

Amy   I've seen the wedding video. He could have married whoever he wanted.

Vira   You shouldn't say things like that.

Amy   Mum doesn't care.

Vira   How come you talk like a newsreader?

Amy   I had lessons. Dad paid.

Vira   Bill doesn't sound like you.

Amy   Bill didn't do extra-curricular activities. He needed looking after at school, didn't you?

Bill   No. No, I did not.

Vira (*to* **Bill**)   Don't dwell on what's past, keep staring in front and create new memories. Me dolled up like a Bollywood star, there's one. You're just beginning Bill, getting ready to cut loose, I can feel it.

Bill   Honestly?

Vira   Yeah. When you start, there's not an army in the world that'll stop you. And Amy, you, you'll set New York alight. Make sure you dance, shout, fall into bed with any beauty that comes your way, be ugly, destroy, scare yourself, be savage, get out of your head . . .

Amy   I am so going to do that.

Vira   Don't you dare be afraid. Of anything.

Amy   I won't be.

Vira *approaches* **Bill**, *eyes his doodle.*

Vira   That's a beautiful picture.

Bill   Why are you saying that?

Vira   Those are nimble hands.

Bill   My hands are just hands like everyone else's hands.

Vira   You're creating magic. I mean look at this nymph . . . you've got the outline of her body . . . perfect.

Bill   I copied it from Wikipedia.

Vira (*points*)   She wants to get that lot waxed. They do that nowadays. You could always rub it out.

Bill   It's meant to be there. The painter believed in showing the truth.

Vira   Twat! Not you, him. All art is a pretty lie.

Bill   Is that what you believe?

Vira   Fakery's what people want, reality reminds them of shit.

Amy   I love the way you talk Auntie. It's so . . . brutal.

Bill   Mum said you came top in English.

Vira   Books are all regurgitated, rehashed shite. I wanted to speak what others couldn't hear.

Bill   That's what I want.

Vira (*indicates picture*)   Sign it then!

Bill (*shy*)   I can't.

Vira   Make your mark!

Bill *reluctantly signs it.*

Vira   Why not use your real name?

Bill   I don't like it. People always laughed.

Vira   Let them. The carers call me Virus. Once you know who you are, you can turn into anybody you like.

Bill *takes this in.*

Vira   Write your real name. Go on.

Bill *writes his name on the picture.*

Vira How does that feel?

Bill Okay.

Vira Now, what's inside you?

Bill I dunno.

Vira Tell the world something. Shout it out.

Bill (*a beat*) Amy hasn't really got a job in America.

Amy Shut up, Bill!

Bill She made it up. She's a liar.

Amy I got carried away, I mean I am going to New York. (*A beat.*) I have to get away from this house.

Vira Yeah, I reckon you do.

Amy Are you going to tell them?

Vira When you've got this blood flowing through your veins, your mouth stays shut.

Amy Thank you.

Deesh *hurries in. She's wearing a beautiful shalwar kameez. She sports too much make-up and her hair's in a tidy bun. She's a rocket of nervous energy.*

Deesh What do you think you're doing?

Amy Talking.

Deesh Well stop it! Put your tie on, Bill. Why isn't anybody ready?

Bill *starts doing his tie.*

Amy We've got ages.

Deesh Course we haven't. What were you talking about?

Amy Nothing.

Deesh Dad's got Dulux emulsion in his hair.

Amy You're joking.

Deesh His head's turned magnolia. He's been painting a ceiling all morning, you have to get it out.

Amy Why me?

Deesh   My hand won't stay still. He's got a bottle of white spirit. Go now. Hurry up!

Amy   I haven't finished my face.

Vira   Sit down Deesh.

Deesh *flutters around anxiously. Inspects* **Bill**'*s tie.*

Deesh   This is wrong, all wrong.

Bill   It's fine.

Deesh   Sort his tie out, Amy.

Amy *does* **Bill**'*s tie.*

Deesh   Do you want a cup of tea, Vira?

Vira   I don't drink tea.

Deesh   Dad's shattered. That kitchen in Manor Road's been a right ordeal, the wife's a beast. They delivered the wrong colour tile and she didn't check. Dad's done all round the cooker up to the fridge. Screaming at him she was down the phone. And he was ever so polite back.

Amy   Dad shouldn't just take it.

Deesh   If he doesn't, he'll be out of a job.

Amy   She might respect him if he stands up for himself.

Deesh   He doesn't want to start an argument.

Amy   Why not start one? Then something might change . . .

Deesh   It won't! You tell her, Vira.

Vira (*to* **Amy**)   Ignore her.

Amy   I am.

Deesh   After the weekend, I mean on Monday, it's time for you to get cracking. Find a new job, a proper job, settle down, make a life. All this flitting, it's senseless.

Amy   Mum, I'm leaving the country next week.

Deesh (*not listening*)   I'm just saying on Monday . . . get cracking.

Amy   I want to destroy, scare myself, be savage, get out of my head . . .

Deesh   Do that on Sunday and then on Monday . . .

Amy   Fucking hell!

Deesh   Don't swear! Do not swear! You know, I think you're hungry.

Amy   I am not.

Deesh   You look like you need a digestive.

Amy (*shouts*)   You know nothing about me.

Bill   Why does everyone always have to shout?

Deesh (*to* **Bill**)   Sorry, babes. Sorry.

Bill *heads out.* **Amy** *follows.*

Deesh   And wash your hands once you're done with Dad. White spirit lingers. You don't want people thinking you work in B&Q.

Vira   Are you lot never quiet?

Deesh   This is what you wanted. (*A beat/tetchy.*) What have you been saying to Amy?

Vira   Nothing. (*A beat.*) I'm missing my programmes.

Deesh *watches her open a can of cider.*

Deesh   You'd better brush your teeth before we go into the hall. And don't move about when you get there. Just . . . stay sitting, in one place! And try not to talk too much. (*Checks watch.*) Once we're there, it'll soon be over. (*Tidies.*)

Vira   How many people again?

Deesh   Two hundred and fifty.

Vira   I'm only used to me in the flat.

Deesh   How did you even get that flat?

Vira   Through the hostel. Half the white girls in there were being punched and kicked by some boyfriend. I kept saying you can meet another bloke but you can't lock eyes with a new family in a nightclub. Those bitches didn't have a clue.

Deesh (*unnerved*)   Did you say something . . . about me and Barry and Mum and Dad? To the Council?

Vira   I had to say something. To get a place.

Deesh   Is it written down?

Vira   Everything like that's confidential.

Deesh (*agitated*)   What if they invent a new law and somebody reads it? Then what will people think?

Vira   They won't care.

Deesh   You're lucky they gave you a place. The rest of us have to work. Me and Barry leave the house at half six. He's not home before eight and then there's Tesco twice a week.

Vira   Make the kids go.

Deesh   They won't go to Tesco.

Vira   Get it delivered.

Deesh   I'm not paying five quid on top of the shopping.

Vira   You can spare a fiver.

Deesh   How do you think people like us got to send those two to that school? Because me and Barry rinse every penny that comes into this house. I wake up day after day and I empty that dishwasher. Every Tuesday morning, I clean one of them detached houses on Marlborough Lane, I pick up fancy knickers and stinking socks and I sweep up toenails. Then I go and sit at my desk and say good morning, nobody ever says good morning back. And I check through their diaries, buy whoever's got a birthday, a cake from Greggs. I never get a cake. Because my birthday always ends up being in half term, when most of them are pretending to have food poisoning, when really they're at Centre Parcs! We can't afford Centre Parcs! (*Tidies.*)

Vira   Sit down.

Deesh   There's no time to sit.

Vira   You're making my head spin. Sit. We've got ages.

Deesh *sits.*

Vira   When you were young Barry used to say you looked like an old woman.

Deesh   Why are you telling me that?

Vira   Just came into my head. Strange thing to say about your young wife.

Deesh   Barry's got a strange sense of humour.

Vira   He seems closer to Amy than he does to Bill.

Deesh   She's her daddy's girl alright.

Vira   Bill's different from her. He's got a way about him. Like he thinks . . . deeply.

Deesh   Well, he's . . . unique.

Vira   Gay?

Deesh   No. I don't know.

Vira   If he is, doesn't matter. There's one on *EastEnders*.

Deesh   I don't care if he is.

Vira   What would Barry say?

Deesh   I don't know.

Vira   Why did he need looking after at school?

Deesh   Who said that?

Vira   Amy mentioned something.

Deesh   She loved the place. Amy fitted right in with the straw boaters and lacrosse sticks. We wanted them to mix with the best people. She told them me and Barry were Consultant Psychiatrists for five years.

Vira   But it didn't suit Bill?

Deesh   No.

Vira   What happened?

Deesh   Bill's my little bird. He's not . . . very confident at being in the world.

Vira   Tell me.

Deesh   They bullied him. Pulled his wings off. So he stays in his cage. It's like we paid them to . . . crush him. We thought he'd be alright if he left so we took him out, but he ended up getting worse.

Vira   How?

Silence.

Vira   How?

Deesh (*a beat*)   He killed a cat. Slit its throat with a knife.

Vira   Why?

Deesh   He never said.

Vira   Whose cat?

Deesh   Some stray. Barry got rid of it.

Vira   You want to take him up the doctor, he might need medication.

Deesh   Don't be stupid. It was years ago.

Vira (*sardonic*)   And you think he's alright now?

Deesh (*fierce*)   Shut up. See, this is why I don't tell you anything. Those bullies ruined his confidence, he just needs us to help him build it back up. (*A beat.*) You remember when he was a baby, he wouldn't let me put him down. Always wanted my arms around him.

Vira   You used to stick him in that cot all the time.

Deesh   Course I didn't.

Vira   I saw you. You left him in there for hours.

Deesh   Well that was a mistake. Now, we try to . . . keep him with us.

Vira   Did Mum ever mention me?

Deesh   Never.

Vira   What happened to her Indian dolls? And the painting of the Golden Temple/

Deesh   /I gave everything to the Cats' Protection League. They bring a van. You don't lift a finger.

Vira   So it's all gone?

Deesh   You could have shown your face at the funeral.

Vira   No I couldn't.

Deesh   They made mistakes.

Vira   Worse than mistakes.

Deesh   Everyone beat kids back then. Wish I'd beaten Amy.

Vira   I didn't mind getting smacked.

Deesh   We had clean clothes, fresh roti on the table. Hot and fresh, every day.

Vira   I told her I couldn't eat *bhengun* [aubergine]. I tried but I couldn't get it past my throat. She stuffed the whole bowl into my mouth. I nearly choked on my sick.

Deesh   It wasn't the whole bowl.

Vira   Can you remember one single moment when we were happy?

Deesh (*thinks*)   That day we went to the Wimpy Bar. There's a photo of you holding the menu. You had a knickerbocker glory. Whipped cream all round your mouth, you tried sticking the long spoon up your nose.

Vira   Where's the photo?

Deesh   Mum got rid of it.

Vira   You're meant to love children, not make them sit there shelling peas and sifting through dhal. Not tell them they're dirt. You're supposed to take them to the park.

Deesh   Who had time for parks? (*A beat.*) They did their best.

Vira   No, they did not. They shut me down. Your parents are supposed to protect you.

Deesh   Thought you wanted to start over. (*A beat.*) You had too much spirit for Mum and Dad. Always complaining about foxhunting and the bloody Bosnian genocide.

Vira   I can't remember . . . who I was before.

Deesh   You just . . . had too much spirit.

Vira   At least I spoke. They never let you speak except to translate at the doctor's or in the Post Office. They hated us Deesh.

Deesh   Hate's a terrible word.

Vira   Mum said she wished we'd never been born. She hoped our female flesh got run over crossing the road.

Deesh   She didn't mean it.

Vira   She meant all of it. Can you imagine breaking your children like they broke us?

Deesh (*a beat*)   No . . .

Vira   And they made Barry their King.

Barry *enters. He wears a smart, ill-fitting suit and ostentatious gold jewellery.*

Deesh   We should get to the hall. Amy's stupid guests'll be waiting. (*Shouts to the exit.*) Come on!

Barry (*to* **Vira**) You gonna be warm enough?

Vira   Yeah. Yeah I am.

Barry   You might want to cover your arms. Borrow a coat if you like. One of Deesh's or one of mine . . .

Deesh (*abrupt.*)   Stop talking Barry!

Barry   What have I said?

Deesh   He's exhausted from doing that ceiling.

Vira   It's okay.

Deesh   When he's tired he waffles on and on. And he was up all night yesterday at the Gurdwara. I mean you try but you can't actually sleep there. Can you?

Barry   Not really.

Deesh   He goes every week. Not everyone makes it for the overnights. They say they will, but they don't show their faces. Barry does the most *Sayva* [service] out of the lot of them. He's never let the committee down once. Everyone knows he's devoted. That he's trying to do what's right.

Barry   I always try.

Deesh   Point is you turn up. Not in spirit like the other idiots, but with your body. That's what people remember, never mind good intentions. Nobody's bothered about your insides, it's what they see on the outside that counts.

Barry   I've been thinking.

Deesh   Barry, they'll be waiting at the hall . . .

Barry   Please! (*A beat.*) I go to the Gurdwara to do *Sayva* [service] . . . I give up my life every week for all of us. That includes you, Vira . . .

Deesh   Barry . . .

Barry   I go for this family. A man can make a mistake and if he chooses the correct action, if he prays with all his heart, and serves the sabji and washes the thalis, then that mistake can go away. Because his good deeds cancel it out. You believe that, don't you, Deesh?

Deesh   Yeah.

Barry   Because if not, if that is not the case, then no man can live on this earth. But I can now. I'm a decent man Vira. You must see that.

Deesh (*a beat*)   That was really good Barry. What you just said, it was really really good.

Barry (*urgent to* **Vira**)   I want you to forgive me.

Deesh   What are you going on about now?

Barry   I want her to say it.

Deesh (*shouts*)   She's got nothing to say!

Barry   At least speak the words, Vira. I must deserve that . . .

Deesh (*at the end her tether*)   Will you please shut your mouth!

Vira   Get a hold of yourself, Deesh. It's fine. Everything's fine.

Amy *and* **Bill** *walk in.* **Amy** *wears a stunning dress, the belle of the ball.* **Bill** *looks more grown up than before in his suit.*

Vira   Oh children! You are sensational.

Barry   Look at my princess.

Amy (*nervous*)   Am I alright? Really?

Barry   Better than alright.

Deesh   You do look lovely, Amy.

Barry *takes* **Amy**'*s hand. He lightly sings Roy Orbison's 'Pretty Woman'. Holds her to him as if they are ballroom dancing. They dance round the room, he spins her and she falls laughing into his arms.*

Vira   Stop!

Amy   It's fun.

He sings/spins her again. She laughs once more with glee.

Vira (*shouts*)   Stop it!

They stop.

Vira   You're making my head spin.

Deesh   It's only a bit of fun, Vira! Right, we're leaving.

As she shoos them out, **Barry** *catches sight of* **Bill**.

Barry   What the hell is that shirt?

Bill   Auntie Vira got it for me.

Barry   Your shirt's the wrong colour, boy.

Bill   It's not.

Barry   You can't wear that. I bought you that white one.

Bill   I like this colour.

Amy   Pink's in fashion, Dad.

Barry   Put the white one on.

Bill   I don't want to.

Deesh   Just leave it, come on, let's go to the car.

Barry   I'm talking to my son.

Deesh   He's dressed Barry, he's ready to go.

Barry   Well, I don't like it. Get changed Bill.

Deesh   It doesn't matter.

Bill   I can stand up for myself, Mum . . .

Deesh   Dad doesn't mean it . . .

Barry   Yes I do! Take it off!

Bill   I decide what goes on my body. And this shirt is staying on my back.

Barry   Listen to me boy.

Deesh   Stop it, Barry.

Barry   You don't look the way you're supposed to look!

Deesh   Shut up!

Suddenly **Barry** *goes to grab* **Bill** *but* **Deesh** *stops him and slaps* **Barry***'s face.*

Amy   Mum!

Deesh   Sorry. I'm sorry.

Amy   What did you do that for?

Deesh   I don't know.

Barry   It's okay.

Amy   It is not okay.

Barry   Forget it.

Deesh   Why don't you wait in the car, Barry?

Barry *doesn't move.*

Vira (*to* **Barry**)   Do as you're told, Barry.

Barry (*a beat*)   You follow me, boy.

Bill *doesn't respond.*

Barry (s*houts*)   I said follow me.

Bill *goes to him, they head out. Silence.*

Amy   My party is not meant to be like this. I'm supposed to be Scarlett O'Hara sauntering down a spiral staircase. Dad's got the Champagne chilled. He pours it into flutes and he toasts me, wishes me the best for the rest of my life and then you hand me a family heirloom, and whisper in my ear what a woman needs to know to survive. And I take your advice and your wisdom and I go out there, into the city, and I sparkle.

Deesh   There'll be Champagne at the hall.

Amy   Cava not Champagne.

Deesh   Yeah.

Amy   Fuck. Fuck Mum. Fuck! You hit Dad!

Deesh   I'm sorry!

Vira   Give her a break, even Jesus lost it with the Pharisees.

Deesh   Everything is for you Amy, every breath of my life, the day after day drudgery of washing and wiping and cleaning and feeding, this jewellery, these nails, bleaching my moustache, it's all, always been for both of you.

Vira   Your Mum might be a twat but she means well. So get to your party. Go and sparkle.

Amy   I don't feel like it.

Deesh   You should see the hall. Red and white roses in vases on each table, long stemmed, just what you asked for. The DJ'll be playing that Steel Banglez song you like and your guests'll be arriving soon. Dripping in gold and diamonds, because they want to give you a proper send off.

Amy   I know I'm a bitch. You embarrass me and I'm ashamed of you. And I do despise you. But I am grateful.

Deesh   Okay. Dad's waiting.

Amy *exits.*

Vira   Oh this is what I came back for. The hate and the love.

Deesh   Thanks.

Vira   For what?

Deesh   For what you said. She listens to you.

Vira   Course she does.

Deesh   Let's go.

Vira   When we're there, can you and me . . . dance?

Deesh   Yeah.

Vira   Do they still play that *Gidhian dhi Rani*?

Deesh   Every bloody time.

Vira   Tonight'll be our cup final Deesh.

Deesh   Oh my dear little elephant. Come on then.

Vira   I'll get a cab in a bit. I want to watch my programme first. Do you mind?

Deesh   Course not. You're home now elephant.

Deesh *exits.* **Vira** *looks in her bag, takes a tablet.*

Scene Three

Hours later. **Vira** *is asleep.* **Barry** *is with her. He watches her. She wakes, sees him, jumps up.*

Vira   Why aren't you at the party?

Barry   I needed to pick up a box of Johnny Walker.

Vira   Where is it?

Barry   In the back of the car. Thought you were getting a cab.

Vira   I fell asleep.

Barry   Yeah. You . . . er . . . you looked sweet.

Vira *uneasily hugs herself.*

Barry   What's the matter?

Vira   It's cold. Heating must have gone off.

Barry *takes his jacket off.*

Barry   Have it, if you're cold.

Vira   No thanks.

Barry *puts the jacket down.*

Barry   Aren't you coming?

Vira   Not yet.

Barry   You grew up.

Vira   Yeah.

Barry   You didn't turn out like I thought. You're more elephant now than you were back then.

He moves towards her. She moves away, sits.

Barry   Where are you going?

Vira   Nowhere.

Barry   Are you scared?

Vira   No.

Barry   I'm not gonna do anything. You heard me before.

Vira   I heard you.

Barry   It's just . . . this is a chance for me to sit with you. I haven't had a chance.

Vira   They'll be waiting for you at the party.

Barry   I'll give you a lift.

Vira *shakes her head.*

Barry   It's no bother.

Vira   It's alright.

Barry   What do you watch apart from the play-offs?

Vira   What?

Barry   On the telly.

Vira   Programmes.

Barry   Which ones?

Vira   I dunno.

Barry   I want to get to know you again. Tell me.

Vira   Er . . . I like when couples go to look at houses in the Caribbean. Some of those houses . . . they've got high ceilings, balconies, with views of the sea.

Barry   I fancy the Caribbean too. Bet it's hot.

Vira   It's humid. Tropical. Rainy season starts in May, goes on till October.

Barry *takes out a quarter bottle of whisky. Takes a swig. Offers it to* **Vira**. *She doesn't take it at first but then takes it. Swigs. Silence.*

Barry   Stupid elephant they used to say. Killed me when I heard them call you names. It . . . killed me. Poor little girl. You didn't deserve that. I'm sorry for the way your mum and dad were. You talked a lot, you talked too much, but I could sense . . . you were lonely. And it was obvious . . . nobody wanted you.

Vira   No.

Barry   You deserved attention.

Vira   They'll be missing you at the party. You should go.

Barry   I will, in a minute. I thought if I showed an interest, it might make you feel better.

Vira   It didn't.

Barry   I was trying to help you, Vira.

Vira   Why didn't you find a prostitute?

Barry   Me?

Vira   Yeah.

Barry   I could never do that. I'm not like that.

Vira   You should have found somebody else.

Barry The Caribbean's supposed to be paradise.

Vira I haven't been yet.

Barry Like the Bounty advert. The one with the palm trees.

Vira I don't recall.

Barry I fell head over heels for you.

Vira I was fourteen.

Barry I remember your pretty face. Big eyes like a frog. You looked better than you do now.

Vira You shouldn't have done anything. You said that before.

Barry I'm trying to explain.

Vira I don't want an explanation.

Barry You remember how happy your mum and dad were, when me and Deesh came to live with you lot. You were happy too.

Vira I trusted you like a brother. You made me feel like I mattered, like I could just sit with you and eat my dinner and not get hit.

Barry That's what I'm talking about. Mum and Dad wanted a man around the place alright. As soon as they heard my key in the door, my roti was on the table, cold beer in my hand, newspaper open at Page 3. Mum used to watch me locking up at night, afterwards she'd put her hand on my shoulder and say – now I can lie my head on that pillow in peace. (*A beat.*) They made me feel like I could do anything.

Vira Don't you blame them.

Barry No matter how I felt, I had to walk through the door like a peacock, pretend I gave a fuck when some relative had a heart attack back home, bomb down the motorway when they needed dropping off at Terminal 3. Nobody ever once asked me what I wanted.

Vira Why are you telling me this?

Barry Because I had to pretend every single day of my life. They knew it, but they weren't bothered because we were all pretending to be this fake family. I put all the real love I had to give, onto you. (*A beat.*) I felt like somebody with you. I still do . . . Deesh, she . . . I can't stand the sight of her.

Vira (*a beat*) The worst thing is, what was in your head about me. From when I was little. You're still little when you're twelve. I'm sure you are.

Barry   You're making it sound like something else. Deesh . . . stank of that formula milk. The thought of you was what kept me alive. Back then, you were nothing to anybody.

Vira   Deesh cared.

Barry   Not after the babies were born. At least I was there. I adored you . . . And then . . . it just . . . happened. These things, just happen. (*A beat.*) The way you're being with me now, the way you sneer at me, talk down to me in front of Amy and Bill. You're making me feel really bad. I can't bear it.

Vira   The second you touched me . . . you broke me.

Barry   God's forgiven me. So you should forgive me . . . then all of us, you and me, Deesh and the kids, we'll be alright.

Vira   How can I forgive you when you don't think you've done anything wrong?

Barry   All men make mistakes.

Vira   Yeah.

Barry   You said before your hate was gone.

Vira   No. I hated you then. And I hate you now. If you feel anything for me . . .

Barry   I do.

Vira   Then please go.

Barry   You liked it Vira. Remember all the stuff I bought you, fruit pastilles, combat trousers, cans of cider.

Vira   I didn't ask for any of it.

Barry   I'm sure you liked it back then.

Vira   No! No, I did not! You made me sick playing your CDs, those sickly sweet songs . . . And you made me cry . . . every time . . . you watched me crying . . .

Barry   All girls cry when they're that age.

He is close to where she is sitting.

Barry   I'm always here for you. Whatever you need. If you just want to talk . . .

Suddenly he pulls her to him and kisses her hard on the cheek. He lets her go and she recoils.

Barry   Even though you turned out different to what I thought, I still love you elephant.

Scene Four

*Sunday morning. A body lies under the duvet on the mattress on the floor. Slowly emerges. It's **Deesh** in jogging bottoms and frumpy long T-shirt. She looks around with concern. Hurriedly checks in **Vira**'s bag, discards it. Then checks again, discards it. **Bill** enters, **Deesh** covers her unease.*

Bill   Dad said I'm a star.

Deesh   You are babes.

Bill   He reckons after last night, I'm born again.

Deesh   Good. Very good.

Bill   Did you see me, Mum?

Deesh   Yeah.

Bill   He told me to run the show and I did. It was so simple.

Deesh   You shone babes. You absolutely shone.

Bill   Has she come back?

Deesh   No sign of her.

Bill (*points*)   She's left her bag. She must come back for her bag.

Deesh   What's inside it?

Bill *hesitates.*

Deesh   Go on. Might be important.

Bill (*opens bag*)   Cigarettes, pants and a vest, a scratch card. It's been used.

Deesh   She won't miss those babes.

Bill   A purse, but it's empty. What if something happened to her?

Deesh   For instance?

Bill   She might have got killed. Run over or stabbed.

Deesh   Who could be bothered to kill Vira?

Bill   Maybe she'll come to the Gurdwara.

Deesh   She was never fussed about God. No, this is how it was meant to be. She's gone back home where she belongs.

Bill   I kind of . . . miss her.

Deesh   I ironed your new jeans. You'll have to put them on soon.

Hungover **Amy** *enters. She's wearing shorts and a T-shirt.*

Deesh   What are you walking around naked for?

Amy   Do I have to go to the Gurdwara?

Deesh   Course you do.

Amy   My head hurts. And I feel sick. I want to watch telly.

Deesh   Everyone'll be there. For your birthday.

Amy   I don't even know them. And the ones I do know, I hate.

Deesh   I told you Dad's already paid for the *langar* [lunch]. Five hundred quid. The ladies'll be in the kitchen slagging each other off, chopping onions, making rotis and rice pudding with pistachio nuts.

Amy   I can't eat rice pudding.

Deesh   People are bound to put cash in the cards. Twenties. A few fifties if you're lucky.

Amy   You bring the cards back. I'll open them in front of the telly.

Deesh   You have to come.

Amy   No.

Barry *enters. He assumes his space, pumped up and in ebullient mood. He holds a bottle of Cava and a carton of orange juice.*

Barry   That . . . that . . . was a fantastic night. No, that . . . was a magnificent night! (*To* **Deesh**.) I told you it'd be worth it and it was, we killed it! Jas said those were the brightest flare lamps he'd ever seen and Harj reckoned the speakers nearly burst his ear drums. And did you watch the crowd when that Bom Diggy Diggy one came on.

Bill   They lost it.

Barry (*to* **Amy**)   I've got this video of you and that girl dancing, and you two . . .

Deesh   Her name's Jasmin.

Barry   You two know all the moves!

Amy   Did you film me when I was standing on the stage?

Barry (*nods*)   Oh yeah. Nobody could take their eyes off you.

Deesh   There was no need to make such a show of yourself.

Amy   I had the crowd in the palm of my hand.

Barry   You did. (*To* **Bill**.) And I watched you boy, turning into a man.

Bill   Really?

Barry   Oh yeah. You've arrived, finally, you are what I always knew you could be.

Bill   I felt like somebody, Dad.

Deesh   Everybody's somebody, babes.

Barry   My boy was filling up whisky glasses to the top, seeing that every table got their boneless chicken, checking there was toilet paper. Our guests were bowled over. Nobody even noticed that homosexual shirt. They said it was the tastiest food, the most bottles of booze. We fattened them up, made sure they left too drunk to drive home.

Deesh   They all drove home.

Amy   There's nothing wrong with being homosexual, Dad.

Barry   Course not sweetheart. (*To* **Bill**.) We showed them.

Bill   Yeah, we showed them.

Barry   There's your power boy. You serving them, making them feel good, earning their respect. You prove yourself and they start to believe in you and suddenly you're the don for the night.

Bill   Right, yeah.

Barry   Always keep an eye on your sister. It's your job to protect her. If you're not looking, some lowlife seizes his chance and then there's gonna be blood.

Bill   I look after you, don't I, Amy?

Amy   I don't need looking after. Oh Auntie Shiro's daughter was asking about Bill.

Deesh   Not that Mindy?

Barry   Hear that, now you're finding your way boy!

Deesh   She drives a Tesco delivery van.

Amy   Don't be such a snob, Mum!

Deesh   Amy says she's not going to the Gurdwara.

Barry   She is going.

Deesh   Tell her then.

Barry *starts tickling* **Amy**.

Barry (*laughing*)   You're going!

Amy (*giggling*)   Alright, alright, I'm going . . .

Deesh   Get your hands off her, Barry! (*He stops.*)

Bill   Mum reckons Auntie's gone home.

Amy   I don't understand why she didn't even show her face.

Barry   I hope she's alright. You wanna give her a call, Deesh?

Deesh   I left a message.

Barry   Maybe it was all too much for her.

Amy   Make me some tea. Please, Mum.

Deesh   There'll be tea at the Gurdwara.

Barry   Who fancies a Bucks Fizz?

Deesh   Not today.

Barry   Come on.

Amy   Sounds perfect.

Bill   I'll have one.

Deesh   I don't want anyone drinking alcohol before we go there.

Barry   It'll keep the buzz going, anyway it's mainly orange juice.

Deesh   We should go there clean.

Barry   One won't hurt. And you could do with a boost to help the
ladies with all that cooking and cleaning.

Deesh   No!

Barry   Relax Deesh, it's Amy's birthday.

Amy   Go on, Mum. Please.

Barry (*to kids*)   And didn't your mum look beautiful last night?

Deesh   Stop being silly.

Barry   I had my eye on you, in case some cheeky youth tried to make a move. (*Pours drinks.*)

Deesh (*laughs*)   Who'd do that?

Amy   You scrubbed up really well.

Bill   I was proud of yo,u Mum.

Deesh   Thanks babes.

Barry (*raises glass*)   To Deesh, my one and only.

All   To Mum. (**Deesh** *laughs, drinks.*)

Vira *enters. She looks a mess. The others stare at her.*

Amy   Do you want a Bucks Fizz?

Vira *shakes her head.* **Deesh** *moves towards her, sniffs.*

Deesh   You smell.

Bill   What happened to you, Auntie?

Vira   I'm not sure. Nothing.

Bill   Are you alright?

Vira   Yeah.

Amy   Why didn't you come?

Vira   Where?

Amy   To my party?

Vira   I forgot there was a party.

Amy   Have you been drinking?

Vira   Yeah.

Amy (*amused*)   You are so bad.

Deesh   You could have said something, left a note. I've been worried.

Edgy **Vira** *sits, takes out a cigarette. Starts smoking.*

Deesh   Do that outside.

Barry   Let her be, Deesh.

They watch her smoke.

Deesh   You're supposed to be coming to the Gurdwara, I've ironed your suit. Where have you been?

Vira   Walking.

Deesh   Are you coming to the Gurdwara?

Vira   No thanks.

Deesh   What are you doing then?

Vira   Going home. I wanted to see the kids. Talk to them before I leave.

Barry   You'd better be quick. We can't be late. Not today.

Deesh   There's no money in your purse.

Vira   I know.

Deesh   How will you get home?

Barry   I've got cash.

Vira (*fierce*)   I don't want your cash.

Deesh   Right, you'd better start getting ready.

Vira (*to* **Amy**)   How was your party, Amy?

Amy   Oh, it was incredible.

Bill   People said it was the best party they'd ever been to.

Deesh   She wants to go, let her go.

Amy   I'll stay here with Auntie.

Deesh (*angry*)   No, you won't!

Barry   Deesh, we can all leave together.

Deesh (*to* **Vira**)   I told you to come but you insisted on watching your stupid programmes. You should have come when I said. (*To kids.*) This is how she behaves. Raises your hopes and makes you think everything's bouncy and then she sticks a pin in and lets the air out.

Vira   I haven't done anything.

Deesh   You shouldn't stay out all night. It's . . . disgraceful.

Amy   Mum, you're beginning to sound like Nani.

Vira   I realise I'm a disappointment.

Deesh   Oh, you are. The biggest.

Amy   Why are you being horrible to her?

Deesh (*to* **Vira**)   Have you once in your life considered what kind of sister you've been? You've been useless! I had nobody when the kids were little.

Vira   You had our mother.

Deesh   My kids were looking forward to you being at the party and you couldn't even be bothered to turn up for the starters.

Amy   I don't mind.

Bill   Come to the Gurdwara, Auntie.

Deesh   She can't.

Bill   What did you want to talk about?

Deesh   We're in a hurry so if it's not important, maybe leave it Vira, until next time.

Vira   I only wanted to say goodbye . . . properly. Time I went.

Starts to go.

Barry   Tell you what, I'll give you a lift.

Vira   No.

Bill   Stay Auntie.

Barry   I can easily drop her.

Deesh   She wants to make her own way, Barry.

Barry   A lift has to be better than a female walking alone on the street.

Amy (*to* **Vira**)   You can't just leave.

Deesh   Course she can.

Barry   I'm happy to take you Vira.

Deesh   We'll be late!

Barry   We don't want anything to happen to her, Deesh. At least if I drop her we'll know she's safe.

Vira (*a beat*)   How . . . how . . . can you dare?

Deesh   Vira . . .

Vira (*shouts*)   How can he dare?

Barry   Okay, okay, sorry, bloody hell, I didn't mean nothing.

Amy   What's the matter?

Deesh   Just let her go, Barry.

Barry   I am, okay, you go.

Bill   Do you want to sit down, Auntie?

Vira (*shaky*)   It's alright, I'm ready. I'm ready . . .

Deesh   You'd better head off now. Go . . .

Vira   I'm trying to turn around and walk out . . . but . . . you see . . . I get this feeling of his breath on me, of his sweaty hands stroking my neck and even though they're not, it feels like it. And no matter where I am . . . I can't get rid of it.

Deesh   What's she on about?

Silence. They all stare at **Vira**.

Vira   I can't get rid of it, Deesh.

Barry   She's lost it.

Amy   What can't you get rid of?

Deesh (*to* **Vira**)   You're not yourself are you, Vira?

Vira   Your mum knows.

Bill   What?

Vira   It's your dad . . . he did something to me . . . when I was young . . .

Amy   Something?

Deesh   Oh God.

Barry   What . . . what . . . why are you saying that?

Deesh   She said she had tablets. Look in her bag, Bill, see if there are any tablets.

Bill *looks through the plastic bag.*

Vira   Last night, he grabbed me, like he grabbed me before . . .

Deesh   Get her outside, maybe just . . . get her outside into the fresh air . . .

Barry   I'm not touching her.

Vira *moves out of their way.*

Vira   Your mum knows and he knows. Say it, Deesh. You say it!

Bill   What is she talking about?

Deesh   Okay, alright, let's, let's get this thing straight . . .

Barry   Wait, Deesh . . .

Deesh   No, we have to. It's started now. (*A beat.*) Dad . . . he . . . he . . . made a mistake.

Amy   A mistake?

Deesh   He'd been drinking and your Auntie Vira was . . . well, she wasn't a child. Not a child like at Infant School.

Barry   She was nearly fifteen.

Amy   You're scaring me.

Deesh   He got carried away . . .

Bill   . . .

Deesh   Just a cuddle. And a kiss. He'd been drinking . . . too much.

Barry   I am so sorry.

Deesh   Vira had problems and she took it badly, but your dad, he's not a bad man. You explain Vira. Tell them what happened.

Barry   Yeah, okay, yeah . . . let's get this out in the open.

Deesh   Go on Vira.

Silence. **Vira** *addresses the children.*

Vira   The truth is, the honest truth is your . . . Barry started buying me stuff when I was twelve. And then when I was fourteen we'd drink cider. The cheapest cider. He said he was my friend and then he stroked me, touched me up all over. Kissed me on the lips, stuck his tongue down my throat. He ripped my tights, and I froze . . . He made me . . . made me bleed all down my leg.

Deesh   No, no . . .

Vira   He tore me right up so I'm broken inside and nobody said nothing. They all kept going, like it was normal and they got used to it.

Deesh   Stop, it's not true!

Vira   I got used to it. And I'm saying it now because nobody is ever going to say it for me. They read the *Metro* and they say they'd spit on Jimmy Savile's grave. But everyone still loves Barry.

Deesh   Oh my God, don't listen, don't listen . . .

Barry   How can you even imagine . . . me . . . ? In front of Amy and Bill?

Vira   You know, Deesh. You heard me crying.

Deesh (*a beat*)   You're mad. She's mad.

Vira   I believed it when you said he was different.

Deesh   Why are you saying this?

Vira   Because he tried it again, last night.

Barry   What? No! No way!

Deesh   He was at the party last night.

Vira   What he did to me is the one true memory I've got.

Deesh   How can you remember? You were always out, drinking cans in the graveyard, hanging around with that lot from the council estate. Whenever me and Mum and Dad walked into the Gurdwara everyone'd be whispering, sniggering behind our backs because you'd been flaunting yourself in a short skirt, talking to some boy. When you left I kept in touch, wrote letters, tracked you down, treated you like a sister when the rest of them called you a bitch and a whore. And now you walk in here and make up these lies about Barry. Stupid, thick Barry who everybody knows wouldn't hurt a bloody fly never mind an elephant.

Vira   You know, Bill. You understand me . . .

Deesh   Leave Bill alone.

Amy   Dad's friendly, he's friendly with everyone.

Bill   Why should I know?

Deesh   Bill, put your jeans on. Amy, get your suit. Take them out, Barry.

Barry   I'm not leaving! She's gonna infect your mind with her poison.

Deesh   No, I'll straighten this out.

Barry   She should go, not me!

Deesh   Amy and Bill don't need to hear any more!

Barry   Deesh, why is she being like this?

Deesh *pushes the children towards* **Barry**.

Deesh (*shouts*)   Get them out of here! All of you, get yourselves dressed. We are going to the Gurdwara. If I have to kill you all and stick you in the boot of the car, we are going!

Barry *shuffles them out.* **Deesh** *stares at* **Vira**.

Deesh   I should murder you.

Vira   Get on with it then.

Deesh (*a beat*)   Why?

Vira   He committed a crime. Crimes.

Deesh   Then go to the police. See what they say.

Vira   What do you think they're gonna do?

Deesh (*gives her phone*)   Dial 999. Do something. Don't bring your . . . mess onto us.

Vira   I never wanted to . . .

Deesh   What if you're remembering it wrong? I mean you can't even remember the Wimpy bar and that knickerbocker glory.

Vira   I'm not wrong.

Deesh   You said he ripped your tights.

Vira   He did.

Deesh   But when you left you said he just touched you, kissed your lips . . .

Vira   Yeah.

Deesh   Well which one is it? Ripping your tights or touching and kissing?

Vira   He had sex with me.

Deesh   Why didn't you speak up back then?

Vira   I didn't . . . I didn't . . . want to hurt your feelings.

Deesh   You're mental. That's why they put you in that hostel. Mental people exaggerate, they tell lies that nobody else would think of, until you can't get their lies out of your head.

Vira   I was alright until he got hold of me. I'm sure I was.

Deesh   You make it sound like he grabbed you in an alley. He's not the Yorkshire Ripper.

Vira   He told me you stopped having sex with him, every time he tried you said you were bleeding.

Deesh   No, Barry's . . . Barry's a decent man. There's a thousand people who know he's a decent man, who are prepared to stand up for him. Who have you got?

Vira   You've learned to live with it, Deesh.

Deesh   You're my blood. I've no choice about you. But me and him have settled on each other. As long as I've got Barry, there's somebody to sit next to me in the car, to check the boiler, to calm me down when Amy calls me names.

Vira   I used to think that people were good.

Deesh   What's the point of saying this now?

Vira   I have to.

Deesh   For what reason?

Vira   Last night, he grabbed me . . . but this time I got away, I got away from him.

Deesh   I should never have let you through the door. Why did you even come?

Vira   I felt a glimmer of hope. You felt it too. Like the first day of secondary school when you squeezed my hand and said it would be alright and I believed you. You're my only family, Deesh.

Deesh   This is family. Real flesh and blood, not out of a catalogue or an Oxo advert. I let you into my house so you could have a bit of company. (*A beat.*) If it's true you should have told me back then.

Vira   I told Mum. Everything. She said if I mentioned anything to you, it'd destroy your life. She said she'd cut my face.

Deesh *takes this in, her breathing quickens.*

Deesh   Barry . . . Barry's . . . a decent man . . . he's always at the Gurdwara. He keeps an eye on the lightbulbs and the drains and . . . and anything they need, he's there like a shot.

Vira   Why is it religious people don't have no God?

Deesh   Course they do.

Vira   Ek on kar, satnam Karta purkh, nir pau, nir vair, akaal murat, ajuni se bhung,

Deesh   Stop!

She tries to cover **Vira***'s mouth but* **Vira** *pushes her out of the way.*

Vira   Gurparsad, jup ad such, jugad such . . .

Deesh *hurriedly covers her head with a* chooni *[scarf].*

Deesh   You have to cover your head when you say those words!

Vira   Heh pee such, Nanak ho see pee such . . . One God, named truth, creator, without fear, without hate . . .

Deesh   I'm not listening . . .

Vira   Timeless, immortal, neither born, nor dies, self-existent, Is revealed by the Grace of the Guru, Truth in the beginning, truth through the ages, truth now . . . Truth shall ever be. They say that in the Gurdwara Deesh. And I always believed them. You say it. He must say it. Why? Why do you all say it?

Deesh (*getting upset*)   They're words from a book Vira. Most of them don't even understand, it's something to say . . . It's just something to say.

Vira   You heard me crying. I know you did.

Deesh *starts to cry.*

Deesh   Oh my elephant. My little baby elephant.

Amy *and* **Bill** *walk back in tentatively. They are dressed for the Gurdwara.*

Amy   Mum, do something. Dad's crying.

Deesh   Leave him.

Bill *approaches* **Vira**.

Bill   Why should I know?

Deesh   Never mind, Bill.

Bill   You said I should know.

Vira   It was a silly thing to say.

Bill   Then what did you say it for?

Deesh   Vira didn't mean anything.

Bill (*to* **Vira**)   Tell me why!

Vira   Because you were in your cot, when he did it to me.

Bill   What?

Vira   He said I should pretend the baby wasn't in the room. You used to cry.

Bill   Babies don't know stuff.

Deesh   This isn't your fault. It's nothing to do with you.

Amy   Please, Auntie, is this . . . is this real, or some joke?

Bill *starts to laugh.*

Vira   Why's he laughing?

Deesh   It's what happens when people hear the worst thing ever.

Bill (*laughing subsides*)   This is . . . one of your stories, one you made up.

Vira   It's not a story. (*Silence.*)

Bill   You made me like you, Auntie. And Amy, she said you were a raver.

Vira   Nothing's changed between us. Not one single thing. We're the same as we were a few minutes ago.

Vira *grabs* **Amy***'s hands and then* **Bill***'s, but their limbs are lifeless.*

Amy (*to* **Vira**)   Thought you were going home.

Deesh   She's staying for a bit.

Amy   But you told us she's mad, that it's just lies.

Deesh   I wish to God it was.

Amy   So you're saying that Dad, our dad is one of those men in the news who does things to children?

Vira   Yeah.

Amy   He abused you, he sexually abused you?

Deesh   Nobody needs any further details, Amy . . .

Amy (*interrupts/shouts*)   I'm asking her, not you! Why didn't you tell Nani?

Vira   I did. She . . . wouldn't listen.

Amy   And Mum?

Deesh   I knew he'd overstepped the mark, but . . . I had no idea . . .

Amy   Overstepped the mark? What mark?

Deesh   I thought he'd touched her. Kissed her.

Amy   Where? On the cheek. On the lips?

Deesh   It doesn't matter now does it? I didn't know the whole story.

Amy   And you carried on like nothing happened?

Deesh   I had two kids and parents who expected me to keep going. I'm surrounded by people who cave in because they feel every tiny thing the world sends their way. Well let me tell you my sweet little snowflake, you want to thank God that some of us show up to look after the rest of you!

Amy   These girls who it happens to. You see them on the telly, they make them sit in shadows or stick curly blonde wigs on their heads. They change their voices so you can't hear how they actually sound. Do they sound like you? (*A beat.*) If it happened, why not leave him?

Deesh   And go where?

Amy   I don't know. Margate, Germany, a mental hospital, a women's refuge . . .

Deesh   Barry never hit me, he wouldn't. And I couldn't take you away from your flesh and blood. And Mum and Dad spent all that money on my wedding. Seven hundred people at the Town Hall . . .

Amy   Money?

Deesh   There weren't choices back then. Just because you lot do as you please . . .

Bill   How do we know she's being honest?

Vira   Your mum heard me crying.

Bill (*to* **Deesh**)   Did you?

Deesh *nods.*

Bill   Did you see it?

Deesh   No . . .

Bill   Why do you trust her more than you trust Dad?

Deesh   I just . . . do . . .

Bill   What if Dad made a mistake? Everyone does. I have.

Deesh   This . . . is something else.

Bill   Just because Dad was like that once, doesn't mean he's like that anymore.

Vira   I thought he wasn't. I would never have told you, never have caused you this hurt, if he hadn't . . . touched me again . . .

Bill   What if she's angry because Nani and Baba loved you more Mum? She might be saying all this to spite you and Dad.

Deesh   No Bill.

Amy   Loads of girls take drugs and get drunk and have sex and then what's happened is a haze and they say they've been attacked.

Deesh   Vira isn't like that.

Amy   You said she was! Before, you said she was drinking cans in the graveyard, because of her, people whispered and sniggered behind your back . . .

Bill   And she was always making up stories. Like Enid Blyton. She said all stories were lies.

Deesh   She is not making it up!

Amy   What about Dad? There are always two sides and you won't even go upstairs and give him a tissue.

Bill   She's your blood Mum. Dad's our blood. Who's gonna stick up for him?

Deesh   This is about . . . what's right. You're in shock, both of you. I know it's hard but you have to accept that this is the truth.

Amy   You have the audacity to talk about truth! You lie all the time

Mum. Little lies, big lies. You tell people you went to the chemist when you've been to the beauty salon. Phone in sick when you've missed *EastEnders* so you can watch it before the next episode's on. And you've taught us to lie, about Bill, about Dad drinking too much. To pretend we like people we hate. Why are you like this? (*A beat.*) I want to know Mum.

Deesh   Because I don't want to hurt people's feelings . . .

Amy   Liar. Speak the truth, for once in your pathetic fucking life!

Deesh (*shouts*)   Because I don't want them thinking we're not good enough. (*A beat.*) Because I don't want my children feeling the same shame that I felt.

Amy   We're stronger than you think, Mum.

Deesh   No, no you are not.

Amy   You never even gave us a chance.

Deesh   I've given you everything.

Amy   You've created this.

Vira   Course she hasn't.

Amy   She's drowned us in her fake world.

Deesh   That's going to stop. Right now. Something terrible happened. And I'm going to show you, for the first time, how to live properly, how to be, and that way, we can all be born again . . .

She finds a plastic bag. Starts sticking whatever she can grab into it.

Bill   What are you doing?

Deesh   Packing up. It might be too late, but it's got to be worth something.

She frantically packs.

Deesh   I'll come to you, Vira.

Vira   Really?

Deesh   To your flat the Council gave you. You're allowed visitors aren't you?

Vira   Yeah, yeah. Stay as long as you like. Stay forever.

Deesh *stops packing.*

Deesh   I'll have to come back for the rest. Stick it in a taxi.

Vira   Don't worry about stuff, we'll buy everything new.

Deesh   Bill will need his bits and pieces.

Amy   Bill?

Deesh   You're alright. You're flying into the clouds in a couple of days.

Amy   What do you want, Bill?

Bill   I don't want Mum to go.

Deesh   You'll be right by my side babes. You must have a camp bed, Vira?

Vira   What's that?

Deesh   A sleeping bag then?

Vira   No. But I'll get one, I'll get as many as you want. Have a tent if you like.

Deesh   Is there an Argos near you?

Vira   There must be.

Deesh   I'll get him a new duvet cover while I'm there.

Amy   What are you going to tell people?

Deesh   I don't know yet. I'll say . . . I'll say Vira's ill.

Vira   And him. You'll have to tell people about him.

Deesh   Give me a chance, I haven't been to Argos yet.

Amy (*to* **Deesh**)   What were you like before . . . him?

Deesh   I have no idea.

Amy (*to* **Vira**)   And you?

Vira *shakes her head.*

Amy   Is that what will happen to me and Bill?

Deesh   No.

Amy   We haven't done anything wrong, it's not fair for you to take our memories.

Bill   I wish we were still at the party. When I woke up this morning, I felt like I'd joined the world.

Vira   You're joining it for real now Bill. (*To* **Amy**.) You . . . you be grateful that you're on your way, you'll be able to leave this shit behind.

Amy   I can't go.

Vira   You have to.

Deesh   What about your job?

Bill   She doesn't care about her job.

Deesh   Then you'll come with us.

Amy   And sleep in a tent in her flat?

Bill   We don't know her.

Amy (*to* **Deesh**)   Why did you keep saying we were lucky, that we had everything?

Deesh   I thought you did. I wanted you to.

Bill   We won't ever have another dad.

Amy   She's stripped us bare.

Vira   If you want me to forgive him, then I'll summon that strength. Amy, please go to America.

Amy   . . .

Vira   You'll come home for Christmas. (*To* **Deesh**.) We'll fill a trolley with all her favourites from Marks. Or we'll go there. Oh yes, we'll arrive at JFK and walk through snowy streets, almost get knocked down by a yellow taxi and we'll sing that song, the one you like Deesh. All of us, we'll sing that one you like . . . (*Sings.*) 'And the boys of the NYPD choir were singing Galway Bay, and the bells were ringing out for Christmas Day.'

Barry *enters. He appears decimated, dishevelled.*

Barry (*to* **Deesh**)   I know you've been talking, she's turned you against me and now you're turning them.

Amy   Dad . . .

Barry (*to* **Deesh**)   You don't know what's in my heart. You're not even interested. You want to blame me for everything. Well I'm human too, alright. I've suffered too!

Deesh   You?

Barry   I tried to be the best man I could. Everybody feels sorry for her. For the story she tells . . .

Deesh   Explain then, Barry. Explain in your own words.

Barry   Whatever I say, she'll make it sound wrong, to suit what's in her head.

Deesh   What has this life, our life been?

Barry   How can you ask me that?

Deesh   I'm asking.

Barry   You and me have built a whole new world out of nothing. From the bare ground to the top of the sky. Given Amy and Bill the best schools, Ted Baker and Gucci on their backs. Any gadget they've wanted. People out there, our neighbours, everyone at the Gurdwara, they know we work hard, they know they can rely on us to show up at the hospital, to help out at a funeral. We are the most solid thing there is round here.

Amy   Please . . . Dad, is it . . . true?

Barry   No. Not like she said it. She's making me out to be something I could never be. I made a mistake. But not like she said.

Deesh   Stop lying, Barry.

Barry   You never listen do you? You don't hear anything. You just believe what you want and now you believe her. When I have given you my whole life!

Vira   They're not with you, Barry. Nobody is with you any more.

Barry   These three are more mine than you can ever understand. After that front door closes and it's just us, this is our home, a happy home. Whatever they want they get. From me. Because of me. Because they know I love them and you . . . not one word you say can touch that.

He starts to cry softly.

Vira   He used to cry like this before. Play sad songs. Whitney and Luther Vandross and Roberta Flack. (*To* **Barry**.) Your tears scare people but they don't fool them anymore. If you tell the truth, there might be hope.

Amy   We're a good family. People know us. They like us and they invite us to join in with their lives. Their normal lives. Us lot mean something round here.

Deesh   Amy, what your dad's done, it's . . . the most wrong thing anybody could imagine.

Amy   We can't suddenly be different Mum, just because you've decided! And we don't know what it was like back then. I mean what if you made Dad be . . . like that. (*A beat.*) And you didn't see anything. It's his words against hers. Because you don't definitely know. You can't.

Deesh   Oh, but I do. I really do.

Bill   Amy's right, Mum. You believe it, but that doesn't mean you know.

Vira (*points at* **Barry**)   This is what he does. Draws you in. Makes you pity him. Makes you feel guilty for doubting that he's good inside. Well Barry is not a decent man! I promise you both . . . you come to my flat and you'll live in more splendour than you've ever known.

Barry   I'll leave if you want.

Amy   No. You stay here.

She goes to **Barry**.

Deesh   Amy . . .

Amy   You want me not to know him like I thought I know him. Well I can't. I can't, Mum.

She hugs him tight.

Amy   You can fuck off to wherever you want, go to her shithole flat with her, but I am not leaving him!

Barry   Whatever darkness you think I've brought on you, Vira, I'm sorry, I'm truly sorry.

Vira   Go to America, Amy. I'm begging you . . .

Barry   All I did was try and be an older brother to her. I did my best. But I failed. I realise I failed. We shouldn't even be here now. I'm supposed to be washing thalis at the Gurdwara. We're meant to be looking after our guests and smiling and praying. There's a hundred people waiting for us and we've let them down because of her. This one malicious woman swans in and wrecks our day. The day Amy was born, the happiest moment of my life.

Deesh   I'm going with Vira.

Barry   What?

Deesh   And Bill's coming.

Barry   You think you can take him, just like that, from the luxury he's lived, from everything you and me have created under this roof?

Deesh   He doesn't need any of it.

Barry   And you? You can't even drive to Tesco on your own.

Deesh   I'll manage. You watch me, Barry. I'm gonna live, like I've never lived. And I'll tell people. I'll tell them everything.

Barry   Nobody cares what you say. You belong with us, Deesh. It's Ranjit's kid's lohri in a few weeks, and then Pali's engagement. You promised to help make rotis, go shopping for her gold.

Deesh   I can still go.

Barry   Not if you leave this house. It's too late for you. Too late for all this shit. What are people gonna think of you?

Bill (*to* **Vira**)   I was worried because I thought you'd been killed.

Vira   I'm more alive than I've ever been.

Bill   I wish you had got killed.

Deesh   Come here, Bill . . .

Deesh *tries to take him but he won't move.*

Bill   No! I'm my Dad's boy.

Vira   Yes, you're his living failure. Born to torture him. He's holding you back. Keeping you weak, so he stays top dog.

Amy   Dad's not like that. You don't even know him.

Vira (*to* **Bill**)   You were a tiny baby when he brought me into the bedroom.

Bill   Shut up!

Vira   You were asleep at first. Then our crying turned into one shitty, broken voice.

Bill   I'm not like you.

Vira   Oh, you are, I can smell the stench of myself. You're in my agony.

Amy   Leave him alone!

Vira   Bill, you were such a beautiful, beautiful baby boy . . . And now, you'll stay frozen, like me . . .

Suddenly **Bill** *starts punching and kicking* **Vira**. *He is much stronger and she quickly crumbles. He beats her up.* **Deesh** *and* **Barry** *pull him off.*

Deesh (*screams*)   Stop it! That's enough. She's had enough.

Battered **Vira** *slowly gets up.*

Barry   You should never have shown your face here. (*To kids.*) Just . . . keep away from her. The worst is over.

Vira   The day I walked through your door has been the best day I've known. If I was somebody on the telly, you might shed a tear. But because I'm here in front of you, you want me out. You lot go to the Gurdwara, all of you, with dark knowledge in your hearts. You collect money and send it to dying babies and white people admire you and say you're decent immigrants and each good word you hear buries your knowledge deeper till it's in your blood and your red blood is polluted with it. (*To* **Barry**.) You chose me, they let you choose me because you were the golden boy and I was filth. I had nobody. And I've still got nobody, I am officially nothing but you know what, whatever you lot think and do, I can speak and I will be heard, because I am somebody! I'd walk through your front door every single day I've got left on this earth, because coming here and being with you shits has given me new life and I'm free, like nobody has ever ever been free . . .

Bill   Mum, get her out!

Vira   The worst isn't over, Barry, it's ahead. Because you know. They all know!

Barry   She's a freak.

Bill   Freak! Get out freak!

Vira   I'm no freak boy. I'm a miracle. I should be dead. Buried or burnt. (*Points at* **Bill**.) I was wrong about you, it's his blood flowing through your veins.

Deesh   Please don't blame him, Vira.

Vira (*to* **Bill**)   You and your terrible, fake art, it's pointless, insincere shit. The same as every particle that surrounds you . . . because there's nothing, nothing real under this roof!

Deesh   Bill's innocent. He's innocent.

Barry   You're a liar! A liar! Get out of my house! (*Opens wallet, chucks notes at her.*) Here's the money you gave them. Have it, as much as you want. Go on holiday to the fucking Caribbean . . .

The money flies everywhere. **Vira** *gets up.* **Barry** *pushes her to the exit.*

Deesh   Please don't!

Vira (*breaks away*)   Oh poor Deesh, you don't understand, do you? Nobody can touch me now. Because they've woken up a thousand armies in my soul. Come with me and you'll feel it . . . Come . . .

Deesh *doesn't move.*

Bill   Mum . . . Mum . . .

The sisters stare at each other for a moment. **Deesh** *turns to* **Bill**.

Vira   You heard me, Deesh. I know you heard me.

Vira *exits.* **Barry**, **Amy** *and* **Bill** *retreat, leaving* **Deesh** *standing.*

Epilogue

Vira *sits in an armchair. She smokes a cigarette and sips a can of cider. She watches a television programme – unseen. She uses the remote to turn up the volume. 'Abide with Me' plays, the start of the FA Cup Final.*

THE END

A Kind of People

A Kind of People was first performed at the Royal Court Jerwood Theatre Downstairs, Sloane Square, on Thursday 5 December 2019.

Cast

Gary	**Richie Campbell**
Mark	**Thomas Coombes**
Nicky	**Claire-Louise Cordwell**
Mo	**Asif Khan**
Karen	**Petra Letang**
Victoria	**Amy Morgan**
Anjum	**Manjinder Virk**

Creatives

Writer	Gurpreet Kaur Bhatti
Director	Michael Buffong
Designer	Anna Fleischle
Lighting Designer	Aideen Malone
Sound Designer	Emma Laxton
Movement Director	Vicki Igbokwe
Vocal Coach	Hazel Holder
Assistant Director	Philip Morris
Design Assistant	Liam Bunster
Casting Director	Amy Ball
Production Manager	Marius Rønning
Costume Supervisor	Lucy Walshaw
Stage Manager	Kate Watkins
Deputy Stage Manager	Caroline Meer
Assistant Stage Manager	Marie-Angelique St. Hill
Stage Management Student Placement	Liane Howatt
Set built by Miraculous Engineering	

Characters

Nicky Sinclair	*late 30s, white female*
Gary Sinclair	*40, Black male*
Victoria	*30s, white female*
Mark	*late 30s, white male*
Karen	*late 30s, Black female*
Anjum	*30s, British Pakistani female*
Mo	*late 30s, British Pakistani male*

The Action takes place in the present day in a city, over two weeks during the Autumn.

The Epilogue takes place in the same city on a summer evening, twenty-five years earlier.

Locations

Gary and Nicky's council flat
Victoria's office
Staff room
A hilltop

Scene One

*Friday. Late September. Evening. Large kitchen diner in Gary and
Nicky's council flat. The place could do with a facelift but it's clean.
Chaotic but not unpleasing.* **Nicky** *is making samosas with* **Anjum** *at an
old Ikea dining table.* **Anjum** *wears a hijab. Agitated* **Mo** *hovers.*

Mo (*indicates phone*)   Not one of them's replied. Not a single one!

Nicky   What?

Mo   They should learn to speak English.

Anjum   I thought you were going home.

Mo   There's no excuse. I mean we learned English.

Anjum   We were born here.

Mo   My mum brought up seven kids and she managed to learn.

Anjum   Mo, your mum can barely read and write.

Mo (*affronted*)   You could quote Shakespeare to my mum and she
might not reply . . .

Nicky (*amused*)   Shakespeare?

Mo   . . . but she'd understand every syllable!

Anjum   No she wouldn't!

Mo   We'll see. (*Finds a number on phone.*)

Karen *enters.*

Karen (*shouts*)   Let's get mashed up!

Nicky   What are you doing here?

Karen (*hands* **Nicky** *a bottle of Prosecco*)   Mark said you're having a
party. (*Makes herself at home.*)

Nicky (*to* **Karen**)   I don't think so, Gary's taking him out.

Mo (*to* **Karen**)   Did you know, not one of those parents replied to my
doodle poll? (*Dials number.*)

Karen   Really?

Anjum   Loads of parents haven't come forward.

Mo   Let's just say if my messages were signed John Smith, we might
have a few bottles of Polski vodka for the raffle.

Karen (*to* **Nicky**)   I told Mark we fancy cocktails.

Nicky   I'm working the early shift tomorrow.

Karen   Fuck the early shift. (*They both laugh.*)

Mo (*into phone/italics indicate broken Urdu*)   Hello Ummi . . . *Yes . . . Yes . . .*

Karen   Make us a coffee Nic.

Nicky (*teasing*)   Make it yourself.

Karen   Please!

Nicky   Thought we were getting mashed.

Karen   Yeah, in a minute.

Mo (*into phone/italics indicate broken Urdu*)   *Mum, I just want to ask you something . . .* (*To the others.*) Give me a Shakespeare quote.

Anjum   What?

Karen   I wandered lonely as a cloud . . .

Nicky   No, that's someone else.

Mo   Got it! (*Into phone/broken Urdu/accent.*) *Ummi . . . what would you say if I said* 'To be or not to be, that is the question' *. . . Yes. Do you know what I'm saying? Yes, yes . . . Thanks Mum, you're the best.* (*Phone off.*) Understood every single word!

Anjum   You should have asked if Zaki's in bed.

Mo   He'll be shattered. Squad swimming tonight.

Nicky   Impressive.

Mo   Zaki usually comes last.

Anjum   How's work Karen?

Karen   Shit. Then I had to pick my car up from the mechanic. He started telling me some fuckery about my alternator. That claart is a thief. (*Observes* **Nicky** *making instant coffee.*) What you doing?

Nicky   Coffee.

Karen   Not instant! I can't drink that . . . piss. I got you that cafetiere.

Nicky   Dunno where it is.

Karen   You wanna buy one of them machines. Then guests can choose from espresso, cappuccino, macchiato . . .

Mo   Ours has got a cup heater and a milk frother.

Karen   Now, that is what I'm talking about! I'm coming round your house! (*They share a laugh.*) Fuck it, open the Prosecco.

Mo   I fancy a Prosecco, Nicky.

Anjum   You're supposed to be getting the fair organised.

Mo   I'm doing it.

Anjum   You said you'd be teetotal this month.

Mo   I can have one!

Anjum   If you get drunk, I'm not telling your mum you've got Salmonella again.

Karen   Let the man live Anj! How's Zaki?

Anjum   We're waiting for his results.

Mo   It's a killer.

Nicky (*to* **Karen**)   He did the exam with Ronnie.

Mo (*checking phone*)   Right, we need new face paints. And brushes. Paper plates, toys for the lucky dip, plastic ducks and a fishing rod, gluten free sweets, cheap wine and chocolates for the Tombola, henna tattoos, hair braids, coloured card, glue, scissors, nine pumpkins, name badges for the choir and . . . goalkeeper gloves.

Anjum   We'll go to the shopping centre. You can get everything there.

Karen   I hate that shopping centre.

Mo   I know what you mean.

Karen   Everyone looks so . . .

Mo   Yeah . . .

Karen   Poor . . .

Mo   Cheap!

Karen   And ill!

Mo   Yeah! Used to be the outdoor market when we were kids, do you remember?

Karen   Course! We went up there every Saturday with my dad.

Mo   We went with our mum.

Karen   Now it's always so . . .

Mo   Packed!

Karen   Full of faces you don't recognise.

Mo   Everywhere's changed.

Karen   Don't get me started . . .

Nicky   I like the shopping centre. Everybody goes there.

Karen   Apparently it's quite popular for suicides.

Mo   Is it?

Karen   People park on Level 3 and jump. Straight down onto the high street.

Anjum   Not in front of Argos?

Gary *breezes in carrying boxes of chicken.*

Gary   Hey you lovely people . . . (*To* **Karen**.) Oh and you.

Gary *affectionately goes to ruffle* **Karen***'s hair.*

Karen   Do not touch my hair!

Gary *and* **Mo** *greet each other.*

Mo   Alright brother.

Karen   Where's Mark?

Gary   Off-licence. (*He kisses/hugs* **Nicky**. *She responds warmly.*)

Nicky   You said you two were going out.

Gary   He fancied coming here.

Nicky   He's here every day.

Gary   Come on Nic, it's his birthday. Chicken?

Mo   I'll have a piece.

Anjum   Which Nando's is it from?

Gary   Warwick Street. (*Sorts chicken.*)

Anjum   Warwick Street isn't halal.

Mo   Course it is.

Anjum   Your mum's made roti.

Mo   We have her roti all the time. (*Sound of a child moaning on a baby monitor.*)

Anjum   Tyler not sleeping again?

Nicky   He's fine.

Gary   I told you, he's too old for this thing.

Karen   You lot want to get him checked out.

Gary   He'll go back to sleep in a minute. (*Turns monitor off.*)

Karen   That boy is not ready for school.

Nicky   Course he is.

Karen   Shall I go?

Nicky   No, it's alright. (*She heads out.*)

Karen   She is killing herself for those kids.

Anjum   That's what happens.

Karen (*to* **Anjum**)   All the girls at school wanted to be Nicola.
Innit, Mo?

Mo   Oh yeah.

Karen   Her hair was always shining, eye-shadow blended just right.
But now, she looks like it's . . . all over.

Gary   What are you saying?

Karen   Doesn't matter. My brother'd worship a toilet seat if he thought
Nicola had sat on it. (*A beat.*) Gary's probably told you, I'm on my own
these days.

Anjum   Er . . . you told us.

Gary   You tell them every week.

Karen   I mean I did everything you're supposed to.

Mo   You did.

Karen   Found the career, waited half my life for Mr Right, married him
in that freezing cold church, started doing the shopping online, went to
Ikea every Bank Holiday, got a massive corner sofa, listened to him
whingeing on about wanting saxophone lessons, had sex with him twice
a week and bam! Wayne walks out, just like that. Said he couldn't cope
with the responsibility.

Gary (*shouts upstairs*)   Nic, get Mark's present!

Anjum   It's a shame.

Karen   Thing is I don't miss him but I do get lonely. Does that make sense?

Mo   Oh yes.

Gary (**Nicky** *enters*)   I forgot to wrap it.

Nicky (*hands him gift*)   Done.

Gary   Now that is why I love this girl.

He puts music on. Pulls her to him. She laughs.

Nicky   You've been drinking.

Gary (*jovial*)   Course I have.

They do a few pretty good dance moves.

Nicky (*light to* **Gary**)   Make sure you take it easy this weekend.

Anjum   Was Tyler alright?

Nicky   Just a bad dream.

Mark *and* **Victoria** *enter with carrier bags.* **Victoria** *is tipsy.*

Mark   Alright.

Gary   Cheers man . . . (*Taking drinks.*)

Victoria   Hello . . .

Nicky   Er . . . Hi . . .

Victoria   I'm Victoria!

Nicky   Oh, I'm . . . Nicky.

Victoria   I've heard so much about you. Really pleased to meet you.

Nicky   Me too. (*She turns off the music.*) Gary, you didn't say Victoria was coming round.

Gary (*casual*)   Everyone was just . . . in the pub.

Victoria   I decided to tag along. Mark said you wouldn't mind.

Nicky   Course not.

Anjum   Happy Birthday Mark.

Mo   Happy Birthday brother. (*They hug.*)

Victoria   I didn't realise you had people round. Gary, you should have said, sorry for interrupting . . .

Nicky   Don't be silly. We've always got people round.

Gary (*to* **Victoria**)   This is Karen, my sister. Mo's an old mate.

Mo   Evening.

Gary   And Anjum, his wife. (*To the others.*) Victoria's . . . the manager at work.

Victoria (*spots samosas*)   What are you making?

Nicky   Samosas.

Victoria   Yummy!

Anjum   We're freezing them for the school fair.

Nicky   We're just finishing up.

Anjum   Er, yeah . . . Mo, we should get going.

Mo   We can stay a bit longer. (*Reluctant* **Anjum** *sits.*)

Nicky (*to* **Victoria**)   Would you like a drink?

Victoria   Oh Prosecco please. Or anything else if you haven't got . . .

Nicky   We've got Prosecco. Gary, take Victoria's jacket.

Victoria (*jacket*)   I see you've got him well trained.

Mo   I'll have a Prosecco.

Karen   Thought we were having cocktails.

Victoria   Oh yeah, oh God, I forgot the spirits! Mark, you should have reminded me.

Mark   I can't drink cocktails, they give me diarrhoea.

Victoria (*to* **Nicky**)   I am so sorry. But I did buy Haribos for your kids. (*Sweets.*)

Nicky   Thank you. They love sweets.

Karen   Tyler can't have those. They send him nuts.

Nicky   Ronnie and Mia can.

Victoria   Could I have lots of ice in my wine?

Nicky   Sure . . . er . . . we've got ice.

Victoria   Lots please. It has to be really cold for me to drink it. Like really really cold.

Nicky   Okay.

Gary (*present*)   Happy Birthday man.

Mark   Cheers brother. (*Opens.*)

Nicky   Open it later Mark.

Gary   It's his birthday!

Victoria   Go on, let's see what you got.

Mark   Ah thanks, Gaz. I've always wanted one of these. Since I was like five years old!

Gary   I know! There's batteries in there an' all.

Mark *puts batteries into the remote control helicopter.*

Mo (*to* **Victoria**)   So how long have you been working with Gary?

Victoria   Too long isn't it Gary? Drive me mad this lot. Especially this one, don't you Mark?

Mark   What have I done?

Mo (*indicating* **Gary** *to* **Victoria**)   Just so you know, they don't make men like this one any more. Proper salt of the earth men.

Mark   Innit.

Gary   Shut up.

Victoria   Tonight I'm nobody's manager, I'm just Victoria. Got that?

Nicky   Sure.

Mo (*checking phone/annoyed*)   Here we go. Finlay's dad says he can't do the bouncy castle now because he has to visit his Grandma in her care home. Tosser.

Victoria (*laughing*)   Finlay's dad a tosser!

Gary   I'll do it.

Nicky   Yeah, stick him down.

Mo   You two are on the Skittles and Splat the Rat.

Karen   You're not doing that shit again.

Gary   We have to.

Nicky   For the kids.

Victoria   Oh, I adore bouncing on a bouncy castle!

Mo   You can't do the whole day.

Gary   I'm not bothered.

Nicky (*to* **Victoria**)   The kids love him. He always lets them stay on longer than they're meant to.

Victoria   Your place is so homely and . . . inviting.

Nicky   Thanks very much.

Victoria   And it's very spacious, you'd never think from outside. Like on *Doctor Who* . . . what's that phone box thing?

Anjum   The Tardis.

Mark *starts flying the helicopter.*

Nicky   Everyone says that, don't they Gary?

Gary (*brings drinks*)   Who?

Victoria   And there's a real sense of community here. I could feel it when we walked from the bus stop . . . it's in the air.

Gary (*food to* **Victoria**)   Is that enough chicken?

Victoria   Oh, I'm a vegetarian. Mine's the beanie wrap.

Suddenly helicopter crashes. **Victoria** *laughs loudly.*

Nicky   Mark! Take it outside!

Mark   I want to eat.

Gary   Eat man!

Nicky   Well put it back in the box for now.

Victoria   We should do this more often, I mean I should do more of this. When you live on your own you end up not bothering, just sitting around and messing about with your phone.

Karen   I do that.

Mo   And me.

Victoria   Have you got karaoke?

Nicky   No, sorry.

Mo (*to* **Anjum**)   Remember when I did 'Eye of the Tiger' at Nav's leaving do?

Anjum   Yes.

Victoria   Let's do Karaoke! (*A beat.*) What's that one we were singing on the bus?

Gary   I wasn't singing.

Mark (*sings*)   369, the goose drank wine . . .

Victoria (*joins in*) . . . the monkey chewed tobacco on the streetcar line. The line broke. The monkey got choked and they all went to heaven in a little row boat. Clap clap . . . Come on everyone!

Mark *and* **Mo** *start to clap.* **Nicky** *joins in.*

Victoria   Come on Gary, let your hair down! (*Sings.*) My mama told me if I was goody, that she would buy me a rubber dolly . . .

Karen (*gets up/shouts*)   Fuck this!

Karen *puts music on. Stefflon Don/Wiley/Sean Paul/Idris' 'Boasty' plays loud, like they are all in a club. They all dance energetically.*

Fuses into Cameo's 'Candy'. They get up, start dancing individually and then, led by **Karen**, *come together to do the Candy Dance.* **Victoria** *can't do it. On the periphery, she downs a bottle of wine, she tries dancing again but still can't get the steps.* **Victoria** *breaks away and the music stops.*

Victoria   God, you lot . . . you lot . . . are like a real community. I mean a proper community. I don't know any of my neighbours. I mean this is so . . . nice, like you're off the telly, like you'd give each other lifts if one of you got cancer and make . . . casseroles . . . Or curries if you don't eat casseroles . . . . But . . . I'm sure you do . . . eat them . . . when you're hungry . . . I bet there's a cosy local round the corner. Serving hotpot. We should go . . . Shall we go?

Gary   Nobody makes hotpot any more.

Victoria (*starting to slur*)   Maybe we should all go camping together.

Mark   My dad took me to a caravan park in Swanage once. That was my one holiday with my dad.

Victoria   Be like a massive sleepover. Has anyone got a really really big tent?

Karen   Children of immigrants don't camp, love. We're trying to get away from that shit.

Victoria   Dirty kids burning marshmallows and smelly people sleeping in bags . . . wankers! (*Laughs.*)

Gary   Nic, get her a cab.

Victoria   No you don't, cheeky! I'm not going anywhere!

Nicky   I can always cancel it.

She gets her phone out, sorts the cab.

Victoria (*to* **Anjum**)   You live on such a nice estate.

Anjum   We don't live here.

Victoria   It doesn't feel like Council.

Nicky   Thanks.

Victoria   My dad told me to stay away from people on estates.

Mark   I reckon the girls on estates are prettier.

Karen (*to* **Mark**)   Have you ever had a girlfriend?

Gary   Leave him alone!

Mark   Course I have. Loads! Ask Gary.

Karen   One who calls you her boyfriend?

Mark   Women expect a lot.

Mo (*friendly punch*)   I'm with you on that one!

Mark   Do you remember when we went to that party in the country? Surrey or some shithole. And Barry from the year below you lot was there and he said his sister fancied me.

Victoria (*to* **Nicky**)   Can you get me a cab?

Nicky   On its way.

Mark   I should have got her number. Why didn't I get her number?

Karen   Nobody cares.

Gary   That was a good night. Ennit babe.

Nicky (*laughs*)   Yeah.

Mark   Except for that neighbour. (*To the others.*) This guy picked a fight with Gaz.

Gary   It got sorted. He went back inside his house.

Mark   Gary never said nothing. The neighbour took a swing at him but Gary shut him up with a sweet right hook.

Gary   I was defending myself.

Mark   I told Gary then. Same as I tell Ronnie and Mia and Ty. If someone hits you, make sure you hit straight back.

Nicky   What you telling them that for? We teach our kids to be better than that.

Mo   You have to speak to people in the language they understand . . .

Victoria (*stands/wobbles/vehement*)   I've tamed these boys. I run this team and we fly. I mean they fly, high up into the sky. I do my best to captain my boys, my red arrows and we are something. I mean if your dishwasher or your washing machine or your microwave or any shit like that breaks down, how are you going to feed your kids? And what are they going to wear? . . . Nothing! . . . I lead these beautiful, strong men and I'm proud . . . because . . . I care about you and you. (*Points to* **Gary** *and* **Mark**.) And I fight for you . . . Like I fought when they tried to make your wages depend on customer feedback . . . I said no, no way, my guys work hard . . . They go out and they fix shit and they make sure your dishes are gleaming and why should they worry about getting five stars for politeness and all that bollocks . . . when they can get your fan oven spinning like the dancefloor after a couple of Jagerbombs? I mean fuck that!

Bewildered silence. **Victoria** *starts to twerk drunkenly. She focusses on* **Gary**.

Victoria   Come on Gary, show me how to . . . I want to learn . . . like properly . . . how . . . like you guys . . . when the girls in the videos . . . you know . . . how you do it . . . with the girls shaking their big fat bottoms . . . Come on Gary, you and me . . .

Gary   Victoria, sit down . . .

Victoria (*to* **Gary**)   I demand that you dance! That's an order from management. Remember, I'm in charge . . . and you don't disobey me

. . . I'm your . . . your superior. Do not disobey your superior! . . . Show me, you show me how to (*Sings the words of Get Ur Freak On by Missy Elliott.*)

Stumbling, she pats **Gary** *on the head like a dog. He sharply moves out of the way.* **Victoria** *teeters and falls over badly into* **Karen**'s *lap.* **Mark** *and* **Anjum** *help her up.*

Nicky   Your cab is here.

Gary   Mark, walk her out.

Victoria (*stumbling*)   It's fine. I'm fine! Gary, your wife is the sweetest thing. And you lot . . . you've all been so . . . welcoming! Are the drivers alright?

Nicky   Yeah.

Victoria   Only I got this one the other week. He was trying it on . . . you know . . .

Mark   They're okay.

Victoria   That wasn't round here. They're probably alright round here.

Victoria *and* **Mark** *head out. Silence.*

Karen (*slowly*)   What a cunt.

Nicky   She was very pissed.

Mo   Certainly a character.

Anjum   You never know what someone like that thinks. I mean what they really think.

Karen   That is how white people stay.

Mo   Some of them.

Anjum   Most of them.

Karen (*to* **Nicky**)   Not you, obviously.

Mo (*to* **Gary**)   Wouldn't worry about it, Gaz.

Gary   How do you mean?

Mo   Well . . . you know . . . her . . . I mean you haven't put a foot wrong.

Gary   I know.

Mo   And she's . . . well, she can't take her alcohol, that's obvious . . .

Gary   She's nothing to me.

Mo (*awkward*)   It's difficult . . . being in that situation . . .

Nicky   Nothing happened.

Karen   Come on Nic, you heard her.

Gary   Leave it.

Mo   I've met women like her before.

Anjum   When?

Karen   Me too. She looks like that slag Wayne took to see Rihanna. Fuck, I'm tired. (*She gets up.*)

Nicky   I've made a bed up for you in the kids' room.

Karen   You're a good woman Nicola. You got a good woman here Gary.

She heads out.

Anjum (*to* **Nicky**)   Er . . . sorry to ask now, but I was thinking about booking this new English tutor for the second round.

Nicky   We don't even know if they've got through yet.

Mo   Your Ronnie'll walk it.

Nicky   I reckon he's had enough.

Anjum   We want to give them the best possible chance. It'd only be a couple of sessions.

Nicky   I should check how much it costs.

Anjum   Never mind about that. Zaki hates going on his own.

Nicky   I dunno.

Mo   We're not quibbling over a few quid! This is both the boys' education.

Nicky   Hmm. Just cos me and Gaz didn't get it right, doesn't mean we can't get it right for the kids.

Mo   That's the spirit.

Anjum   Have a think. I'll come and see you after the weekend. (*Gets up.*) We'd better go, he's opening the shop in the morning.

Nicky   How come?

Anjum   Mo and his brothers take it in turns these days.

Mo (*gets up*)   My dad can't bend down to open the shutters any more. Been doing it too many years. His spine's wrecked.

Nicky   I'm sorry.

Mo (*shrugs/to* **Gary**)   Our dads came here with so much fire in their bellies. People go on about what Britain's given us, well what about what's it's taken away.

Gary   Yeah.

Mo   They're not crushing us lot with their sticks and stones because we know to throw them back. It's up to the likes of you and me now, Gaz. You go in on Monday and grab what's yours brother.

They leave. **Gary** *and* **Nicky** *tidy up.* **Nicky** *stops, eyes* **Gary** *tentatively.*

Nicky   You okay?

Gary   Yeah.

Nicky (*a beat*)   Tyler wet himself again last night. I was up at three in the morning, changing the bed. Then I couldn't get back to sleep.

Gary   He wants to stop that stupidness.

Nicky   I might start putting a nappy on him, only at night-time . . .

Gary   No! I've told you . . . he has to feel it, otherwise he won't learn.

Nicky   She was off her head and/

Gary   So Mo and Anjum are paying for this other tutor now?

Nicky   I haven't said yes.

Gary   I can afford it. Whatever he needs, I'm paying for it.

Nicky   Okay.

Gary   What did you mean, you and me got it wrong?

Nicky   Eh?

Gary   You said we got it wrong, but we can get it right for the kids.

Nicky   I didn't say that. We never bothered with maths or science did we? But Ron's shining. Remember when the teacher said he was two years ahead?

Gary   That was a couple of years ago.

Nicky   You heard Anjum, we have to make sure he has the best chance. You and me, we should be doing everything we can.

Gary   We got him a tutor for this eleven plus, didn't we?

Nicky   Only because Mo and Anjum told us.

Gary   What else is there?

Nicky   We set an example, show the kids it's important to get on. They see me working every shift I can and now you're going for this promotion.

Gary   I don't wanna go for it.

They both stop.

Nicky   Why?

Gary   I just don't.

Nicky (*a beat*)   I could kill Mark for bringing her round. Why didn't you stop him?

Gary   I didn't think she'd stay more than five minutes! (*A beat.*) You were going on like she was your best mate.

Nicky   She was a guest in our house!

Gary   I didn't like what she said.

Nicky   Nobody did. She was out of it.

Gary   She was out of order Nic.

Nicky   You just said you were okay.

Gary   Well I'm not.

Nicky   She was that drunk she probably won't even remember.

Gary   No, I don't expect she will.

Nicky   I don't like serving Pinot Grigio to yummy mummies every day but I do it. (*A beat.*) You have to go for the interview Gary. We've been talking about it for months. Think of the money, five hundred quid extra a month. Imagine the possibilities, I mean we can start to save up. Why should she stop us? Why should anybody stop us from having what other people take for granted? (*A beat.*) We said we might buy this place.

Gary   What if that time's gone?

Nicky   We have to try. And if we can't do it, who says we have to stay in the city, we could find a little semi outside. With a garden. Ronnie could get the train to school. Loads of people move to the countryside.

Gary   People like us?

Nicky   Why not people like us?

Gary   We never got anything wrong Nic.

Nicky (*a beat*)   There is nobody better for that job than you.

Gary   I know.

Nicky   Plus the kids are all excited that you might become a manager.

Gary   Team leader.

Nicky   We never had any choices Gaz. So maybe we have to take what we can. (*A beat.*) If Ronnie gets into the grammar, he'll have more freedom than us.

Gary   You saying someone locked you up?

Nicky   No, but if he does well, his whole world'll open out.

Gary (*pulls her to him*)   We've done good. Yeah? If this is it and there's nothing more, we've done good. There isn't a single thing that can touch us. Not ever. And if we end up on the street, you, me and the kids, we'll still be okay.

Nicky   I am not living on no street.

Gary   Man can't say nothing these days.

Nicky (*a beat*)   So, are you gonna go for it?

Scene Two

Monday. Victoria's office. **Victoria** *is gathering papers after the interview. She catches sight of* **Gary** *walking past the door.*

Victoria (*calls*)   Er, Gary . . .

She beckons him. He enters. He wears a smart suit.

Gary   Yeah?

Victoria   This is . . . a bit embarrassing . . . but I wanted to apologise about the other night. I normally go straight home on a Friday. When I was at your house, I think I may have had too much to drink.

Gary   Right.

Victoria   Far too much. I can't quite remember what I said, but . . . I am really sorry . . . I know I fell over and banged my knee . . . I hope I didn't . . . er . . . spoil Mark's birthday.

Gary   Don't worry about Mark.

Victoria   I'm not sure what happened. I hardly ever drink. (*A beat.*) Your wife is lovely. Very pretty. Is she okay?

Gary   Nic?

Victoria   Mark mentioned she was looking tired.

Gary   No.

Victoria (*a beat*)   Well, thanks. We should make a decision reasonably quickly.

Gary *lingers.*

Gary   Victoria . . . Can I ask you something?

Victoria   Fire away.

Gary   You do reckon I can do this?

Victoria   What?

Gary   The job.

Victoria   Of course. You wouldn't have been invited for interview otherwise.

Gary   I was just wondering . . .

Victoria   Yes?

Gary   If I'm here to make up the numbers?

Victoria   Certainly not. No way.

Gary   Good.

Victoria   You mustn't doubt yourself Gary.

Gary   What about Brian?

Victoria   Brian?

Gary   Does he know I already cover if one of the team leaders is away?

Victoria   Of course.

Gary   I mean you always ask me . . .

Victoria   It's absolutely been noted.

Gary   Only you see . . . there's a rumour going round.

Victoria   Go on.

Gary   I heard . . . that Brian's decided it's Des.

Victoria   No, no that's wrong.

Gary   A couple of people have been saying . . .

Victoria   Nothing's been decided. We're in the middle of a process, we'll sit down, go through our notes and then we come to a decision . . .

Gary   Okay.

Victoria   Good.

Gary (*light*)   Victoria, what do you think when you see me?

Victoria   You're Gary. Gaz. Someone I can rely on.

Gary   It's just . . . when we chat, you and me . . .

Victoria   Yes?

Gary   When the kettle's boiling in the morning. Mark noticed.

Victoria   Mark has a few issues.

Gary (*light*)   Thing is . . . all you talk to me about, every morning, is . . . Black shit.

Victoria   Black shit?

Gary   Yeah. Like when they said Stormzy bought a can of Red Bull in the Costcutter or what Alesha was wearing on *Britain's Got Talent*. Or that time you had rice 'n' peas . . .

Victoria   I don't know what to say . . .

Gary   It's true.

Victoria   What you're describing is us having a bit of small talk while the tea's brewing. We have a natter about what's on the front page of the *Metro* . . .

Gary   Why did you ask if I'd seen *Twelve Years a Slave*?

Victoria   Did I?

Gary   You've never asked if I've seen any other film.

Victoria   Haven't I?

Gary   Not once.

Victoria   I suppose . . . as your line manager, I'm expected to connect with my team so . . . I'm being a . . . human being.

Gary   I see.

Victoria   Do you know what I mean?

Gary   I think so.

Victoria   Going for a new job can be stressful. For all of us. It's one of those times in life when our personal demons can rise up and attack. Just . . . try and stay positive. Yeah?

Gary   So me and Des definitely have the same opportunity?

Victoria   Absolutely! Look, you've just done an interview and now you're feeling vulnerable. Gary, this sort of thing . . . it happens. (*A beat.*) My parents got divorced when I was nine so I never believe it when couples say they're happy. I mean I can see they are but I don't believe it, because how can they be? Because sooner or later one of them's going to do something terrible.

Gary   You think that?

Victoria   It's irrational but it's my first reaction, because I suffered when I was a child. The same as you must have suffered because of your . . . skin colour. But times have changed. Thank goodness times have changed.

Gary   Right.

Victoria   I should probably get on.

Gary *nods.*

Victoria   I'm really pleased we've been able to have an honest conversation.

Gary   Me too.

Scene Three

Tuesday. **Nicky** *is coming in from work.* **Anjum** *is following her and showing* **Nicky** *some papers.*

Nicky   *Jane Eyre*?

Anjum   That's the standard they're expecting. The creative writing section's even worse. 'Write a letter to Mr Rochester, questioning his treatment of Bertha.'

Nicky   They're ten years old.

Anjum   Apparently this tutor has a formula to improve speed without losing marks on SPAG.

Nicky   SPAG, I want him to have a rest.

Anjum   Nicky, three thousand children take the exam. After the second round, they only take the top sixty-five. Plus Ronnie started the tutoring late so he needs all the help he can get.

Nicky   I'm not sure.

Anjum   We have to take charge. Remember when the school put Ronnie in the lowest reading group, he was bored out of his skull, until you spoke to them.

Nicky   Maybe.

Anjum   Be Mia next. You'll be an expert by the time it's Tyler's turn.

Nicky   Might not be right for Tyler.

Anjum   If he's anything like his brother and sister/

Nicky   He's not. You know he's not.

Anjum   No.

Nicky   He's more . . . sensitive.

Anjum   That's good. Sensitivity's a . . . soft skill. And those are going to be extremely important in the future.

Nicky (*a beat*)   What have I done wrong with him, Anjum?

Anjum   Nothing. I wish Zaki talked to me the way your kids do to you. You're a brilliant mum. The best.

Nicky   Tyler just . . . wants my arms round him, all the time. It's like he doesn't believe in the rest of the world.

Anjum   Then, for now, you give him your arms.

Nicky *nods.* **Anjum** *senses her anxiety.*

Anjum   He's going to be fine.

Nicky   I hope so.

Anjum   School doesn't work for everyone. Sometimes I'm not sure it's been right for Zaki. (*Gets text.*) Oh, go away Mo!

Nicky   What's happened?

Anjum   He's bought a candy floss machine for the Fair. I asked him to hire one but he doesn't listen. Now he's told Zaki if he passes the eleven plus he can have candy floss every day for the rest of his life.

Nicky   And if he doesn't pass?

Anjum   Exactly.

Nicky   I suppose you can afford private.

Anjum   Mo's not keen on touching the savings account. He says we've paid our taxes so we're entitled. He's so tough on Zaki.

Nicky   Because he cares, Gary hasn't got a clue.

Anjum   He's probably been anxious about the interview. How did he get on yesterday?

Nicky   He said it went really well.

Anjum   Great.

Nicky   He finds out tomorrow. They have to choose him. I mean, he's perfect.

Anjum   We've got everything crossed for him. I mean he was totally prepared. That's how you need Ronnie to be – exam ready.

Nicky   Right.

Anjum   Did I mention we went to have a look at St Joseph's? We're just in the catchment.

Nicky   That's a Catholic School.

Anjum   They take twenty-five per cent other faiths or no faith. Classrooms are state of the art. Their IT's sponsored by Apple and they have their own theatre.

Nicky   Wow.

Anjum   We're not applying.

Nicky   How come?

Anjum   The staff. They were smiling but only with their lips. They tried not to, but they were all staring at my scarf. Trying to make sense of it. Wishing us well and hoping we'd settle on another school. They were nice enough. We're all nice enough. As long as there's a safe distance.

Nicky   You never used to wear that scarf.

Anjum   I used to drink Bacardi Breezers.

Nicky   Why did you stop?

Anjum   I didn't know you that well when I first got married. After Zaki was born, Mo's mum looked after the baby and I went shopping. I joined a book club and had make up tutorials and lunches with other women. We were all into . . . self improvement. And soya lattes. We'd do yoga five mornings a week but never ask each other how we were. I hardly spoke to my mum, I hated Mo's family. I had it all and I wanted to die. Then his cousin handed me a book about women and Islam. I read it and my heart lifted. My parents didn't teach us anything, we just had to go to mosque and nod our heads even when we didn't understand, learn words parrot fashion without interrogating or learning the beauty of what was on offer. I joined a few forums and became part of something. Faced the fact that I'd been pretending my whole life until the moment I put this on my head.

Nicky   It's changed things that much?

Anjum   My mum never had a drop of faith, she walked the streets with her head down, scared that some skinhead might chuck a stone at her or the neighbours would complain about the smell of the keema. I walk tall. This (*Points at hijab.*) is the message that I don't have to please anybody, that I'm in control of my womanhood. That I'm not prepared to demean myself. People can think what they like. But I am free.

Nicky   Do you reckon I demean myself?

Anjum   I'm not judging anyone. This is your culture. We do our own thing because people here won't ever really accept us.

Nicky   People round here . . . they're alright.

Anjum   Britain isn't about equality.

Nicky   England's not perfect but we have decent teachers and free hospitals, we can do whatever we want, we can say whatever we want.

Anjum   I wish it was like that. Do you honestly believe your Ronnie, your brilliant, bright boy has the same chances as some thick middle-class kid?

Nicky   If he works hard, yeah.

Anjum   We prefer to rely on ourselves. If my car breaks down, I ask Mo's uncle. If we need an accountant, there's Mo's cousin and when we go shopping we support our own businesses.

Nicky   You're lucky with your family and that. We've only got Karen and Mark. (*A beat.*) Why not go for a Muslim school?

Anjum   We want Zaki to be able to compete with everyone else. Education is a weapon and we need our children to be armed. Make sure they have the say that we never did.

Nicky   But you're . . . well-off.

Anjum   Doesn't mean we belong. After I started wearing this, not one of that yoga lot ever spoke to me again. But you're my friend Nicky, that's why we can be open with each other. We both want the same thing for our boys. And to get what you want, you always need a plan.

Nicky   Yeah.

Anjum   Shall we give this tutor a go then?

Nicky   I don't suppose one or two sessions will hurt.

Anjum   I'll text her now. (*Texts.*)

Nicky   I wouldn't have a clue about secondaries if it wasn't for you.

Anjum (*a beat*)   I hope I haven't said anything that's offended you.

Nicky   Don't be stupid, Mo's like family to us. That means you are too.

Scene Four

Wednesday. Staff room. **Mark** *sits at a small table finishing a pasty.* **Gary** *gets a can of Coke from a vending machine.* **Gary** *comes to sit. Drinks.*

Mark   What are you gonna do?

Gary   Do?

Mark   They think they can treat us like shit. Like nothing.

Gary   Us?

Mark   I'm on your side. Always. Know that.

Gary   I know.

Mark   You got jobs this afternoon?

Gary   Yeah.

Mark   How do you feel?

Gary   I imagined this moment in my head. This moment, right here. I thought it would come, but I didn't realise it would break me up so bad.

Mark   Gaz, you . . . you'll never be broken. You sitting here, stewing, it's what they want.

Victoria *enters, goes to the vending machine, gets a Diet Coke. Silence.*

Victoria   Can I get anyone anything?

She approaches awkwardly.

I'm sorry it didn't work out.

Gary   I'm a better engineer than Des.

Victoria   You are a first-rate engineer. And your feedback score is right up there. None of that means you can manage a team.

Gary   He's never covered the job before, I have.

Victoria   It's our role to have an instinct for the future . . .

Mark   Instinct . . .

Victoria   . . . to imagine how each interviewee might perform in a given situation.

Gary   What's your instinct based on?

Victoria   Experience.

Gary   Of what?

Victoria   Business, life, people . . .

Gary   Do you know any other Black people?

Victoria (*a beat*)   Yes.

Gary   I've been here ten years. All the managers and team leaders we've had, every single one has been white. Why is that?

Victoria   It might just be that there are more white people in the field. I . . . don't know. (*A beat.*) If you want any . . . feedback . . .

Gary   I don't want feedback.

Victoria   Might help to get some perspective . . .

Gary   You don't think I've got perspective?

Victoria   It's only a suggestion. I'm sure there'll be another chance in the future, at a different office. I'll let you know. (*A beat.*) Nobody gets the first thing they go for.

Mark   Did you?

Victoria   You did your best Gary. That's all you can ask of yourself. And you can carry on with your jobs now. I mean nothing's really changed.

Gary   Everything's changed.

Victoria   What?

Gary   This shit. Your shit . . .

Victoria   There's no need for bad language.

Mark (*amused*)   Language.

Gary   . . . And now you come down here pretending you're gonna drink that Diet Coke.

Victoria   You're bound to feel . . . disappointed.

Gary   They said it was Des and it is. Just like we both knew it would be.

Victoria   Nobody knew.

Gary   Then I'm an astrologer, seeing the future. Why can't you speak the truth?

Victoria   Truth?

Gary   The thing you don't say but you know is there.

Victoria   I don't . . .

Gary   I'd like to know what you really feel when you look at me.

Victoria   My role is to be impartial, my feelings are not relevant.

Gary   But they affect your choices.

Victoria   Not in my professional life. People should be judged by their actions.

Gary   You mean the way you acted on Mark's birthday?

Victoria   I was drunk!

Gary (*angry*)   Speak the truth! You liar.

She goes to leave, **Mark** *gets in her way.*

Victoria   What are you doing?

Mark   What are you doing? Gary's got a right to have his say.

Victoria   It's nothing to do with you Mark.

Mark   This man is my blood. Tell her Gaz.

Gary (*to* **Victoria**)   All you lot. You colour us with failure.

Mark   You're no failure, brother.

Victoria   You're too angry right now.

Gary   I am angry. So angry. But my anger is clean and clear. It's washed off all the shit you put on me. Like there's new skin on my flesh.

Victoria   This is not appropriate . . .

Gary   What you see, what you feel about us, goes into your bloodstream and then you make your move. You come to my house and you humiliate me . . .

Victoria   I tried to explain . . .

Gary   You said you were superior, you patted me on the head like a dog . . .

Victoria   I'd have done the same to Mark if he'd been sitting in front of me! I was out of it. You're taking my words out of context.

Gary   You made fun of Black women.

Victoria   No!

Gary   And you used a word. Begins with an N.

Victoria   It was a line from a song . . . you can't think I meant . . . how can you think?

Gary   Thought you couldn't remember.

Silence.

Gary   I'm glad you said it. Now we can have an honest conversation.

Victoria   How many times do I have to say sorry?

Gary   Wherever you go, you take the trace of that feeling.

Victoria   You won't believe it but I tried to fight for you. I honestly did make your case.

Gary   No. When you lot sing, it sounds like one voice.

Victoria   Rubbish me all you like but your take on this whole situation is convenient, it's how you want to perceive me . . .

Mark   She's not listening. You should listen to people.

Victoria   I've been up front with you, I've tried really hard to understand/

Gary   You don't know how it feels to be in my skin.

Victoria   Of course I don't, what's that got to do with anything?

Gary   These white eyes you see through . . .

Victoria   White eyes? You analyse life in these weird terms and it's not real. What about Mark? He's white and he's a nobody.

Mark   What?

Gary   Now you're disrespecting him?

Victoria   Disrespect? Listen to how you're talking to me, I'm your manager.

Mark   You think you're better than us. (*Moves closer to* **Victoria**/*loud.*) Who's nobody now?

Victoria   You wouldn't dare speak like this if I was a man.

Mark   What's that got to do with it?

Victoria   You both, you . . . you have certain power.

Gary   Who am I? I can't change nothing. I can't do nothing. All you lot, you use your words and play with our heads.

Victoria   No . . .

Gary   You give your jobs to people who you feel comfortable with, who look like you, who feel like you. Because you can't understand things any other way. What's really fucked up is, you think you understand everything.

Victoria   Listen to me, I do not see the colour of your skin.

Gary   That's the problem. Saying I don't exist . . . you're shutting down who I am . . . I want you to see it.

Victoria   I thought you didn't. Make up your mind.

Gary   It's how you see it. I want you to try and look at me without thinking I'm inferior.

Victoria   This is ridiculous. You're just . . . playing the race card now.

Mark   Race card?

Gary   That's your card. Your get out of jail free. You're using it now so you can blame me, so you don't have to face yourself. You put us in your ticked boxes. Well I'm not in your box now!

Victoria *is getting upset.*

Gary   And when we speak up, you can't cope. You start crying. Admit what you are.

Victoria *shakes her head.*

Gary   Racist.

Victoria   I am not. Bully me however much you like.

Gary   See how she turns it around. So I'm the bully now?

Victoria   Yes, yes you are!

Mark   He's not doing nothing.

Gary   You're the power here Victoria. You. Racist. Fucking powerful racist. Fuck you Victoria. Fuck you.

Gary *kicks over the chair.*

Scene Five

Same day. The Flat. **Nicky** *is painting* **Mo**'s *face – what she's doing cannot be seen.* **Anjum**'s *face is painted like a cat. She fills assorted jam jars with various sweets.*

Mo   How's your skin?

Anjum   Okay, I think. Though I don't see why you couldn't just buy the branded paints.

Mo   Brands won't save the school money. Anyway you haven't come out in a rash, so these are almost definitely non toxic.

Anjum   I'm sure Nicky's got better things to do.

Nicky   I don't mind.

Mo   When you're faced with a queue of little alpha females demanding to be butterflies, you'll be glad of the practice.

Nicky   Done. (*Hands* **Mo** *mirror. She packs the paints away.*) As he looks up, we see that she's painted a dog face on him.

Mo   That is very . . . lifelike. It's funny . . . I actually feel . . . canine.

(*To* **Anjum**.) Do you know what I mean?

Anjum   No. You're supposed to be helping me fill these jars.

Mo   You should be putting two sweets in, not four.

Anjum   We're charging a quid per jar.

Mo   If people can afford Iphones and Playstations, they can afford a quid to support the school.

Anjum   Still no word from Gary?

Nicky   He's not answering his phone. Hopefully he's out celebrating.

Mo   He probably wants to tell you in person. If it's good news, and I reckon it will be, Mark's gonna babysit and we're taking you both into town. We'll find one of those rooftop restaurants and rub shoulders with the oligarchs and the Chinese and those bearded bastards from Shoreditch.

Nicky   You don't have to.

Mo   I need a night out. Waiting for these results is gonna give me a brain haemorrhage.

Nicky   It is stressful.

Mo   There has to be some sort of test. How else do you separate the men from the boys?

Anjum   Girls take the eleven plus too.

Mo   It's a metaphor. (*To* **Nicky**.) Zaki needs spoonfeeding. Did you know in one of the mocks, he left half the multiple choice questions blank?

Anjum   He ran out of time.

Mo   Who leaves multiple choice questions blank? You wouldn't would you?

Nicky   I suppose not.

Anjum   How's Ronnie coping?

Nicky   Alright.

Mo   Well he's clever isn't he? Natural intelligence. Our problem is, Zaki's thick. That's why I keep telling him he has to work twice as hard. I mean the second round's in three weeks and he still hasn't come to terms with apostrophes . . .

Anjum   Zaki knows exactly where apostrophes go!

Mo   Not after irregular nouns.

Anjum (*to* **Nicky**)   He's been sick most mornings.

Nicky   Poor thing.

Mo   I keep telling him, he's got to develop resilience. We're beginning to suffer now. (*Indicates* **Anjum**.) She's hardly sleeping. And I've got a mouth ulcer the size of a 50p piece. Look . . . (*Starts to show* **Nicky**.)

Anjum   She doesn't want to see! (*A beat.*) It doesn't help that you're always shouting.

Mo   Not always.

Anjum   This morning.

Mo   Because he keeps confusing prepositions with fronted adverbials! (*To* **Nicky**.) He knows I just want what's best for him.

Nicky   At least we find out soon.

Mo   What if Zaki's sick for the second round?

Anjum   We're not there yet Mo.

Mo   Well if he gets through, he's sitting the exam no matter what. Asif's daughter shit herself at the start of the verbal reasoning and she still managed to finish the synonyms and antonyms. (*A beat.*) And he doesn't concentrate. I keep telling him. I bought him that meditation app for £2.99. I could have got a free one, but I chose to pay.

Anjum   He did better in the last comprehension.

Mo   Better is not good enough. (*A beat.*) Something drastic needs to happen. I could . . . tell him I've got cancer.

Nicky   Have you?

Mo   No. But if he thinks I have, he might try harder.

Anjum   Mo, will you stop!

Mo   It'll only be for a week or so, once the exam's out of the way the consultant can give me the all clear.

Anjum   I'm not listening.

Mo   He has to want it Anj. Ronnie wants it doesn't he?

Nicky   I think so.

Anjum   Give him a chance!

Mo   We've already given him too much. (*To* **Nicky**.) Anything he wants. When I was his age, I was in charge of my Dad's stock, jointing chickens, chucking drunks out onto the street.

Anjum   That was wrong.

Mo   It was a better time.

Anjum   It wasn't.

Mark *and* **Gary** *bustle in.* **Gary** *picks* **Nicky** *up, swings her round.*

Mo   Somebody's happy.

Gary   Happy, oh yes.

Mark   You should have seen him. Gary's . . . he's a hero.

Nicky   Thank God.

Anjum   Congratulations.

Gary   I didn't get it.

Nicky   What?

Mo   Oh mate, no way.

Nicky   Why are you smiling?

Gary   Because you're all . . . beautiful.

Nicky   Gary?

Mark *takes a packet of fruit sweets from his pocket, shows* **Nicky**.

Mark   Got these for Tyler. I thought they might stop him screaming on the way to school.

Gary   If my boy wants to scream, let him scream.

Nicky   Why didn't you ring me?

Anjum   I'm really sorry Gary.

Gary   I don't care.

Mark   Victoria's a joker. You know how these people stay. One minute they're round your house necking your last Red Stripe and next they're stabbing you in the back with your own kitchen knife.

Anjum   I knew it. Your manager is why a good school is essential. You don't want Ronnie's destiny in hands like hers.

Nicky   What do you mean?

Mark   She's a racist Nic. Victoria is a racist.

Silence.

Anjum (*to* **Mo**)   Let's go and pick up the boys. (*To* **Nicky**.) Ronnie can come back to ours for dinner. (*Packs up fair stuff in a bag which she takes.*)

Mo   Your day will come brother. (*They exit.*)

Gary   I'm living it right now Mo.

Nicky   Thought you said the interview went well.

Gary   It did.

Nicky   We should have had another practice run. I kept telling you to practise.

Gary   It's nothing to do with that. Victoria doesn't think a Black man can run a team.

Nicky   She said that?

Gary   She doesn't have to.

Nicky   Go and check Tyler for me, Mark.

Mark *heads out.*

Nicky   What did you do exactly?

Gary   I told her about herself. If I hadn't spoken up, then she'd carry on like that for the rest of her life and nothing, nothing would change. (*A* *beat.*) I've realised that I've never had a proper chance. And now, I feel like . . . I'm born again. The boys, all of them, Mark and Si and Chas, they're calling me the don.

Nicky   You told me the interview went well.

Gary   Because it did.

Nicky   Did she give you any reason?

Gary   What's she gonna say? That I wore the wrong suit or I couldn't spell thermostat. Whatever it is, it's gonna be a lie.

Nicky   Right . . . well, we'll put it behind us and move on.

Gary   I walked out Nic. I'm not going back.

Nicky   What? (*A beat.*) You can't leave work!

Gary   You saw how she was that night.

Nicky   You're punishing us because you felt humiliated.

Gary   This is down to her, I pointed certain things out and she's slapped me down.

Nicky   But what did she say?

Gary   The problem is what she doesn't say, it's what she thinks but leaves out of her sentences.

Nicky   Fucking hell, do you realise how paranoid you sound?

Gary   It's real.

Nicky   Why didn't you chuck her out on Mark's birthday?

Gary   Because you wanted me to get this fucking job!

Nicky   You took her shit then, why not take it now?

Gary   I should never have taken it. I can't go to that place day after day and come home and face Ron and Mia and Ty and have respect for myself.

Nicky   Victoria is . . . she's nothing. You concentrate on what's best for you. Forget your pride . . .

Gary   My pride means something, it makes me who I am.

Nicky   Did you lose it with her?

Gary   She was taking the piss.

Nicky   Shit.

Gary   Aren't I allowed to be angry?

Nicky   Listen Gary, you and me . . . we haven't got a house or savings or all the things you're supposed to. And now, we can't catch up, there's a price to pay. We wasted so much time. Going out, getting high, night after night . . .

Gary   That was before the kids.

Nicky   And when Ron and Mia were little.

Gary   They were the golden days. We saw our mates ennit. The kids loved it.

Nicky   We never made plans, never thought about getting on.

Gary   So?

Nicky   I don't want the kids to end up . . . (*Falters.*)

Gary   What? Like us? Like me? (*No response.*) So you get Ron into this fancy school, and then what?

Nicky   At least he'll have a chance.

Gary   And what about the kids who go to the local shithole like we did?

Nicky   They're not my kids.

Gary   So fuck them! You reckon they don't feel or think like the brainboxes who pass the exams.

Nicky   I didn't say that!

Gary   That they won't make enough money to be any use to fucking society.

Nicky   I won't apologise for putting my children first.

Gary   There's no point in any of it Nic. Why are you so desperate?

Nicky   We can't give them any money and they're not gonna get flats off the council. (*A beat.*) There must be some way to sort this out.

Gary   Tell me something. Where can I just be a man? A man, like any other geezer.

Nicky (*a beat*)   You should never have gone for the promotion.

Gary   You're wrong. I'm glad this happened. I've been burying myself alive Nic. I'd have carried on, pushing the feelings into my blood, poisoning myself. Now she realises who she's dealing with.

Nicky   You have to see sense. Because I need you and the kids need you.

Gary   I'm gonna set up on my own.

Nicky   You tried that once.

Gary   That's me done then is it? On the scrap heap?

Nicky   Ring up the other firms.

Gary   I told you I'm setting up my own business.

Nicky   We can't manage without that job. Are you're happy living this life? (*Indicates the flat.*) In this place? Five of us in two bedrooms.

Gary   Have we ever had rent arrears?

Nicky *half shakes her head.*

Gary   Is that fridge ever empty? Name me a time when my kids haven't had new shoes on their feet, leather shoes. Legoland once a year, whatever Nintendo they want at Christmas/

Nicky   This isn't about stuff. People are supposed to grow together. To want things together. (*A beat.*) Why did you chase me down at school?

Gary   I wanted you. You wanted me an' all. (*A beat.*) Nic, if I go back to work, will you be happy?

Nicky   Yeah.

Gary   You want me to tolerate Victoria's shit so you can have a bigger kitchen.

Nicky   You're making it sound like something else.

Gary   After all these years, you don't understand.

Nicky   Fucking hell, Gary, how can you say that? Do you remember my dad dragging me home by my hair when he caught us on that bus? Broke two of my ribs after he got me home. He shut the door on me the day I went to show my mum our baby.

Gary   At least your dad and his kind said what they felt.

Nicky   They talked shit. My dad and yours.

Gary   They had their reasons.

Nicky   My dad said you weren't capable, that you'd let me down.

Gary   Now I have.

Scene Six

One week later. Wednesday. Victoria's office. **Nicky** *is opposite* **Victoria**.

Victoria   Unfortunately Head Office didn't feel it was his time. (*Checks papers.*) He scored very low on the organisational section in the interview.

Nicky   And that was the reason?

Victoria   One of the reasons. How is he?

Nicky   A bit . . . low. He's not used to sitting around.

Victoria   Sure. Gary's a . . . pretty fair worker.

Nicky   He's thinking of setting up on his own. But . . . I dunno . . .

Victoria   That's going to be hard.

Nicky   He was happy here for a long time.

Victoria   I thought he was happy.

Nicky   I'm wondering if there's any way things can go back to how they were. Before.

Victoria   Nothing can go back to how it was, can it? Not if the moment has passed.

Nicky   But an engineer, like him, with his experience . . .

Victoria   What do you do Nicola?

Nicky   I work in a pub.

Victoria   Manager?

Nicky   I do lunches. So I can pick the kids up.

Victoria   Right.

Nicky   I fit in as many shifts as I can. It's the rent that scares me. They might cut our benefits because Gary walked out. He's taken out a couple of credit cards.

Victoria   If somebody came into your pub and verbally abused you, what would happen?

Nicky   They'd have to leave. Might get barred.

Victoria   On the day he walked out, Gary shouted and swore. He got right up in my face. As you know he's a big man, a powerful man. It was really horrible. Hurtful.

Nicky   We all say things we regret.

Victoria   Does he regret it?

Nicky   I think so. Is there a chance of moving on?

Victoria   Possibly . . . he'd . . . have to retract everything. Publicly apologise.

Nicky   I'll talk to him.

Victoria   I mean if he still believes . . . what he said . . . why would he want to come back?

Nicky   He misses the job, I can tell.

Victoria   So he'd apologise and mean it?

Nicky (*nods/low*)   Yeah.

Victoria   Does he know you're here?

Nicky (*a beat*)   No.

Victoria (*stands up*)   I'm sorry things are tough but I can't help you.

Nicky   Has Gary once let you down at work?

Victoria   That's not the point . . .

Nicky   What if you said it was all forgotten . . .

Victoria   It's not forgotten.

Nicky   Please. We don't need much.

Victoria   You? Poor victimised Gary doesn't get his promotion, he abuses me and then he walks out leaving a trail of rumours and labels. He's planted seeds of doubt in the minds of the men who used to trust me!

Nicky   He was upset that day.

Victoria   He chose to quit! Gary pinned his own failure on me. What he did was cheap. Lazy.

Nicky   He's not lazy.

Victoria   I'm talking about the excuse.

Nicky   Why did you use that word?

Victoria   Because that's what his excuse is. It's really not helpful seeing problems that aren't there.

Nicky   What?

Victoria   I had no idea he had all these . . . feelings, because he never said. You know, the kind of behaviour Gary displayed breeds resentment. I've been left feeling really . . . anxious, unsafe.

Nicky   Unsafe?

Victoria   Yes.

Nicky   My dad believed black people were dangerous. Inferior. He stopped talking to me because he said I'd polluted his bloodline. He had nothing to base it on, it's just what he picked up from around him.

Victoria   That's not relevant to me.

Nicky   What if we all do that, just pick up stuff . . .

Victoria   If people are constantly separated into these sub-groups, then that's how they start to see themselves and that's how they behave. That's why I treat everyone the same. Isn't that what you do?

Nicky   Me?

Victoria   You don't share your father's views.

Nicky   No. But maybe I did. Or maybe I do, somewhere.

Victoria   I applaud the fact that you're a hard working family and you're here because you're trying to build a life. And I can imagine it's difficult to keep someone like Gary under control.

Nicky (*a beat*)   He's not a dog.

Victoria   I didn't mean it like that. Come on Nicola, you're a white woman. You and I aren't so different.

Nicky   I'm not like you.

Victoria   Because you're more aware?

Nicky   More something.

Victoria   So what exactly do you think, deep in your heart? I mean you're here, asking for his job. You must doubt his version.

Nicky   No.

Victoria   You must know . . . that he just . . . goes too far sometimes. His behaviour was totally irrational.

Nicky   Because of how he felt he was being treated.

Victoria   He put everything he's ever been through because of his colour onto me. And I'm not responsible . . . The way he was that day . . . was disgusting. You'd have been ashamed. I could have got him arrested.

Nicky   For what?

Victoria   Being threatening.

Nicky   He wasn't . . .

Victoria   You weren't there.

Nicky   Mark was with him. You gonna call the police on him an' all?

No response.

Nicky   I think Gary opened his mouth and made you listen to the truth. You're the real criminal.

Victoria   There are laws to protect individuals like Gary. I don't break the law.

Nicky   Tell me for real Victoria, please, why didn't he get the job?

Victoria   The truth is, Brian and I were going to give him the job. But that day, after the interview, Gary asked certain questions which were . . . not appropriate. He messed it up for himself.

Nicky   You were never gonna give him that job.

Victoria (*a beat*)   Like I said, head office decided it's not his time yet.

Nicky   When will it be his time? Fucking when?

Victoria   You ought to leave.

Nicky   I'm gone.

Victoria   I'm sorry it's ended like this.

Nicky   Ended where? You're still the boss. Three grand's still hitting your account at the end of the month. People like you . . . you're always the winners.

Victoria   If money's tight, we do need cleaners. Although, it is a very early start . . .

Nicky   Have you told head office you came round our house? Pissed out of your brain. That you insulted us and disgraced yourself. Mark had to pour you into that cab. (*A beat.*) Did you discuss that with Brian?

Victoria *is knocked.*

Nicky   I didn't think so.

Scene Seven

Thursday. Early evening. **Karen** *is with* **Gary** *who is constructing a Splat the Rat.*

Karen   Fresh air! Come on, I'll buy you a dirty burger and a rum and Coke.

Gary   Nah.

Karen   Then you two go and I'll stay with the kids.

Gary   I'm alright here.

Karen   Now or never Gary, I'm off out later.

Gary   Wayne?

Karen   I do have friends.

Gary   Off the internet?

Karen (*a beat*)   Yeah.

Gary   Is he Black?

Karen   Why?

Gary   He's not is he?

Karen   None of your business.

Gary   Maybe he should be.

Karen   All that fucked up shit you just said, I'm gonna pretend you never said it. (*Observes the construction.*) What is that?

Gary   Splat the Rat. For the school.

Karen   You turn into house husband now?

Gary   Shut your mouth.

Karen   Thought you were setting up a business.

Gary   I'm taking care of my kids.

Karen   They're at school all day! You can't go on like this. Daddy put up with worse. Much worse.

Gary   And he made sure we knew about it. I'm not dealing with the same shit.

Karen   It isn't the same.

Gary   She treated me like some house nigger.

Karen   Do you have to use that word?

Gary   Am I wrong?

Karen   It was better than no job. Just because you didn't get what you wanted.

Gary   No. Because/

Karen   Stop, I don't wanna hear it again. What did the other firms say?

Gary   I'm not working for nobody. I can't let them do that to me any more. Either you turn into one of their victims or you end up thinking like them.

Karen   Forget them, just be yourself.

Gary   I'm working out who I am.

Karen   You're too old for this Malcolm X shit, Gary.

Gary   Think of all the times we've been held back, all the opportunities we never had. Mr Franks at school, he told us boys to sit in the bath and scrub our skins with nailbrushes because it might wash the black off.

Karen   Mr Franks was a cunt.

Gary   We pretended we didn't care but we did Karen. We cared about all of it. They've damaged us with their looks and their words, they've made little cuts into our souls.

Karen   You can't keep looking back.

Gary   Why did we accept it?

Karen   I dunno. To fit in, to not get beat up, to keep going.

Gary   Well it wasn't worth it. There's generations of us, lost, we could have become big people, somebodies. I'm not staying silent any more. They have to listen.

Karen   To what? You're sat indoors twatting around with this rat thing.

Gary   I'm taking time, to think.

Karen   About what?

Gary   I got stopped every week from when I was fifteen, for years. Stopped, for just . . . walking from one place to another. And I never even checked it, because it became normal. That's got to make you think about yourself in a certain way. I knew what Victoria was like, I know what they're all like, I felt it for years. On the news they go on about how different things are now, and they're so pleased with themselves. But nobody ever asks us how it was or what it's done. (*A beat.*) Remember when the police grabbed Daddy off the street.

Karen   Daddy was a drunk.

Gary   They didn't have to beat him up. (*A beat.*) Just because he was there.

Karen   Why are you doing this?

Gary   It happened Karen. And if we don't say it, who will? Daddy said they always treat you like the invader. The alien.

Karen   Daddy said Kunta Kinte was his Great-Uncle.

Gary   You know what I mean.

Karen   We're here, yeah, so we've got to find a way of living together.

Gary   Living? Us lot, we've hardly survived. Do you know the Caribbean population in this country is dying out? The Africans are taking over. One more generation and we'll be gone.

Karen   Like you ever dated a sister. Your wife's white. Your best friend's white . . .

Gary   I'm talking about the bigger picture.

Karen   I'm practically the only Black person you know!

Gary   You won't listen. Because you won't face it.

Karen   I face it every day. You think you're educating me? I'm not letting them stop me. I'm not letting anybody stop me. Because I'm gonna fucking well live my life. And I wanna live more than I want to join your fight. (*A beat.*) What if the other geezer, who got the job, was better?

Gary   He wasn't.

Karen   How do you know he didn't do a killer interview, lick her out afterwards, make her come seven times?

Gary   You are disgusting!

Karen   Shit happens at work. Shit happens with white people. You should have ignored it.

Gary   It wasn't fair.

Karen   Are you five years old? What's fair? Wayne walked out, shamed me, destroyed everything I thought was true. But I'm not fiddling with razor blades in front of *Come Dine With Me*, am I? Because I know I'm worth something, no matter what some white woman thinks.

Gary   Wayne followed his instinct.

Karen   You're a Dad and a husband. Fucking get on with it. You should be out there.

Gary   If I stay in here, they can't touch me. And I can plan on making my next move.

Karen   So make it, Gary!

Nicky *enters with clothes. Finds a basin under the sink. Soaks the clothes.*

Karen   What's that smell?

Nicky   Tyler had an accident.

Gary   He's getting too old for this. If that was me, Daddy would have beaten my sorry arse till it bled.

Nicky   Something's going on at school. He said the other kids won't let him play on the slide.

Gary   Boy should stand up for himself. I'll talk to him.

Nicky   Be gentle. He's a bit . . . anxious.

Gary   And who's made him like that? You treat him like a baby.

Nicky   He's under the weather . . .

Gary   You're on him the whole time. It's like it's just you and him.

Karen   Nic knows what she's doing.

Gary   Really? She's got Ron doing these tests day and night.

Nicky   He wants to do them.

Gary   And Mia's eyes are stuck to that phone. You should talk to the girl.

Nicky   You talk to her. They'll all need new coats soon.

Gary   My kids have got everything they need.

Nicky   You dressed them recently? Been in their bedroom?

Gary   Course I have. You wanna get rid of them stupid Harry Potter books. Start teaching them some Black history.

Karen   You do it.

Gary   I'm teaching them stuff every day. Preparing them for how they're gonna be treated.

Karen   That sounds like fun.

Mark *enters carrying beers.*

Mark   Present.

Gary (*downs tools*)   Nice one. Thought you were going out with that Lisa.

Mark   She can't make it.

Nicky   Rio's mum?

Mark   Yeah.

Karen   Lisa's got a boyfriend you div.

Mark   He ditched her. Said Rio was rude. Told her off for not slapping him.

Gary   Order a couple of pizzas, Nic. (*To* **Mark**.) Or do you fancy Indian?

Mark   Pizza. Yeah, Pizza.

Nicky   I found a pack of mince in the freezer. Thought I'd make Bolognese.

Gary   That'll take hours.

Nicky   I haven't got any cash.

Mark   I can get pizzas! (*Produces cash.*)

Gary   Shut up man, put that away!

He takes a twenty pound note out of his wallet, hands it to **Nicky**. *She stands still for a moment, holding the money.*

Karen   Fucking hell, this is a joke!

Gary   If you don't wanna be here, go.

Nicky   It's okay, Karen.

Gary *opens a can of beer.* **Mark** *follows suit.*

Gary   Lisa's a nice girl. Keep knocking that door.

Mark   I ain't bothered about her.

Nicky (*to* **Gary**)   You're supposed to be collecting Mia from gymnastics.

Gary   One beer!

Mark   We'll pick her up Nic. Sit down, have a drink.

Karen (*pointed*)   How's work Mark?

Mark   Half our jobs got cancelled this afternoon. Victoria's messed up the rota.

Gary   What?

Mark   She's not concentrating properly. Si and Chas say they saw her crying at her desk. Them lot are starting to feel sorry for her.

Gary   Sorry for Victoria?

Mark   And she went off sick yesterday.

Gary   There's nothing wrong with her.

Mark   Innit. She made up some nonsense about a migraine after Nic came to see her.

Nicky *freezes.* **Gary** *takes this in. Silence.*

Gary (*to* **Nicky**)   You went into the office? (*A beat.*) Why . . . why would you do that?

Nicky   I wanted to talk to her. To see if there was any way . . .

Gary   Any way?

Nicky   I just wanted to see if you . . . if you might be able to get your job back.

Gary   Fucking hell Nicola. Fuck!

Nicky   To make her realise . . .

Gary   Behind my back!

Nicky *can't respond.*

Gary   Why didn't you tell me?

Nicky   I only went because I thought it might help . . .

Gary   Because you have to take care of me? Because you don't think I'm capable of providing for this family?

Nicky   Go and do it then.

Gary   And what did she say? I mean when do I start back?

Nicky   She wouldn't listen to me.

Gary   Am I this problem you and Victoria need to sort out?

Nicky   No . . .

Gary   Can't leave anything alone can you? You think sticking one of your dibby plasters over an open wound's gonna make a difference? Well it's not, cos this one's gonna bleed and bleed . . . You've got the same infection in your head as the rest of them.

Nicky   I haven't.

Gary   Victoria's fine if we're cleaners or serving in the canteen or driving a van. I don't even want that job. I want more than what she decides I'm allowed to do. And you, you're dragging me backwards.

Karen   Calm down Gary!

Gary (*to* **Karen** *and* **Nicky**) Both of you . . . you don't see it . . . you don't believe me.

Nicky   I believe you.

Gary   Is me crawling back there what you want the kids to see their dad doing?

Nicky *shakes her head.*

Gary   Who do you even think they are?

Nicky   They are our children!

Gary   Black children, but you keep trying to make them like you. You English . . . and your little England. Using your Henry the eighth education to whiten our boy.

Nicky   Stop talking like this!

Gary   You're my girl Nic. My girl. You're supposed to be mine and I'm supposed to be yours . . . And you went down on your knees in front of her.

Nicky   No, I didn't.

Scene Eight

Later that night. **Mark** *finishes tidying up.* **Nicky** *enters.*

Mark   I done the washing up.

Nicky   Thanks.

Mark   Is he asleep?

Nicky *nods blankly.*

Mark   You alright?

Nicky   He's been hitting kids in his class. Ronnie and Mia never did anything like that. Gary's mood . . . he can sense it.

Mark   Course.

Nicky   Those kids are my hope. Feels like they're slipping through my fingers.

Mark   No. You're their everything.

Nicky   You know, when Tyler cries. I don't even mind. Because as soon as I hold him, he stops and then when he closes his eyes, I could lie there forever . . .

Mark (*a beat*)   Do you want me to get you a take away?

Nicky *shakes her head.*

Nicky   Karen reckons Gary needs time. What do you think?

Mark   He's . . . changing.

Nicky   Why does everyone think I should give him minutes and moments and space? He should understand that I was doing my best . . . at least I was doing my best.

Mark   You were.

Nicky   Mark, can you make him see sense?

Mark   Try and forget it, yeah. Just for now.

He takes out his wallet, removes notes, holds them out.

Here.

Nicky   Don't be stupid.

Mark   I want you to have it. You deserve it. Go on! When was the last time you bought a fancy perfume or a new pair of boots or one of them coffees with cream on top?

Nicky   Can't remember.

Mark *leaves the money on the table.*

Mark   A girl like you, you shouldn't let yourself go. Gary wouldn't want that.

Nicky (*a beat*)   Can I tell you something?

Mark *nods.*

Nicky   Don't say nothing to Gary.

Mark   Okay.

Nicky   Promise.

Mark   I won't.

Nicky   I told Gary that Tyler wet himself.

She starts to laugh.

But he actually stood up and pissed on his uniform.
On purpose.

Mark *joins in the laughter.*

Nicky   It's not funny. But it is funny, he just stood there and . . .

They laugh some more.

Mark   You're a survivor, Nic.

Nicky   Thanks.

Mark   I told Gaz, you know. That your intentions were good.

Nicky   And?

Mark   Gary's . . . he's a good man. But he doesn't get it.

Nicky   Has he said anything?

Mark   No. I dunno.

Nicky   What? Tell me.

Mark   He's . . . not sure.

Nicky   About me?

Mark *nods.*

Nicky   But . . . that's because he's angry isn't it?

Mark   How do you feel?

Nicky *half shrugs.*

Mark (*a beat*)   What if . . . what if you and him are done?

Nicky   We can't be.

Mark   He's on the edge with this, Nic. I mean he's really on the edge.

Nicky   He'll come back.

Mark   What if he doesn't? What if he doesn't want to?

Nicky (*a beat*)   Is that what he said?

Mark *doesn't respond.*

Nicky   He'll calm down, eventually he will.

Mark (*a beat*)   If I had a girl like you, I'd never shout or do nothing bad. I wouldn't sit around all day.

Nicky   You?

Mark   Yeah. (*A beat.*) Your Dad . . . you remember . . . your dad always liked me ennit.

Nicky   No he didn't.

Mark   He liked me better than Gaz.

Nicky (*slowly*)   Why are you always here, Mark?

Mark   For you lot, for the kids . . .

Nicky (*realising*)   No . . .

Mark   You're a special girl Nic. Gary doesn't realise how lucky he is. And you always make my tea just how I like it. Two and a half sugars. Dash of milk. You're kind to the kids, even when Ty dropped your phone down the toilet, you never raised your voice . . .

Nicky   Don't . . .

Mark   I'm here Nic. I've always been here.

Nicky (*a beat*)   I don't want you coming round no more.

Mark   But I wanna help . . .

Nicky   Go Mark.

Mark   Nic . . .

Nicky   You need to be in your own place.

Mark   Hang on, you've got this wrong/

Nicky   Get out and don't come back.

Mark   Are you serious?

Nicky   Leave your keys.

Mark *doesn't move.*

Nicky   Leave them!

He chucks the keys on the table. Exits. Shocked **Nicky** *beholds them.*

Scene Nine

The next day. Friday. **Nicky** *stares at an envelope. She tears it open. Reads. Breathes. Reads again. Agitated* **Anjum** *hurries in. She holds a letter. The two women stare at each other. They exchange letters and read.*

Anjum   I don't believe it . . . I was sure. Point nought two decimal points. That's . . . cruel.

Nicky   It is.

Anjum   At least he was close, Zaki was nowhere. You should definitely appeal.

Nicky   They say appeals are a waste of time.

Anjum   Did he go in today?

Nicky   Yeah.

Anjum   Our letter came first thing so I kept Zaki at home.

Nicky   How is he?

Anjum   Won't stop crying. Mo's made it clear that he won't pay for private school because that money's our pension, and his air fare to the cricket World Cup. He's insisted Zaki calculate how much we spent on past papers and tutors, oh and petrol. Mo reckons it's good maths practice. I said there's no point torturing him, but Mo's adamant, Zaki needs to reflect on how much effort we've put in. (*A beat.*) How's Gary?

Nicky   Quiet.

Anjum   He took a stand, that's something to be proud of.

Nicky   This is all . . . it's . . . out of control.

Anjum   There's an element here that . . . you can't understand.

Nicky   I've shared a bed with him since I was sixteen, felt his heart beat next to mine every night, watched him get fat, held him in my arms while he cried like a baby when we buried his Mum. Me and Gary are more the same than any other two people in this world.

Anjum   Right.

Nicky   When a man like him doesn't work, it's not good.

Anjum   Once he finds something that'll change.

Nicky   Are there any jobs going with Mo? Gary might say yes if you asked . . .

Anjum   I'm not sure . . .

Nicky   Or I could help, unpacking, checking the stock, cleaning. Cash in hand. Whatever you need . . .

Anjum   I'll ask, but Mo . . . tends to employ relatives.

Nicky   Okay.

Anjum   I will ask though.

Nicky   Thanks.

Anjum   Mo couldn't have picked a worse weekend for the Autumn Fair. He's such an idiot.

Nicky   I don't know if Gary's gonna manage to do the bouncy castle and all that.

Anjum   Don't worry.

Nicky (*a beat*)   What will you do about secondary school?

Anjum   Er . . . it's not ideal, but . . . we're going for Ashfield.

Nicky   That's . . . that's miles away.

Anjum   Well, we prepared for the worst-case scenario.

Nicky   How?

Anjum   We rented a flat opposite the school six months ago. It isn't quite what we want but it is one of the best comprehensives.

Nicky (*knocked*)   You mean . . . you're alright?

Anjum   Mo sorted it. They ask for a utility bill so we went round there every Saturday night to watch telly and heat up a few pizzas. We're hoping we don't have to move in, but if it's necessary . . .

Nicky   So . . . Zaki was always gonna be alright.

Anjum   We needed a Plan B.

Nicky   Why didn't you say anything?

Anjum (*a beat*)   Mo and I are really glad we were able to support Ronnie and get him to this point.

Nicky   Zaki wouldn't have gone to the tutor without Ron.

Anjum   Nicky, that's a slight exaggeration.

Nicky   He told him!

Anjum   Zaki says all sorts of silly things.

Nicky   My boy was only there to help yours. (*A beat.*) I can't believe you actually rented a place. Some people can't afford to pay the rent on their own flats.

Anjum   We've worked hard.

Nicky   Anjum, you haven't even got a job! You're taking a school place that doesn't belong to you, handing your boy another kid's future.

Anjum   Most parents would do the same if they had the chance.

Nicky   I hope to fuck I wouldn't.

Anjum   Education is a game and you don't know how to play. You only went for the eleven plus because I reached out to you. So now you're no worse off than you would have been before.

Nicky   Course we are, we've seen the other side.

Anjum   What side?

Nicky   The life that's out there if you pay for it.

Anjum   You had no back up for Ronnie. That's where you failed.

Nicky   You've dished out the same shit as the system you complain about.

Anjum   Would you be saying that if Ronnie had got in? You knew exactly what you were doing and you were perfectly happy to take part in the competition.

Nicky   Because he's clever.

Anjum   Because women like us worship our children Nicola, because they deserve to have what we never did.

Nicky   I can't . . . take this in . . .

Anjum   You have to be focussed, call the school, ask them to give him a shot in the second round.

Nicky   I'm not listening to you any more.

Anjum   Do you think this is easy? People like you, you expect things to happen because you haven't been taught how to think. You end up believing whatever lies you're being told.

Nicky   People like me?

Anjum   I'm trying to help you. You need to fight for what you want, to keep going till you fall to your knees and then you grab whatever you can. You're lucky, your son is outstanding, he'll be fine wherever he goes.

Nicky   That's the biggest lie.

Anjum   It's not my fault there aren't enough places at decent schools. Perhaps Mo's right, this country is full to the brim.

Nicky   Why shouldn't they come? Your family did.

Anjum   Britain owes us.

Nicky   And what does it owe me? (*A beat.*) That scarf's a mask. Underneath it, you're a liar.

Anjum (*a beat*)   You don't know who you are.

Nicky   What?

Anjum   You take a slice of Black culture, a piece of white, this, that and whatever else you can grasp. There's no solid base. It's bound to fall apart.

Nicky   You think you're stronger because you've got a culture?

Anjum   If anything happens to me, a hundred people stand up. If you went to hospital this second . . . who'd come for you?

Nicky *can't reply.*

Anjum   Mo was the one who wanted us to be friends. He kept saying, Gary and Nicky, they're alright. But I had an idea about the kind of people you are. It's sad the way your community lives . . . you're all so . . . lost.

Nicky Stop . . .

Anjum You can't help being broken Nicky, I get it, it's not your fault . . . You haven't got a clue about the world. You don't even understand your own kids.

Nicky What?

Anjum They're different from you.

Nicky No, they're not.

Anjum You know they are. You'll never know what they experience, how they feel. (*A beat.*) I'm sorry for you Nicky.

Anjum *exits. Through the baby monitor, the sound of Tyler crying.*

Scene Ten

Hours later. **Nicky**, *almost trancelike, sorts through a pile of books and hands various ones to* **Mo** *who is nervously holding a list.*

Mo There are no . . . er . . . acts for the talent show, so the stage won't need building.

Nicky Maths Made Easy?

Mo (*checks list*) Yeah.

She hands it to him.

Mo And . . . I think . . . face painting might be more of a . . . summer activity. But you are coming? I mean, you must come.

Nicky (*books*) Eleven Plus Success.

Gary *comes in carrying a few clothes. He and* **Nicky** *don't acknowledge each other.*

Mo Thanks. (*Checks list.*) Anj thinks you might have our 'How to master Verbal Reasoning' as well.

Nicky Must be in his room. (*She heads out.*)

Mo *beholds* **Gary** *who is getting a carrier bag for the clothes.*

Mo Zaki's beginning to realise the massive toll this has taken on me. I've never asked that boy for anything. All he had to do was answer a few questions on percentages and compound words, I mean we all speak the English language don't we? These kids . . . We should stick them in Gaza, see how they cope with Israeli bombs falling out of the sky. (*A beat.*) Your Ronnie'll survive. Our Zaki's weak. We've made him weak. He needs us to keep him together. (*A beat.*) Every move I make is for that family, there's nothing, not one thing left over for me. I know I pushed Zaki to his limit, but it was for his own good. Do you believe me?

Gary *nods.*

Mo   I feel like . . .

Gary   What?

Mo   Like . . . I've killed a part of him . . . I mean I haven't . . . Honestly, I love him so much, more than my own breath.

Gary   I know.

Mo   I don't want him to end up in the shop.

Gary   What's wrong with the shop?

Mo   People think I'm this . . . something . . . But I'm not. (*A beat.*) Gary, I know what you're gonna do.

Gary   Yeah?

Mo   When us lot were at school and you and Nicky used to come into the shop, I couldn't take my eyes off you two. She looked at you in this way and I wished I had someone who looked at me like that. She still does it. Gaz, you love someone who loves you back. That's the real thing. (*A beat.*) You turning your back on all this, is what they expect, out there. Don't be that man Gary. (*A beat.*) If you trash this, then we're all trashed.

Nicky *enters.*

Nicky   Here. (*Hands him book.*)

Mo   I'll see you tomorrow. (*Exits.*)

Gary *takes clothes out of a plastic tub. Folds them.*

Nicky   That lot's not dry.

Gary (*carries on*)   Which school will he go to now?

Nicky   Doesn't matter. The nearest ones are shit.

Gary   What's the choice?

Nicky   There is no choice.

Gary   You must have some idea.

Nicky   You never showed an interest before.

Gary   You never gave me the chance!

Nicky   He's better than the lot of them. He should be there. (*Observing* **Gary** *putting clothes into bag.*) What are you doing?

Gary (*carries on*)   I'm going to stay with Mark.

Nicky   For how long?

Gary   I dunno.

Nicky   What about the kids?

Gary   What did you take his keys for?

Nicky   I wanted them back.

Gary   That's my spar, I gave him those keys.

Nicky   Mark . . . doesn't belong here!

Gary   He hasn't got anybody else.

Nicky   This flat is our patch. There should be a boundary between him and us. Why do you need him hanging off you anyway?

Gary   He's family to us.

Nicky   Not to me! Where's his own life, his own people? We're not at school any more. (*A beat.*) He said something to me.

Gary   What?

Nicky   Something he shouldn't have.

Gary   Tell me.

Nicky   Like . . . Like he wanted to know.

Gary   Mark? (*A beat.*) No, no . . .

Nicky   You don't believe me?

Gary   Maybe you got it wrong.

Nicky   I haven't.

Gary *freezes, takes this in.*

Nicky   Gary, I'm really scared. We need money . . .

Gary   I never wanted to apply for that job Nic.

Nicky   You said you did.

Gary   I should have stopped the whole thing after she came round. I only carried on because it was your dream.

Nicky   Gary, there are things I don't . . . can't understand but you can't go because I made one mistake.

Gary   What if you and me's the mistake?

Nicky   Leave then. Go and drown in your anger. Blame me, the kids, everyone except you. You don't want to see reality.

Gary   I can't bear what I see. I can't, okay? If that means I'm not the man you want me to be . . . then I'm not.

Nicky   You are. You were right. About setting up on your own. I'll help.

Gary   You're always pushing, aren't you? Me and Ron . . .

Nicky   So he wouldn't have to go through shit.

Gary   Don't you realise how this thing works? If he becomes a lawyer do you reckon he'll ever become a judge? And if he's a doctor, he ain't gonna be no consultant.

Nicky   We can't let the kids think like that.

Gary   If he got in to the grammar school, it wouldn't make a difference. You know it Nic. You feel it when you walk down the road with them. People might say they're beautiful and admire their hair but they're gonna treat them like they're less, they're gonna expect them to be less. That's why you keep pushing, but it's no use.

Nicky   I just . . . want to protect them.

Gary   You have to protect our kids because they're Black?

Silence.

Gary   I used to think this was enough.

Nicky   It was, it is. Stay, please. I promise I'll stop dreaming.

Gary   You just tried to do your best. And you were right, this life, the way we've been living, it isn't enough. But not for the reasons you said.

Nicky   We're going through a shit time, it'll change.

Gary   It's done Nic.

Nicky   Everything that's happened, it's made you see us as different, you never used to. That's what Victoria does.

Gary   You don't understand . . .

Nicky   She's made you see it, when before, you and me, we were free.

Gary   No, I'm more free than I've ever been. This is me, now.

Nicky   How do we get from you, back to us?

Gary *takes his bag and heads out.* **Nicky** *watches him go. Silence. She tries to compose herself but starts to shake. She tries tidying but drops a cup.*

Suddenly through the baby monitor, the muffled sound of a boy urinating on clothes. Then two children coming into the room, laughing and screaming.

Shouts of 'Mum . . . Tyler'.

Nicky   For fuck's sake.

Nicky *hurries upstairs. Through the monitor, we hear a bedroom door open. Then we hear her grab Tyler.*

Nicky (*monitor/muffled*)   I told you before . . . you don't mess up your uniform. You . . . disgusting . . . You're supposed to be proud of it!

Sound of **Nicky** *beating Tyler hard with slaps and punches. Sound of Tyler crying and Mia and Ronnie shouting at her to stop.*

Nicky (*monitor/muffled*)   I'm sorry . . . I'm sorry . . .

Sounds stop dead.

Assorted children's toys – small cars, Lego pieces, action figures, cuddly animals fall from the ceiling onto the floor of the living area.

Scene Eleven

The next morning. Saturday. **Gary** *watches a shaken* **Karen** *pick up the toys. She packs them into a holdall.*

Gary   I'm here now.

Karen   What use is now?

Gary   Karen . . .

Karen   Be quiet. It's you that's made this happen. You and your pride . . . your arrogance . . . Couldn't just go back to work, could you?

Gary   That's . . . that's my boy you're taking!

Karen   Would you rather it was social workers packing his rucksack? Because once a GP sees the state of him, that's you and Nic done with all of them.

Nicky *enters, observes them both. She is dazed, numb.*

Nicky   I . . . I didn't mean to . . .

Karen *continues to pick up the toys.*

Karen   You two . . . you two were it. Fucking it!

Nicky   What's happened to me?

Karen   You should have gone to see someone.

Nicky   I don't know . . . what happened to me . . .

Karen   You should have got pills from the doctor or . . . or . . . something. Why didn't you?

Nicky (*a beat*)   They're supposed to be going to the fair. Gary, tell her . . .

Gary   They have to go with Karen.

Nicky   No, they don't.

Gary   They want to. All of them.

Silence as **Nicky** *takes this in.*

Nicky   I won't do anything like that. Ever again. I swear. If you like I'll walk into the police station or whatever you say . . . I'm alright now. Back to who I was. (*To* **Karen**.) You . . . you . . . don't know what pasta Tyler eats or what story to read him or how much bubble bath to use.

Karen   I'll figure it out.

Nicky   They didn't come out of your body.

Gary   It's only for a while.

Karen *zips up the bag, she's ready to go.*

Nicky (*to* **Gary**)   You actually want them to leave? How can you want that? Where are they?

Karen   In the car.

Nicky   Have you left the them alone, outside? Fucking hell!

Karen   The kids are with me, yeah? Me.

Nicky   I can't stay away from them.

Karen *leaves.* **Nicky** *crumbles almost into a heap.* **Gary** *goes to hold her.*

Gary   It's gonna be alright.

Nicky *shakes her head.*

Gary   Stay close to me Nic . . . just be close . . . and this . . . this'll come good.

Nicky   No . . . no . . .

Gary   You and me . . . we'll stay inside . . . shut the door . . . lock ourselves up . . . and then . . . then we'll be free.

Lights fade.

Epilogue

1994. **Gary**, *15, and* **Nicky**, *14, are on top of a hill in the park. They share a cigarette and a can of cider. It's after school but they have taken their ties off, so they wear black trousers/skirt and white shirts.* **Nicky** *is lying down.*

Nicky   Sun's burning my eyes.

Gary   Move then girl.

Nicky   I like it.

Gary   You're mad.

Nicky *sings a few lines from Whitney Houston's 'I Have Nothing'.*

Gary   You singing to me?

Nicky   No.

Gary   Yeah you are . . .

Nicky   They keep playing it on the radio.

Gary   And you close your eyes and see me . . .

Nicky   Don't be stupid.

They laugh nervously, stare at each other. **Gary** *kisses her.*

Gary   Was that alright?

Nicky   Yeah.

Gary   I feel like I can say anything to you.

Nicky   You can.

They retreat, not quite knowing what to do. They look down the hill.

Nicky   Little Mark just fell off his bike. See? (*They laugh.*)

Gary   That's the whole world down there.

Nicky   Shut up, it's only the estate. Concrete flats and green fields somewhere far.

Gary   And those big houses the other side. Where all them big people live.

Nicky   Oh yeah.

Gary   You'll be living in one of them in a few years. I'll turn up in my MG, double breasted suit, brand new Rolex round my wrist. Knock the door and you'll sing to me. (*A beat.*) Look, people are going indoors.

Nicky   Wonder what they're doing.

Gary   Cooking, cleaning, shouting, screaming . . . I don't care.

Nicky   I'll have to go soon.

Gary   Do you wanna go home?

Nicky   No.

Gary   Will your dad come looking for you?

Nicky   Doubt it.

Gary   Thought he would.

Nicky   Nothing's what you think. (*A beat.*) He doesn't care about me. It's your blood he's after.

Gary   Then you don't have to go.

He kisses her again. They retreat awkwardly.

Nicky   What shall we do?

Gary   Stay up here.

Nicky   For how long?

Gary   Forever.

She laughs.

Gary   Why not?

They laugh, look down again.

Gary   The city's beautiful isn't it?

Nicky   From here, yeah.

Gary   I like it. It's a good place. Keep watching. And one day it'll be ours.

Nicky   You reckon?

Gary   Yeah . . . yeah, it's gonna be . . . all ours.

THE END

Scenes from Lost Mothers

First performed at the University of Hertfordshire on 6th February 2025.

A Clean Break and University of Hertfordshire co-commission, based on Dr Laura Abbott's research project Lost Mothers.

Cast

A	**Shabina Cannon**
B	**Ro Florence**
C	**Claire Bayley**

Creatives

Writer	Gurpreet Kaur Bhatti
Director	Anna Herrmann
Designer	Jida Akil
Composer & Sound Designer	Holly Khan
Assistant Director	Neetu Singh
Movement Director	Corinne Meredith
Workshop Facilitators	Andrea Lowe, Shona Babayemi

Scene One – Baby Sweets

A woman, **A***, is in prison. She puts sweets on her pregnant tummy.*

A   Your mummy's here, baby. Right here. You have your sweets. All the sweets in the whole wide world. Red, yellow, green, orange. I want you to taste the rainbow colours, savour every single flavour. I'm gonna make being your mum the greatest thing I've ever done. I'll get you tiny trainers and wipe your cheeks clean. I'll treasure every sound that comes out of your mouth and you'll make a mess and I won't say a word. And you and me . . . you and me, we'll ride on a roundabout and eat chicken nuggets and sing stupid songs and we'll party together. Dance so hard. So free. I can tell you're a mover. I know it. And when I feel you kicking, I know a bit of me can still dream.

Scene Two – The Body

Two women, **B** *and* **C***, sit on the floor.*

B   My body's stretched to hold this life that turns from a speck into human fruit. A strange bump sticking out. I'm carrying a new message.

C   Thick, swollen feet. My uterus presses hard on my bladder, I need to keep closing toilet doors. Pissing and pissing. I don't care because when it presses down, it's letting me know it's here.

B   Sick in my mouth and the sight of beige prison food makes it worse. My breasts hurt. I can take all of it. Precious agony. This will be the healing that saves me.

They stretch out and hold one another's hands. But they are still in their own worlds.

C   And then the real pain comes.

B   It's the day. The actual day.

C   I can't bear it . . .

B   You haven't got a choice.

C   So much pain.

B   Like someone hitting you on the back with a cement mixer.

C   Again and again . . .

B   I can't . . .

C   You have to.

B   And then . . .

C   And then . . .

B   Like fucking magic.

C   This beauty appears.

B   Out of me.

C   And there is a moment of bliss.

B   Pure bliss.

C   Better than any drug you ever touched.

B   And I'm holding him.

C   Her. Our eyes lock.

B   And nothing else matters.

C   That one second is my perfect eternity.

B   He's my jewel.

C   She's my jewel.

B   And then I don't know what to do.

C   The stitches make new wounds that tear me up.

B   When I get back, do I have to take him into the shower with me? Is that normal?

C   Is this normal?

B   Is he okay with the water and the steam in the shower? Is he okay? Tell me!

C   I have to keep this jewel safe.

B   What if he breaks or I smash something.

C   What am I supposed to do?

B   I don't know how . . . to even breathe . . .

C   I'm jangling inside . . .

B   And my mind's gone dark.

C   I don't know.

B   Anything.

C   Please, I really don't fucking know.

B   And nobody tells me.

Scene Three – No Room at the Inn

B   Social worker just said I can't go. I don't get it . . . Why not me? I mean, aren't me and the baby what the place is for? . . . But I just stand there with my big wide-open mouth and take it in . . .

The officer smiles and sort of plays with loud clunky keys, she keeps playing with them and I can't cope with the sound and I say to her . . . whatever her name is . . . Miss Whatever . . . you've got negative energy. You wanna . . . burn some sage or something. Clean the air you've been polluting. She's eyeing me and it's like my baby's done something wrong. So it has to be punished.

No space for a girl like me. I'm that Mary from the Bible. Only there's no donkey or stable and definitely no pissing Joseph.

I . . . go to work. Grab a few seconds of sleep. Listen to madness day after day. Wear a big baggy top so that no-one guesses, so that no-one tries to fuck me up. Eat this nothing food. Then she calls me podgy for a laugh and I don't know why but tears start pouring down my cheeks and I can't stop and Miss Whatever's like . . . Sorry. Sorry . . . Sorry. And I'm . . . like . . . what's your sorry gonna do? You gonna help me? You wanna help. Help me? Help me!

I'm carrying this baby inside but just under my womb, deep in my flesh, I can feel my shame, swimming in its own amniotic. Why not me? Why never me?

You wait, when I get out, I'll have another baby. And then another and another. I'll carry on until . . . until they let me keep one. They must let me keep just one . . .

Burn the sage, Miss Whatever. Go on. Burn it. Let us both burn.

Scene Four – In the Hospital

C *puts her hands together as though they are in handcuffs.*

C   People are staring. And not because they recognise me off

EastEnders. They see the cuffs and they're frightened. I'm frightened too. What is this thing? This animal I've been made that requires a leash in the hospital around nurses and doctors. Kittens and puppies get six weeks with their mummies. My baby'll get three days. When I had the first scan, one of the zookeepers said I was in for a special treat. Long cuffs. I thought they weren't supposed to use them, but he took them out anyway. Long cuffs. He said I could still move but not run away. Like when I went to the toilet. He was the first man to see my baby on the monitor. I wanted my partner, but they sent the wrong appointment time. Computer error. When I was in labour, I kept asking them to call him, but the zookeepers said they needed authorisation. I asked and asked, started shouting. In the end, the doctor rang him. He got stuck in traffic. I was gonna breastfeed but the zookeeper was watching over me, so I asked for a bottle. Afterwards, I walk out of the hospital with three zookeepers and no cub. No cub. I catch sight of us all in a mirror and it's a picture of a moving cage. It's weird. People are staring. They can't stop. I don't blame them.

Scene Five – Getting Stuff

A woman, **B***, approaches a prison officer,* **A***.*

B   Where's Miss?

A   Off sick. I'm covering.

B   Oh . . . er . . . I need something.

A   What's that?

B   I'm leaking.

A   Leaking?

B   Yeah.

A   Like a faulty tap?

B   The milk.

A   Oh. Oh . . .

B   There are breast pads. To soak it up.

A   Right . . .

A *leaves.* **B** *waits.* **A** *returns, holds out a sanitary towel.*

B   That's a . . . for periods. Miss always gives me the proper things.

A   I couldn't find them. So I used my imagination. Thought you could tear it in half.

B *takes it.*

A   Use the other half next time. Then there's no waste.

B   But it's not . . . it isn't the right thing.

A   I did look. You saw me.

B   Yeah.

A   I can't be ransacking the place. Can I?

B   No.

A   It's better than nothing. Would you rather have nothing?

B *shakes her head.*

A   There you go then. There you go . . .

Scene Six – Mother and Baby

Three women, **A**, **B** *and* **C** *are playing with their babies.*

A   She won't sleep. Midwife said it should be easier to have a routine in prison . . . but she won't do what she's supposed to when they want.

B   Be glad.

C   Ennit. The girl's got spirit. Nobody's got the right to put her under manners.

B   Not a little baby girl.

A   She doesn't even cry. When she's awake she keeps looking around.

C   Her soul's inquisitive. Curious. This one wants to travel the world.

B   Have an adventure.

A   This must be what happy is.

B   I'm gonna rub HMP out from the birth certificate.

A   They type it in ink.

B   Tippex then. I don't want him always to be from this place.

C   Fuck it. It's a bit of paper. Let him dazzle you with his fresh eyes. No old ideas about you. Just that you're his mum.

B   I can't wait to hear him say it.

C   They say Dada first.

B   What the actual?

C   It's easier. Something to do with the tongue. Plosives and all that.

B   How are you gonna manage when the time comes?

A   Time?

B   Eighteen months.

C   I'll be out before then.

A   Lucky.

B   I'll still be here. (*A beat.*) I hope he gets a nice family. A doctor mum or dad. Then if he catches flu or breaks his leg they'll see to it straight away. And there'll always be plasters in a bright box in a shiny bathroom.

A   You gonna let him go? Just like that.

B   I don't want him seeing me sad. So I'm getting ready. And when it's my turn. I'll be there for him.

A   I'm not letting her go.

B *and* **C** *laugh awkwardly.*

B   You?

A   Yeah.

C   You got anyone outside?

A   No-one.

C   Then don't be weak. Don't ever be weak. That's when you suffer the most.

B   Who knew tiny hands could hold your fingers so tight? Like they'll break one of your bones.

A   Makes you remember you're a real human.

They gently sing a nursery rhyme together to the babies.

Scene Seven – The Board Decides

A *is the same character from the previous scene.* **B** *is the* PMBLO, **C** *is the Chair of the Board.*

A   Is that it?

C   Yes.

A   Right.

C   I appreciate this isn't the decision you were hoping for. You are free to appeal.

A   Appeal?

C   Your Liaison Officer can explain.

B   You can ask if they'll change their minds. In the future.

A   The future.

C   That's all for today.

A   Can I ask a question? Please.

C   Of course.

A   What do I need to do?

C   I don't follow.

A   So you change your mind about her staying with me.

B   That's something we can talk about.

A   Sorry . . . but . . . I'm asking her, because it's her mind that's important.

C   This isn't a matter for today.

A   I know you don't believe in me . . . But . . . (*touches her heart*) in here . . . you know, all I want is a chance for my life to be different. For her. Because she's like . . . my . . . and I really think I can love her. I can love her in a way that nobody else can because . . . because she's my daughter. You know, she's my actual daughter. So . . . I get it . . . from your point of view . . . But if you can just give me an idea of what I need to do, then I can make a start . . .

C   As I said, this is not the appropriate moment . . .

A   I'm begging you . . .

C   I think it's time to go.

A   No, I'm not moving . . . you have to tell me.

B   This situation is bound to take time to process.

A (*shouts*)   I said I'm not moving!

Silence.

A   I'm on my knees. Rockbottom. I know that. I just need . . . a leg up
. . . from somebody . . . then I might be able . . .

C   I'm afraid you're going to have to go.

A   No.

B   You have to.

B *and* **C** *move* **A** *from the space.*

Scene Eight – Separation

A *and* **B** *are the same characters from the previous scene.* **C** *is a social
worker.*

A *'s baby is in a car seat, the back of which faces the audience.*

A *stares at the car seat.*

C   Are you okay?

A *nods.*

C   You can leave, if you'd prefer.

A   I'm alright.

B   There isn't much time left.

A   I just . . . I . . . don't want to miss a moment.

Silence.

C   I have to go now. Do you understand?

A   Yeah.

C *reaches for the car seat. Suddenly* **A** *goes to hug it.*

B *and* **C** *watch uneasily.*

C   It's time.

B *edges* **A** *away as* **C** *takes the car seat off.*

A *is centre stage. She opens her mouth to scream. Her scream is silent.*

B *looks on, disturbed.*

A *crumbles, drops to the floor.*

B *watches* **A** *slowly curl up into a small ball.*

Scene Nine – The Officer afterwards

C *is a prison officer, she is writing notes.* PMBLO **B** *(from the previous scene) enters.*

B   Did you call them?

C   Course I called them.

B   What did they say?

C   They'll come when they can.

B   When they can?

C   They're busy. Handing out medication or something.

B   Did you tell them she's upset?

C   Yeah.

B   That she's screaming? That she won't stop?

C   Cows cry when their calves are taken away. And they're alright after a few days.

B   She doesn't look alright.

C   How she looks is not your problem.

B   I know but . . . it just was . . . a lot, you know.

C   Prison's a lot. You'll get used to it.

B   She said it was like having her heart ripped out and slammed against the wall.

C   That's quite an extreme image.

B   Those were the words she used.

C   Extreme words don't help. Not in a situation like this.

B *seems to get upset.*

C   Are you . . . are you crying?

B   No . . .

C   You bloody are. Why are you crying?

B   I dunno . . .

C   Nobody's taken your baby away.

B   No, you're right . . . I think . . . I think I'm stressed.

C   You get stressed, they get stressed.

B   I'm sorry, yeah. I'm tired. I haven't had a break.

C   Should have taken the weekend off.

B   Yeah.

C   Why didn't you?

B   Can't turn anything extra down at the moment.

C   Don't worry about her. She'll be okay.

B   The screams are so loud. I can't stop hearing them in my head.

C   And what are you going to do about it?

Silence.

C   You've got a job. An important job that nobody out there wants to do. That girl needs you to be on it.

B   I know.

C   So stop the drama and fucking well pull yourself together.

Scene Ten – Where There Is Breath There Is Hope

*A social worker **B** is with **A** (from Scene 8). They are looking at a box. A few baby items are strewn around. **A** is quiet, emotional.*

B   It's a tender time.

A   Yeah.

*Silence. **A** picks up a baby blanket, inhales the scent.*

B   This could be a way of keeping a connection.

A   Maybe.

B   Only if you want to.

A   I think . . . I do . . .

B   What would you like to put inside?

A *picks up a hospital name tag. Examines it.*

A   Her wrist was so tiny . . . I can hardly remember . . .

She puts it in the box. Finds a cuddly rabbit.

A   This was the first toy she touched.

She puts a book in.

A   I read these words every night. Dog. Cat. Bear. Night after night. Do you think she recognised my voice?

B   Of course. She's been listening to you since she took her first breath.

A   I just . . . want her to remember the best of me.

B   She will.

A *closes the box.*

A   How does the pain stop?

B   Slowly.

A   What if it feels like it's gonna be never?

B   Slowly. Very slowly.

Scene Eleven – The Telling

PMBLO, **B**, *from Scene 9 is with a journalist,* **C**, *who is taking notes on her phone.*

B   There are things they say shouldn't be happening, but they happen anyway.

C   Why?

B   Because . . . that's how it is in there.

C   So this female prisoner was screaming for her child?

B   It was piercing.

C   And nobody went to help?

B   No

C   Why didn't you go?

B   I was called to another wing.

C   So she was left alone?

B   Yeah.

C   For how long?

B   I'm not sure.

C   Five minutes? Five hours?

B   I can't say exactly.

C   If this story is going to fly, I need details.

B   I can't remember! But the noises she made . . . were unbearable. Like an animal.

C   An animal?

B   You have to see it. Then you feel it. Plus, we don't have the right stuff. Sometimes we don't have any stuff. And the food's not good enough. Not for the ones who are growing babies. It's like we're giving them a bad start, the wrong start.

C   And you're prepared to go on the record?

B   My name?

C   Yes.

Silence.

C   You said this was important.

B   We're not allowed . . . we're not supposed to . . . say stuff.

C   What do you want me to do?

B   Make sure people know. That's what you do, isn't it?

C   I need your name.

B   This is my job.

C   How brave are you? Actually brave?

B *shakes her head.* **C** *slowly walks off.*

B   I want to do a good job. (*A beat/loud.*) That's all I want.

B *is left alone on stage. On the verge of breaking down.*

Scene Twelve – My Son

A woman, **C**, *addresses the audience.*

C   They say my boy can come to live inside with me. The liaison officer and the social worker and the prison officers, all of them. They're being really kind. My little one's with my auntie. She's had him from when he was tiny. I couldn't cope at the start. I couldn't . . . do anything . . . Now, I reckon I can. But my auntie, she wants to keep him. Says this isn't a decent environment. What do I think I'm doing bringing him into this? She says he knows her, trusts her, they've . . . bonded. She doesn't want him damaged any more. I told her, thanks, yeah. But . . . these people here, they say I can do something, I can be something. Thanks yeah, but he's my baby. My son. It's not perfect, I'm not perfect. But show me some respect, yeah? Let me have a tiny spot of dignity . . . Because . . . because there's a gap in my arms, where he belongs.

Scene Thirteen – Twice a Month

B, *a woman in prison, is with her social worker, played by* **A**.

A   Do you understand the implications?

B   Yes.

A   Are you sure?

B   Yes.

A   You might feel differently in a couple of weeks.

B   I won't.

A   I'm going to be honest, if you refuse to see your son now, it's likely to affect your chances further down the line.

B   Chances?

A   I need to make you aware. I mean . . . he's only being brought in twice a month . . .

B   I refuse.

A   I realise how difficult this must be . . .

B   Really.

A   Yes.

B   Do you live in my brain?

A   No . . .

B   Inside my skin, with my blood and my bones rattling around.
Every time he comes, he cries and I cry and my mum's in front of me,
bouncing him on her lap, trying not to pay attention to our tears and the
snot and she's shaking her head and not speaking but I know she's
sitting there thinking what the actual fuck and what did I do wrong to
make you like this and you know I'm struggling and stop making noise
because you are such a fucking disappointment. You're the devil. You
are the devil.

A   I don't believe your mother thinks that. Not at all.

B   The thing is . . . I actually . . . can't bear it. Every time he goes it's
like there's a knife left inside me . . . like when the surgeons on Casualty
mislay a scalpel after cutting you open.

Silence.

B   I know I made a mistake. Have you made a mistake ever?

A   Of course.

B   I thought so. Who hasn't, right?

A   Nobody.

B   Nobody. So . . . you could tell them to let me have him all the time?
(*A beat.*) What do you think?

A   That's not possible.

B   How about every Monday, Tuesday and Wednesday? Or every
Friday, Saturday and Sunday?

A   Not in this setting.

B   What's wrong with this setting? I mean I'm in here. We're all in
here. You lot put us in here.

Silence.

A   Twice a month is a positive start. I'd urge you to reconsider.

B   Thanks but . . . I'd rather not.

Scene Fourteen – Calling for help

A *and* **B** *are on a policy committee.* **C** *is a campaigner, reading through a document. She puts it down.*

A   Well?

C   I don't know what to say.

B   You agree with the recommendations?

Silence.

A   Speak.

C   I've read all this . . . stuff . . . before.

B   It's a slow process. Too slow . . . .

A   Which is why we have to keep making the case.

B   Public opinion is continually evolving and progress has been made.

A (*to* **C**)   Your campaigning has contributed to that.

B   The effort you've put in is so admirable.

A   And the fact that you've got lived experience of prison . . .

B   It's changed the tone of the report.

A   Definitely, government reports are not usually this . . . deeply informed.

C   The thing is . . . whatever the changes are . . . I'm just . . . I'm left with this question . . . and it keeps going round and round in my head . . . .

A   Go on.

C   Why are we sticking pregnant women in prison in the first place?

B   That is a longer conversation . . .

C   So, let's have it . . . where are the ideas?

A   We've got ideas.

C   I mean . . . halfway houses, weekend visits, mother and baby units in the community.

B   Those are all valid thoughts.

C   I'm tired of thoughts. There's too much damage being done. To women, to kids, to staff. We are sentencing whole families . . . and it's hard to recover. Some people do not recover.

A   This report is an offer, okay, it's an offer . . . so that institutions can make small changes that lead to bigger changes.

C   Or it means that nothing ever moves on for anybody . . .

A   It's easier for you, you're on the outside.

C   I wasn't before. The loss is . . . it's like an amputation . . .

A   We have to deal with the realities of the actual system – structures that we have no control over.

C   You have seen, you have heard . . . you know I'm right, you just won't say it.

B   Come on, you know we are doing our best.

C   This is shit.

A   I think we've talked enough for today.

C   You know!

B   Please, let's stay calm . . .

C   Nobody should be calm about this . . . not for one second longer. I'm asking you . . . I'm telling you . . . we cannot do this again and again . . . I cannot bear witness . . . We have to stop doing it. We have to stop. Just stop . . .

B *and* **A** *retreat, leaving* **C** *on the stage on her own.*

Scene Fifteen – A New Dream

B *sits with her liaison officer* **C***, who is on a computer.*

C   I emailed them again. Should get a response any minute.

B   I'm excited.

C   You deserve to be. It's all ahead of you.

B   How do you mean?

C   Life.

B I'm gonna get a job. Coffee shop or Morrisons or something. I don't care what but I'm taking my space in this world. Gonna ride a bike again. I might even join a choir.

C *checks computer.*

B Has it come?

C Not yet. (*A beat.*) What are you looking forward to the most?

B Us being on our own in the flat. Plus, I wanna push her down a slide and watch her fly.

C The way you are with your daughter is golden.

B Thanks.

C Ah . . . here it is. Hang on . . .

She reads on her computer.

B Have they given a date?

C *takes a deep breath.*

C This isn't . . . what I was expecting. It seems the housing association haven't received the checks from the police and social services.

B What's happened?

C I'm not sure. They had all the documents weeks ago. I'll have to send everything again. So . . . frustrating. I'm . . . I'm really sorry.

B I don't get it.

C Unfortunately, the housing require the checks. They don't want a void so they've passed the accommodation on.

B On?

C To someone else.

A long silence.

B And what do we do?

C Wait until another property comes up.

B Where do I wait?

C Here. In prison . . .

B No . . .

C   It hopefully won't be much longer.

B   No!

She gets up, points at **C**.

B   And you mucked up my ROTL that time. You mucked it up and I never said anything.

C   I realise this isn't fair.

B   Fuck your fair! Out there, you get badges that say Baby On Board. People stand up to give you a seat. They're happy for you, ask you what you're gonna call it and what car seat are you getting . . . It's like your new possibility is their possibility and I've never known none of that. None of it! Because this place squashes every single tiny piece of hope . . .

C   Listen, this . . . sometimes the way agencies communicate is . . . chaotic and not joined up.

B   You are setting my girl up for failure.

C   No. This is a setback, yes . . . I appreciate it's a setback.

B   Yeah.

C   But do not let it defeat you. (*A beat.*) I'm going to do everything I can to sort this out.

B   Really?

C   People do care. And they are fighting for this . . . whole thing to be better.

B   Okay.

C   The best is yet to come for you. And for your daughter.

B   Yeah, right . . .

C   Please . . . hold onto that.

B   Yeah . . . yeah . . .

Scene Sixteen – The Touch of Kindness

Two women, **B** *and* **C** *bring on* **A**'s *box*

They start singing softly before leading **A** *in.*

They all sit together and sing. **A** *takes items out of the box and the others look on.*

When all the things are out of the box, **B** *and* **C** *put their arms around* **A** *and cradle her as if they are holding a baby.*

The singing gently subsides.

THE END

Marriage Material

This version of *Marriage Material* was first performed at the Lyric Hammersmith Theatre, London on 22 May 2025 with the following cast:

Cast

Jim/Bill/Tommy	**Tommy Belshaw**
Mr Bains/Arjan	**Jaz Singh Deol**
Surinder	**Anoushka Deshmukh**
Miss Flanagan/Claire/Reporter	**Celeste Dodwell**
Mrs Bains	**Avita Jay**
Kamaljit	**Kiran Landa**
Tanvir/Ranjit	**Omar Malik**
Dhanda	**Irfan Shamji**

Creative and Production Team

Writer	Gurpreet Kaur Bhatti
Adapted from the novel by	Sathnam Sanghera
Director	Iqbal Khan
Set & Costume Design	Good Teeth
Lighting Design	Simeon Miller
Composition & Sound Design	Holly Khan
Movement Direction	Anjali Mehra
Casting	Jatinder Chera
Associate Sound Design	Anna Wood
Associate Movement Direction	Rakhee Sharma
Voice & Dialect Coach	Gurkiran Kaur
Fight & Intimacy Direction	Dani Mac
Assistant Director	Harper K Hefferon
Company Stage Manager	Claire Bryan
Deputy Stage Manager	Georgia Rose
Assistant Stage Manager	Sarah Back
Production Manager	Lil Dickson
WHAM Supervisor	Sophia Khan
WHAM Head of Department	Christina Semertzaki
Lighting Programmer	Dan Miller
Lighting Operator	Alistair Warr
Sound Operator	Dan Ronayne/Scott Bradley
Fly Person	Tom McCreadie/Will Collins

Stage Crew — Charlotte Gregory
Wardrobe Assistant — Lola Kezunovic
Costume Consultant — Meghana Shah

Costume Supervision & Making — Lyric Costume Department
Turbans — Sukhvinder Singh Bamrah
Set Built — Liverpool Scenic Workshop
Lighting equipment supplied — White Light

Audio Description — Ruth James & Willie Elliot
Open Captioning — Miranda Yates
BSL Interpretation — Theatresign

PR — Bread & Butter PR
Rehearsal & production photography — Helen Murray
Poster image design — FEAST Creative
Poster image photography — Rich Southgate
Programme design — Hannah Yates

Characters

Mr Bains/Arjan	*South Asian male*
Mrs Bains	*South Asian female*
Dhanda	*South Asian male*
Tanvir/Ranjit	*South Asian male*
Surinder	*South Asian female*
Kamaljit	*South Asian female*
Jim/Bill/Tommy	*White male*
Miss Flanagan/Reporter/Claire	*White female*

Locations

Past

Bains' Living Area
Shop
Street
Restaurant
Bedsit

Present

Bains' Living Area
Shop
Shed
Street
Club
Flat
Lobby
Park
Wedding Hall

Tanvir *enters carrying a rack made out of wood.*

Tanvir   Uncle, I finished!

He holds a wooden rack, alongside bread, paper and string.

Tanvir   For the bread.

Mr Bains   Nice work, Tanvir.

Tanvir   Thank you, Uncle. And I made space for the brown paper and string. You take the bread, then the paper . . .

He tries to show them but keeps messing up. **Mrs Bains** *gets up and takes the items from him.*

Mrs Bains (*demonstrates*)   You take the bread, then the paper and tie it up in a bow.

Tanvir   That's right!

Mrs Bains   A loaf wrapped in brown paper and tied with string always looks fresh.

Tanvir   Extremely fresh!

Dhanda (*indicating rack*)   I could have bought you one of these from the market?

Tanvir   Only cheapie people purchase essential hardware from the market. I made this with my bare hands.

He proudly hands it to **Mr Bains**.

Tanvir   Built to last, like the London Bridge!

As **Mr Bains** *examines it, the structure immediately falls apart. They all stare at it.* **Tanvir** *tries to put it back together.*

Dhanda (*to* **Tanvir**)   You know Bill was a thief?

Mr Bains *has a coughing fit.*

Tanvir   That fellow is why Uncle's lungs are running out of breath.

Dhanda   The police must be throwing away the key, heh Birji?

Mrs Bains   The police let him go.

Dhanda   I will inform our Association.

Dhanda *gets up to leave.*

Prologue

1960s. Midlands. **Bains**' *living area – the Baithak – the area between the shop front and the kitchen. The shop counter is visible at one side, as is the kitchen on the other side, there should be a flow of activity between the different spaces. Cardboard boxes, filled with stock, are piled high.* **Mrs Bains** *kneels on the floor, pricing bars of soap.* **Mr Bains** *sits on a chair.* **Dhanda** *is on a low stool, both men are drinking tea.*

Dhanda   What do you expect? From a gora [*white man*]?

Mr Bains   Bill was my friend.

Dhanda   No, no, no! They are not our friends, Birji. My Charna came home from school crying because one of his 'friends' tried to cut off his topknot with a pen knife.

He turns to **Mrs Bains***.*

Dhanda   Remember what I said to you, Bhanji, about Bill.

Mrs Bains   You say lots of things, Prahji.

Dhanda (*not listening/points towards shop*)   He sat there eating humbugs, then once every hour he would take the newspaper into the toilet and I would be left on the counter. That kutha [*dog*] would leave the door open. The smell, Birji, the smell! These goreh do not smell like other humans. (*A beat.*) I knew he was lazy, a bad egg. But I never suspected he was rotten. Stealing! From you! After all you did for him. I blame myself.

Mr Bains   You?

Dhanda   You pay me to be your eyes, Birji. How could I let him deceive me?

Mrs Bains   Bill was too sneaky.

Mr Bains   Charging always full price but putting only half the money in the till.

Mrs Bains   And he was taking food, mainly custard creams and tinned peaches. Hiding them down his jean and under his bobble hat.

Dhanda   Kutha [*Dog*] . . . Haramjadah [*Bastard*] . . . Bhenjot [*Sisterfucker*]! Soon he will be getting into bed with Enoch. Mark my words, that one is getting ready to chuck a brick through your window.

Mrs Bains   Bill wouldn't.

Dhanda   They listen to me. You deserve justice.

Mr Bains   In this des [*country*]? Men like us?

Dhanda   If we organise ourselves correctly, these goreh will realise we are here to stay.

Mr Bains   Those Association idiots can't do nothing.

Dhanda   Let us see. (*Observes* **Tanvir** *trying to fix the broken rack.*) Leave that, Tanvir. I will buy you a new one, Birji. From the market.

He heads out.

Mr Bains   Patwant! Don't you want my blessing?

Dhanda *stops.* **Mr Bains** *turns to the others.*

Mr Bains   Patwant is opening a shop.

Mrs Bains   Kee [*what*]?

Mr Bains   Number 78 Victoria Road. The old butcher has a bad hip and his son wants to be a pop star, so they need someone to rent the lease. Patwant has been saving his pennies.

Dhanda (*a beat*)   You have been my everything, Birji. Father, mother, brother. You took in a poor boy and showed him how to be a man. I will never compete with you.

Mrs Bains   So why are you opening a shop?

Dhanda   I am planning to sell different stock. Pandeh [*dishes*], plugs, beer, whisky and the suchlike.

Mrs Bains   They say you make more money from beer than from white loaves and pear drops.

Dhanda   Bhanji, sharab is a hard business! The drunks are your best friends during the day but at closing time they pull down their trousers, show you their bottoms and call you Paki.

Dhanda *puts his hands together, half pleading, half apologetic to* **Mr Bains**.

Dhanda   Your blessing will give me and my missus hope for a life.

Mr Bains   You talk too much and too loudly, Patwant. But you are a hard worker and you have warmed my blood in this cold country. (*A beat.*) Give me your first bottle of Johnnie Walker when you open.

Dhanda *touches* **Mr Bains**'s *feet.*

Dhanda   When I look at my Charna, I wish I could give you half of my boy.

Mrs Bains   There are two children already under this roof!

Dhanda   Kismet has burdened you badly, Birji, by surrounding you with females. You will see, this shop will be your son.

Surinder *can be seen doing schoolwork in the shop.* **Kamaljit** *is cooking in the kitchen.*

Dhanda (*indicates shop*)   It will make your fortune. And then your daughters will marry great men and have sons who will have more sons. Outside, these goreh might spit at our faces, but inside these walls, we will be kings of England. And we will make this place our place. These goreh, we will show them. We will show them!

A movement section showing **Mr Bains**'s *decline. He goes from his seat to lying on a makeshift bed.*

Act One

Scene One

Years later. The Baithak has been smartened up, with a telephone in the corner. **Tanvir** *is sweeping the kitchen and* **Mrs Bains** *is busy in the shop.* **Mr Bains** *lies on the makeshift bed.* **Kamaljit** *feeds him with a spoon.* **Surinder** *approaches with a stainless steel beaker of water.*

Kamaljit   Well done, Daddy.

Surinder   He's not a baby, Kamaljit!

The two girls sit with him, each holding one of his hands lovingly.

Mr Bains   I'm going to race you in the park, Surinder. And I'm going to beat you.

Mr Bains *holds his hand out for the water.* **Surinder** *helps him drink.*

Mr Bains   My boy. My good boy.

Surinder   I'm a girl.

Kamaljit   Stop upsetting him!

Mr Bains   One day he will be Prime Minister.

Surinder   And I'll get a short back and sides.

Kamaljit   You wash your mouth out!

Mr Bains *and* **Surinder** *laugh.*

Mr Bains   Be quiet, Kamaljit, we are just having the fun. (*A beat.*) I sleep now.

He shuts his eyes.

Surinder   Later we'll go to the park, Daddy.

They watch him fall asleep.

But you'll never catch me.

She stands up, wheels **Mr Bains**' *bed towards the shop area.*

Kamaljit   What are you doing?

Surinder   Moving him closer to the till, he likes to sniff the pound notes.

She finds a magazine, positions a stool in the centre of the room. Puts newspaper down on the floor. **Tanvir** *enters.*

Tanvir   Ready?

Surinder   Almost.

He sits on the stool. **Surinder** *finds a page in a magazine. Takes out scissors.*

Kamaljit   I'm telling Mum.

Surinder   She doesn't care.

Kamaljit   Try cutting yours and see.

Surinder *brandishes the scissors.* **Kamaljit** *takes the dishes into the kitchen, tidies up.*

Surinder   Once I've finished with you, people are gonna think you're that Tony Curtis.

Tanvir   You said Shashi Kapoor.

Surinder   You won't be you any more, that's the point.

Kamaljit   Thought you were growing it, Tanvir.

Tanvir   I can always grow it again after I've had it cut.

Surinder   Exactly! We're not in the village now, Kamaljit. There are people in Wolverhampton with colour tellies.

She dances around the space.

Kamaljit   You should be fasting today, not dancing around like you're on Top of the Pops.

Surinder   Wish I was!

She reads the magazine.

Kamaljit   Where's your sharam [*shame*]?

Surinder   Forgot the towel.

She rushes out. **Tanvir** *gets up, he and* **Kamaljit** *behold one another nervously. Draw closer to one another.*

Kamaljit   Are you really going to have it done like Shashi Kapoor?

Tanvir   Er . . . well . . . I want to do whatever I can to . . . improve myself. (*A beat.*) What do you think?

They tentatively move closer and closer when **Surinder** *comes back.*
They hurriedly part. **Tanvir** *sits back down and* **Surinder** *puts a towel*
round his shoulders and checks the magazine.

Surinder (*reads*)   Make sectional partings across the head. And cut
from the nape.

Kamaljit   I could do it.

Surinder   What do you know about fashion?

She starts cutting his hair.

Kamaljit   I can follow instructions!

Surinder   You're not brave enough to touch another human.

Kamaljit   Who wipes Dad every morning?

Surinder   I'm not talking about Dad.

Mrs Bains *enters carrying boxes. She puts them down, starts pricing.*

Mrs Bains   The driver delivered two boxes of marrowfat peas by
mistake.

Surinder   How can they actually eat those?

Mrs Bains   They have different tastes. It's not for us to judge what
people put in their mouths.

Tanvir   Imagine if goreh tried tandoori chicken.

They all laugh.

Kamaljit   They never would.

Surinder (*indicating boxes*)   You should have given these back, Mum.

Mrs Bains   I asked. The kutha laughed in my face. (*To* **Surinder**.)
What are you doing?

Kamaljit   Turning Tanvir into a skinhead.

Mrs Bains   You've got no sharam, Surinder.

Surinder   Miss Flanagan says, when we're not revising, we should be
expanding our horizons, maybe learn a new skill.

Kamaljit   Mum, tell her to stop.

Mrs Bains   Who listens to me?

Surinder   I'm smartening him up.

Tanvir   I want to look nice, Auntie, for the customers.

Mrs Bains   The customers don't look at you, Tanvir.

She eyes **Surinder**.

Mrs Bains   Put your chunni [*scarf*] on properly, Surinder.

Surinder   But I'm not going anywhere.

Mrs Bains   Just do it.

Surinder *reluctantly rearranges her chunni.* **Mrs Bains** *turns to* **Kamaljit**.

Mrs Bains   Have you fed Daddy?

Kamaljit   Yes.

Mrs Bains   Tidied the kitchen?

Kamaljit   Yes.

Mrs Bains (*to* **Surinder**)   Once you've finished your nonsense you can goon the atta [*knead the dough*] . . .

Surinder   Mum, these next exams are my actual O-levels!

Mrs Bains   What's more important, feeding your family or feeding your brain with stupid facts that you're never going to use?

Surinder   I might use them.

Tanvir   Did the man selling the chocolate come, Auntie?

Mrs Bains   Not today.

Kamaljit   What's that?

Tanvir   A salesman's bringing a new selection of bars. They sent a letter.

Kamaljit   Do we get to taste?

Mrs Bains   No you do not!

She goes to put the boxes in the shop corner. **Surinder** *takes off her chunni.*

Surinder   Save us some, won't you, Tan?

Kamaljit   He's not supposed to.

Tanvir   Course I will.

Kamaljit   If there's one with soft mint cream in the middle, can I have it?

Tanvir   I'll make sure.

Mrs Bains *returns with more boxes. At the same time, a buoyant* **Dhanda** *bustles in from the kitchen. He has the air of a man who has become accustomed to success, he carries a small box.*

Dhanda   Bhanji!

Mrs Bains   Prahji.

Dhanda *regards* **Tanvir** *with his half-shorn hair.*

Dhanda   What is this?

Mrs Bains   Er . . . poor Tanvir has . . . fleas.

Dhanda   Hai, hai . . .

Mrs Bains   So we are disinfecting the fleabag. Aren't we, kurreeyoh [*girls*]?

Surinder   Hanji [*Yes*].

Mrs Bains   You two, clean him up and make chah for Uncle.

The girls instantly clean up around **Tanvir** *and spring into a well-oiled routine, almost like a dance where they assemble a tea tray with biscuits.* **Tanvir** *gets up,* **Dhanda** *dodges him and goes to crouch at* **Mr Bains**' *feet.* **Tanvir** *heads into the shop.*

Dhanda   How is my Birji today?

Mrs Bains   Same as usual.

The girls bring his tea.

Dhanda   When he wakes, I will tell him the football scores. You like that Georgie Best, isn't it, Birji? Oh, and I brought him some barfi.

Mrs Bains (*takes box*)   He'll enjoy this.

The girls bring in flour and dhal.

Dhanda   Soon he will be behind the counter again. Punching and kicking the paper boys when they are late for their rounds.

Surinder   No, he won't.

Awkward silence. **Kamaljit** *sorts through the dhal while* **Surinder** *kneads the dough.*

Dhanda   Such good girls you have.

Mrs Bains   Yes. Is Bhanji keeping well, Prahji?

Dhanda   My missus is heading back to India next month. My Beji [*mother*] is suffering with her toilet trouble and Sarjit will be looking after her.

Mrs Bains   What about little Charna?

Dhanda   Going with his mummy. A man can't take care of a child on his own.

Mrs Bains   Certainly not. Who will be making your roti?

Dhanda   I will be relying on the kindness of the ladies from the Gurdwara.

Mrs Bains   There will always be roti here, waiting for you, whenever you need it.

Dhanda   I shall remember that, Bhanji. But I am not here to discuss my roti . . .

Tanvir *brings in more boxes. Prices the stock.*

Surinder   Why are you here, Uncle?

Dhanda   Because Surinder, these goreh, always these goreh are trying to break the Sardar [*Sikh man*]!

Tanvir   How are they doing that?

Dhanda   They are happy for us to wear the turban when we are fighting wars for their British Empire, but now they are saying we cannot wear our religious attire when we work on the buses of Wolverhampton.

Kamaljit   That doesn't sound fair.

Dhanda   Exactly, Kamaljit beta [*dear*]. Men like me are being stripped of our human rights.

Surinder   But you don't wear a turban.

Dhanda *takes a biscuit.*

Dhanda   The point here, is the case of Sohan Singh Jolly.

Mrs Bains   That man talks too much.

Dhanda   Jolly Sahib is no fool, Bhanji. The fellow lost an arm while fighting Kikuyu during the Mau Mau revolt. He has denounced

Wolverhampton Transport Committee as the worst racialists in the world.

Kamaljit   I reckon he's right.

Dhanda   If the turban ban is not lifted, Sohan Singh Jolly has declared that he will burn himself alive on 13 April.

Mrs Bains   But that's Basaikhi [*Sikh festival*].

Dhanda   Quite.

Mrs Bains   Are you allowed to burn yourself alive on Basaikhi?

Dhanda   I'm not sure. (*A beat.*) Unfortunately that bandar [*twit*] Tommy Higginbottom is making matters worse.

Kamaljit   Tommy Higginbottom who does cut and blow dries on the precinct?

Dhanda   Hanji. He is threatening to burn himself alive if the committee give in to Jolly's demands. Following this, Jarman Singh Parmar, editor of the Indian Observer has vowed to also set himself on fire fifteen days after Jolly Sahib. One of us will do the same every fifteen days until this racialist policy is reversed. (*A beat.*) Jolly Sahib needs us to show the citizens of Wolverhampton that we mean business. So, we, the Gurdwara committee, are planning a protest in the city centre in two weeks. Can we count on your support?

Uneasy silence.

Surinder   My teacher says we should be spending as much time as possible studying.

Mrs Bains (*a beat*)   We will be there for sure, Prahji.

Tanvir   What about the shop?

Mrs Bains   We will manage.

Surinder   Someone'll have to stay with Daddy.

Kamaljit   That's true.

Surinder   I can. I'll keep an eye on the counter as well.

Dhanda   You are a young girl . . .

Surinder   I'm old enough.

Dhanda   You should not be here alone.

Surinder   Daddy's here.

Dhanda   Your father cannot protect you.

Surinder   He's not dead yet!

Suddenly **Mrs Bains** *slaps* **Surinder** *round the face.*

Mrs Bains   You don't talk to Uncle like that. (*A beat.*) She is sad because of her daddy, you understand.

Dhanda   This young one has always had spirit.

Mrs Bains   Soon she will learn.

Dhanda   You should teach her, before she gets married.

Mrs Bains   We are not planning their marriages yet.

Dhanda   I will discuss with Birji next time.

He goes to leave.

Mrs Bains   Tanvir, go and give Prahji the moolis [*horseradishes*] from the vegetable box.

Tanvir *jumps up, heads towards the shop.*

Mrs Bains   I thought perhaps Sarjit Bhanji would like to make paratheh?

Dhanda   I will ask but my missus is not the cleverest in the kitchen. Sat siri akal.

Mrs Bains   Sat siri akal.

They watch **Dhanda** *follow* **Tanvir** *into the shop. As soon as he's out of sight,* **Mrs Bains** *turns to* **Surinder***, grabs her by the hair.*

Kamaljit   Mum, leave her please!

She shields her sister. They both fall to the floor. **Surinder***'s hair comes loose.*

Mrs Bains   Now he will tell everyone at the Gurdwara that you are doing O-levels!

Surinder   We're not really getting married, are we?

Kamaljit   Course not.

Mrs Bains   What else do you think you're going to do?

The girls take this in. **Mrs Bains** *points at* **Surinder***.*

Mrs Bains   And tonight you're doing the night shift with Daddy.

Surinder   I did it yesterday.

Mrs Bains   Well you're doing it again. And every single night this week. Until you learn not to be a stupid!

She walks into the kitchen. The girls sit in silence.

Surinder   Why does he always come round?

Kamaljit   Uncle's alright.

Surinder   You know he isn't. (*A beat.*) I just want to do well at school . . .

Kamaljit   You might be able to, if you shut your mouth.

Surinder (*a beat*)   What do you want?

Kamaljit   Me?

Surinder   There must be something. (*Indicates her heart.*) Inside . . . here.

Kamaljit (*a beat*)   Find someone special who thinks I'm special too and have a load of kids. Five or seven. A gang of us. We'd go up the high street to the shops . . . and then come home and . . . they'd play hopscotch and I'd eat black forest gateau. I saw a picture of it in a magazine. It's from Germany.

Surinder   Are you ready to get married, Kamaljit? Actually married.

Kamaljit   It's not up to us.

Surinder   Wish it was.

Kamaljit   Shut up now. Try learning to have some sharam.

She cradles her sister in her arms, starts smoothing down **Surinder**'s *hair.*

Surinder   I do try.

Kamaljit *starts to sing* Build me Up Buttercup. *They both sing together.*

Scene Two

Later that night. **Surinder** *sits with her father who lies on his bed. She massages his legs.*

Mr Bains   Newspapers?

Surinder   A handful.

Mr Bains   Bread?

Surinder   Gone.

Mr Bains   Butter?

Surinder   Sold out.

Mr Bains   More coming?

Surinder   Tanvir said first thing in the morning.

Mr Bains   Acha [*right*]. Is important to keep up stock levels. If a man has stock he will never go out of business.

Surinder   Yes, Daddy.

Mr Bains   Tanvir must learn.

Surinder   He manages to run the shop.

Mr Bains   I run my shop! You people better not bloody forget it.

Surinder   We won't.

Mr Bains   Stop doing the malash [*massage*]. You are sending too much blood into my circulation.

She gently retreats.

Surinder   There's new chocolate coming.

Mr Bains   Keep the bars away from Kamaljit. I know she steals the Creme Eggs. Stuffed a whole one in her mouth the other day. She thought I didn't see. But I did.

Surinder   That girl dreams about chocolate.

Mr Bains   She should stop. No mother-in-law wants her son's bride to have spots on her face and a fatty tummy.

Surinder (*a beat*)   What . . . do you dream about, Daddy?

Mr Bains   I don't have no dreams no more.

Surinder   Did you used to?

Mr Bains   When I was young. Your age.

Surinder   Go on.

Mr Bains   Leave the village. Come to Belayt. Start a business. Live in a castle. Drive a Mercedes Benz. Become a somebody. Have a beautiful wife to make my roti and hold my hand at night. One daughter and one son to call me Daddy.

Surinder   I call you Daddy.

Mr Bains   Did I ever tell you your grandmother left you in the sun when you were born?

Surinder   Tell me again.

Mr Bains   All the old women in the village said you don't need another girl. Leave her outside for one day and see if she lives or dies. Your mummy screamed when they took you from her arms. And you didn't stop crying for a single second. After two hours, I grabbed you, told them to stop playing games with my flesh and blood. You know, your mummy only started to love me from that day. And then . . . and then . . . we never let you go.

Surinder   I must have wanted to live.

Mr Bains   Oh yes.

Surinder   I've got dreams, Daddy.

Mr Bains   Acha?

Surinder   I'm doing well at school. Not like Kamaljit. My teacher said I should stay on, do A-levels.

Mr Bains   For what?

Surinder   If I get an education, I can learn more stuff to help with the shop. We could expand.

Mr Bains   You are telling me about my business?

Surinder   To support my family. I like working.

Mr Bains   You are a hard worker.

Surinder   I might . . . even get a job. I'd still cook and clean and everything. But I'd . . . be a somebody. (*A beat.*) What do you think?

Mr Bains   You think too much. What job you like?

Surinder   Maybe a nurse or a teacher . . .

Mr Bains (*amused*)   My daughter wants to be a somebody.

Surinder   Like you.

Mr Bains   We will find a somebody for you to marry.

Surinder   But what about . . . my life.

Mr Bains   You think this is your life?

Surinder   It's me in this body.

Mr Bains   You is my girl. What are you, thirteen, fourteen?

Surinder   Sixteen.

Mr Bains   You think the goreh will let you take one of their jobs?

Surinder   They're not all bad.

Mr Bains   I didn't say they were bad. But they will always look at you like you are different. Make you feel different.

Surinder   Thought you wanted to get away from the village.

Mr Bains   You know what the goreh did when they came to my country? Made us learn English, took our women, built their own little Belayt. They never became Indian because they thought they were better. You think I'm going to let my family be infected with English ways. Not on your bloody nelly.

Surinder   You brought us here, Daddy. What are we supposed to do?

Mr Bains   What I say!

Surinder *recoils slightly.* **Mr Bains** *feels bad.*

Mr Bains   You think I don't see the boys looking at you through the shop window. Kamaljit will be lucky to find a boy that is even breathing. You, you will be able to choose.

No response.

You want to make me happy or not?

Surinder *half nods.*

Mr Bains   My good boy.

He slowly sleeps. **Surinder** *retreats.*

Scene Three

Living area. **Kamaljit** *is tidying up.* **Tanvir** *runs in holding a radio.*

Tanvir   They're playing it now.

Kamaljit   Really?

He nods vigorously.

What about the shop?

Tanvir   It'll only be two minutes.

The first few notes of Sugar, Sugar *play. They both start dancing clumsily but joyfully and sing along to one another. A woman,* **Miss Flanagan**, *enters. She watches them jumping around, somewhat bemused.* **Kamaljit** *notices her. Grabs the radio, turns it off. They all stare at one another.*

Kamaljit   Are you?

Miss Flanagan   That's right.

Kamaljit   You look older.

Miss Flanagan   I remember you from school. The children used to call you . . . er . . .

Kamaljit   Camel Shit.

Miss Flanagan   The door was open.

Tanvir   Er . . . thank you for reconnecting the loose wires inside the radio, Kamaljit.

Kamaljit   You're very welcome, Tanvir. I hope it works now.

Tanvir   I'm sure it's perfect.

He awkwardly retreats into the shop area. **Kamaljit** *eyes* **Miss Flanagan** *nervously.*

Miss Flanagan   He seems like a nice young man.

Kamaljit   He's not. (*Shouts.*) Mum, come here (*in Punjabi*).

Mrs Bains *and* **Surinder** *approach from the kitchen.*

Miss Flanagan   Hello, Surinder.

Surinder   You're early, Miss.

Miss Flanagan   Good afternoon, Mrs Bains, I'm Miss Flanagan, Surinder's English teacher and head of fifth year. I sent a note saying I'd be popping round.

Surinder   She read the note.

Mrs Bains   I have a mouth! (*A beat.*) I read the note. Is she in trouble?

Miss Flanagan   No. No trouble.

Mrs Bains   Please sit. (*Nods to* **Kamaljit**.) Kamaljit, chah.

Kamaljit *hurries to the kitchen.* **Mrs Bains**, **Miss Flanagan** *and* **Surinder** *sit. Awkward silence.* **Miss Flanagan** *picks up a magazine next to her. She scans the picture of the Viking warrior on the front.*

Miss Flanagan   The Vikings! They were immigrants. From Scandinavia. People always describe them as bloodthirsty and murderous. And they did wear unusual hats and pillage churches but apparently they were excellent handymen. Nobody's all bad, are they?

Mrs Bains   Who?

Miss Flanagan   Er, the Vikings.

Surinder   It's a joke, Mum.

Mrs Bains *forces polite laughter.*

Miss Flanagan   Who are the British anyway? I mean, there are two million people living in this country who were not born here. The problem with the likes of Enoch Powell is that he has no historical awareness. Not even first year standard. Your daughter could teach him a thing or two?

Mrs Bains   Kamaljit?

Miss Flanagan   No, Surinder.

Mrs Bains   Oh.

Miss Flanagan   I don't want to embarrass you, but she is bright. Ridiculously bright.

Mrs Bains (*yells*)   Kamaljit, chah!

Kamaljit (*from kitchen*)   I'm coming!

Mrs Bains   You ever tried a samosa?

Miss Flanagan   Er . . . yes. So, I'm here . . .

Kamaljit *brings in the chah.*

Miss Flanagan   . . . to talk about Surinder.

Mrs Bains   Have a samosa. With the imli chutney.

Miss Flanagan   Oh . . . er . . . I will . . .

Mrs Bains   They are tasty. With the chutney. Homemade. By me.

Miss Flanagan   Right.

Mrs Bains   Eat!

Miss Flanagan *takes a samosa, munches it.* **Mrs Bains** *eyes her.*

Mrs Bains   You want to know the secret to making a superior samosa?

Miss Flanagan   Okay.

Mrs Bains   My secret is to fry on low gas. So the samosa cooks evenly from the inside out. Makes the pastry crispy. Not greasy. Is it crispy?

Miss Flanagan   Yes.

Mrs Bains   How crispy?

Miss Flanagan   Very.

Mrs Bains   Is it the crispiest samosa you have ever eaten?

Miss Flanagan   Possibly.

Mrs Bains   Because I am patient. With the gas. And patience is paradise, Miss Flan.

Miss Flanagan (*a beat*)   I wouldn't be surprised if she gets top grades in all her O-levels.

Mrs Bains   Who?

Miss Flanagan   Surinder.

Mrs Bains   Drink your chah. You want to know the secret to making superior chah?

Miss Flanagan   Well . . .

Mrs Bains   Put whole spices in cold water with a big spoon of tea, bring to a rolling boil and then you add the milk!

Miss Flanagan   Mrs Bains . . .

Mrs Bains   You want to know the secret to making extra superior tarka dhal?

Miss Flanagan (*firm*)   Mrs Bains, I think it would be a pity if Surinder didn't stay on at school.

Mrs Bains   Too much education makes people's brains get mixed up, they don't sleep at night and then they have to force their toilet out in the morning.

Miss Flanagan   Or they learn new ways of thinking. Do astonishing things like build bridges and skyscrapers. Surinder absorbs knowledge and turns it into something incisive and sometimes . . . extraordinary.

Mrs Bains *regards her with suspicion.*

Miss Flanagan   My parents came here from Ireland. They wanted a better life, but my mother was terrified about me going into this place that was foreign . . . she'd been spat at, had her hair pulled . . . and worse. I don't have to tell you . . . The point is . . . (*Falters.*)

Mrs Bains   What is the point, Miss Flan?

Miss Flanagan   My mother realised this better life would only come if she was brave . . . so she decided to let me go.

Mrs Bains   You want me to allow my daughter out into your world.

Miss Flanagan   Our world, Mrs Bains. And it's going to be hers.

Mrs Bains   You . . . you think my Surinder might build a bridge?

Miss Flanagan   Your daughter can do things that nobody else in her class can do.

Mrs Bains   Clever?

Miss Flanagan   Yes.

Mrs Bains (*sinking in*)   She is clever . . .

Miss Flanagan   The cleverest. But she needs someone to believe in her.

Mrs Bains   You . . .

Miss Flanagan   No, not me.

Mrs Bains *gets up.*

Mrs Bains   I have to go to the toilet.

Surinder   Mum . . .

Mrs Bains *heads out.* **Miss Flanagan** *gets up.*

Miss Flanagan   Will you consider it?

Surinder   I'm begging you, Mum. I swear I'll do whatever you say, if I can carry on . . .

Mrs Bains   Okay, okay.

Surinder *goes to hug her mother but* **Mrs Bains** *continues on.*

Mrs Bains   If you love school so much, go and get your history, chemistry blah blah books.

Surinder (*delighted*)   I will.

Mrs Bains (*going*)   And tell your teacher to eat more samoseh . . . and buy fish and chips on the way home. She is too bloody well thin.

Scene Four

Bains' *living area*. **Mr Bains** *lies on his makeshift bed*. **Surinder** *sits nearby doing her homework*. **Dhanda**, **Mrs Bains**, **Kamaljit** *and* **Tanvir** *are dressed up to the nines*.

Kamaljit *and* **Tanvir** *unfurl a long white sheet which reads* – *TURBANS BELONG ON WOLVERHAMPTON BUSES*.

Dhanda   Impressive heh, Birji. We will be thousands in the town centre. Coaches of apneh [*our people*] are arriving from Walsall, Slough, Southall.

Mr Bains   I should come and give the chairman of the Transport Committee a big fat thupurr. (*Mimes slap.*)

Mr Bains *has a bad coughing attack. The women go to him, gently stroke his shoulder.*

Tanvir   Maybe we shouldn't leave him.

Mr Bains   Him? Who is him you bhenjot [*sisterfucker*]? Don't forget you are my representatives. This family needs to have a presence on a day like this. (*To* **Dhanda**.) I let them close my shop. For one day only!

Mrs Bains (*to* **Mr Bains**)   Surinder will be with you.

Mr Bains   I don't need no girl looking after me.

Mrs Bains (*to* **Dhanda**)   She is becoming more and more devoted to her daddy.

Dhanda   Her spirit is certainly calmer. I can see she is a very simple girl nowadays.

Kamaljit   Will there be a riot, Uncle?

Dhanda   We are a peaceful people, beta [*dear*]. But if they antagonise us, we must be prepared.

Mrs Bains   Finish up in the shop Surinder. And then sit with Daddy. His dhal and roti's on the stove.

Surinder *heads into the shop.*

Dhanda   Chullo everybody!

Mrs Bains   Let me get my shawl. I will catch up.

Dhanda, **Tanvir** *and* **Kamaljit** *head out.* **Mrs Bains** *beholds her husband.*

Mrs Bains   Sure you are okay?

She finds her shawl. Pointedly picks up a book.

Mr Bains   Yes, woman. Stop fussing.

He takes the book from her hands.

Mr Bains   Who is this . . . Tess of the d'Urbervilles?

Mrs Bains   It's for Surinder's exams.

Mr Bains   She reads too many books.

Mrs Bains   Girls in this country read. Do things. School says she's intelligent, cleverest in the class. (*A beat.*) Perhaps we should give her a chance.

Mr Bains   No more school.

Mrs Bains   It's only two more years.

Mr Bains   Enough time for her to become someone who is not like us.

Mrs Bains   Why not give her a few more months of a life?

Mr Bains   A woman like you can't make a decision about my child.

Mrs Bains   Surinder has a quick brain and a spirit of iron. She can do better for herself.

Mr Bains   Better than what?

Mrs Bains   You know.

Mr Bains *takes* **Mrs Bains***'s hand.*

Mr Bains   You always dreamed big. That's why you still set me on fire.

He pulls her towards him. They kiss.

Mr Bains   I want to see Surinder's wedding.

Mrs Bains   Better not go blind then. (*A beat.*) Kamaljit is kind and she can clean but not much else. Plus she is older so she should go first.

Mr Bains   They will all want Surinder. That girl was born with some magic . . .

Mrs Bains   If she leaves, who will help me run the shop?

Mr Bains   My shop.

Mrs Bains   You know I can just decide. And you can't do nothing!

Mr Bains (*laughs*)   Woman, you love me too much to insult me.

Mrs Bains   Would it be so bad if we let her go?

Mr Bains   My girls are my izzat [*honour*]!

Mrs Bains   Your izzat doesn't wake at 4 am to get the papers ready! It doesn't make saag and keema and muttar paneer. It doesn't say nothing when the goreh shout at us to get out of their country. You sit here like a king. Order us around like servants. We take it, we do what you say. But that teacher said my daughter is special. And this chance . . . this is what I want for her.

Mr Bains   You are going to bring trouble into this house. Big trouble.

Mrs Bains   Well?

Mr Bains   When have I ever not given you what you want?

Mrs Bains *strokes his shoulder lovingly. He closes his eyes.*

Scene Five

The march. A street. A dhol plays a loud bhangra beat. And the sound of Punjabi folk music blares out. The actors advance on stage dressed as protestors holding placards. Defiant shouts can be heard over the music.

Protestors   Sikhs have rights! . . . You brought us to this country to do your dirty work! We are here to stay! . . . Shame on you, Transport Committee!

The music and shouts blend into a rendition of 'We Shall Not Be Moved', *which culminates in a climactic bellowing of* 'Bole So Nihal. Sat Siri Akal'.

A reporter takes out a microphone. Shoves it in front of **Tanvir** *and* **Kamaljit.**

Reporter   Surely when in Rome, you should do as the Romans do?

Tanvir   Thing is, we are actually in Wolverhampton.

Loud cheers. **Kamaljit** *applauds fervently.*

Reporter   Would you both describe yourselves as devout Sikhs?

Tanvir   Certainly.

Kamaljit   Absolutely.

Reporter   But you're not wearing a turban.

Tanvir   My faith is in my soul.

Kamaljit   That's lovely, Tanvir.

Reporter   Right.

Kamaljit   We're here to support our brothers. Their fight is our fight.

Tanvir   Very true, Kamaljit. This is a question of freedom, not religion. If we protect people's rights to be who they are, then they'll feel part of society. And there'll be more connection between all of us.

Kamaljit *regards* **Tanvir**, *bowled over by his words.*

Kamaljit   It's all about . . . connection.

Reporter   Is this going to end with a man burning himself alive?

Tanvir   Not if the transport lot make the correct decision.

Reporter   So what should they do if a Turkish member of staff suddenly decides he wants to wear a fez?

Kamaljit   Why not? Live and let live, like the hippies say!

Reporter   Isn't this is a bit of a palaver for what is essentially a type of hat?

Tanvir   The turban is not a hat, it's a symbol of holiness, sacrifice, courage. In the last two world wars, thousands of Sikhs fought for this country with no other protection but their turbans. You take our turbans away, you take away our hearts. And a man is nothing without his heart.

Kamaljit   Well said, Tanvir.

Tanvir   Thank you, Kamaljit.

As the **Reporter** *retreats,* **Tanvir** *and* **Kamaljit** *look at each other, transfixed. The other protestors start a chant of 'Sikhs have rights' around them.*

Kamaljit*'s chooni falls.* **Tanvir** *picks it up. Puts it back gently round her neck.*

Their eyes locked, **Tanvir** *and* **Kamaljit** *slowly join in the chanting as the protestors retreat.*

Scene Six

The shop. **Surinder** *reads her book whilst cleaning the counter. She tidies up and turns the sign on the door to CLOSED.*

Surinder (*reads to herself*)   Never in her life had she intended to do wrong; yet these hard judgements had come . . .

She closes the book. Starts to write with a pen.

Thomas Hardy indicates that life is not fair. But his decision to execute Tess after all that she has suffered, is an act of literary cruelty. Why not let his heroine live . . .

Suddenly **Jim** *bounds in, carrying a briefcase.*

Jim   Sorry I'm late . . . There's a right carry on going on out there. Massive crowd. TV cameras and everything.

Surinder   I should have locked the door. We're closed.

Jim   But I've got an appointment. With Mr Banga. Mr Tanvir Banga. About the chocolates. I'm Jim Wilson. What's your name?

Surinder   Surinder Bains.

Jim   Sue – rinder. How lovely. Sue Bains.

Jim *is entranced by her but covers and quickly composes himself.*

Do you like chocolate?

Surinder   Who doesn't?

Jim (*opening briefcase*)   You are in for a treat. I've been doing this job six months, and this is the best product I've had.

He takes out a box of chocolate bars.

It's all the rage in London. That's where I used to live. You ever been?

Surinder   No. Where do you live now?

Jim   Er, well . . . all over the place, a rep has to be nimble, travelling up and down. Means I've seen a bit of the world. Coventry, Gravesend, Swindon.

Surinder   Wow.

Jim   But London's the place. Full of artists, writers, musicians. They sit around in pubs and restaurants and discuss life, you know. How to make it kinder, softer . . .

He takes out the chocolate.

Surinder   Perhaps you should wait for Tanvir. I haven't got the money.

Jim   I can pop back another time. I'm always passing this way in the motor.

He holds a bar in front of her.

Surinder   I'd better not.

Jim   At least let me try out the patter. I need to practise.

She eyes the chocolate as though it's forbidden fruit.

Surinder   Alright.

A loud thudding sound from the back.

Jim   What was that?

Surinder   Probably my books falling off the kitchen table again. I always pile them too high.

Jim   You like books?

Surinder   Yeah.

Jim   So do I. They make my insides soar. Like a jumbo jet.

Surinder   Oh.

Jim   Shall I start?

Surinder *nods.* **Jim** *nervously clears his throat.*

Jim   Would you like to try the chocolate, Miss?

Surinder   Yeah.

Jim   Unwrap it. Let your eyes feast on the shiny foil and anticipate the adventure. Taste isn't the only sense that matters when it comes to flavour. Do you know what else . . .

Surinder (*interrupts*)   Smell.

Jim   That's what I was gonna say . . .

Surinder *sniffs the chocolate.*

Surinder   Smells a bit funny.

Jim   Funny can be new, different. Funny might be . . . sensational.

She eats a piece.

Surinder   It's got raisins in it.

Jim   Can you tell what the raisins taste of?

Surinder   Coke?

Jim *begins to sing* Jamaican Farewell.

Surinder   Tizer?

Jim *continues to sing.*

Beat.

Jim   Jamaican rum.

Surinder *spits it out, coughs and splutters.*

Surinder   I'm not allowed to drink.

Jim   You won't get drunk. Not from a couple of raisins.

Surinder   It's against my religion to drink.

Jim   I'm sorry, Sue. It's not real rum, only the flavour. They make it in the factory in Bromsgrove.

Surinder *composes herself. He stares at her, doesn't want to leave.*

Jim   You ever been to Catacombs?

Surinder   I sometimes walk through the graveyard on the way home from school.

Jim   It's a nightclub. In town.

Surinder   Not my kind of place.

Jim   What is your kind of place?

Surinder   Shop. Gurdwara. Laundrette.

Jim   There's a big world out there.

Surinder   Sounds like it.

Jim   In a speck of a second, the universe turns like a coin, from darkness to light and his being becomes whole . . .

Surinder   Eh?

Jim   Fact is, I'm a poet Sue. And I'm suddenly feeling . . . rather poetic. (*A beat.*) Because you're so sweet. Forgive me, I shouldn't have said that.

Embarrassed, he retreats to the door.

But you are Sue. You really are.

He heads out. **Surinder** *beholds the half-eaten chocolate bar and eats it, ravenously.*

She then picks up the radio, turns it on. The Monkees' Daydream Believer *plays.* **Surinder** *sings and dances as she cleans and organises the shop.*

Lost in her own world, she doesn't notice **Mrs Bains**, **Tanvir** *and* **Kamaljit** *enter. She continues swaying to the music.* **Mrs Bains** *turns the radio off.* **Surinder** *notices them, stops dead.*

Mrs Bains   Why didn't you lock the door?

Surinder   I thought I did.

Mrs Bains   Stupid!

Mrs Bains *locks the door.*

Kamaljit   You missed out, Surinder. Practically every single Sikh in England was there . . .

Tanvir   Felt like we were at Man United. All of us cheering at the Stretford End.

Kamaljit   And Tanvir's gonna be on the news.

Surinder How come?

Tanvir Reporter asked for my opinion.

Kamaljit He was very eloquent. And . . . passionate.

Tanvir No . . .

Kamaljit You were . . . commanding.

Tanvir Was I?

Mrs Bains Has Daddy had his chah?

Surinder I was just going to put the pan on.

Mrs Bains I'll do it.

Mrs Bains *heads off.* **Kamaljit** *looks in the box, she beams.*

Kamaljit Chocolate!

Surinder The rep dropped it off.

Tanvir I forgot about him!

Surinder He dropped it off and left. Immediately. He was here for two minutes, actually only one minute . . .

Kamaljit Suppose I'd better try one, then I can tell the customers how they taste.

Surinder Don't! They're alcoholic.

Kamaljit You've had one!

Surinder I didn't realise.

Tanvir She can have a piece!

Suddenly **Mrs Bains** *screams from the back.* **Tanvir** *rushes out.* **Kamaljit** *follows.*

Terror consumes **Surinder***, she is frozen to the spot.*

After a few moments, **Kamaljit** *re-enters, she's in shock.*

Kamaljit What were you doing?

Surinder Nothing . . . I was here . . . what . . . what's happened?

Silence.

Surinder   Kamaljit?

Kamaljit   Did you check on Daddy?

No response.

Kamaljit (*loud*)   Did you check on him?

Surinder (*nods*)   I was about to get the pan. For his chah.

Kamaljit *slowly sits on the floor. She's in a daze.*

Surinder   Is he alright? He was alright a minute ago. Kamaljit, he was alright . . . He was.

She starts to cry as she drops to the floor, next to her sister.

On the other side of the stage, we see **Mrs Bains** *kissing and hugging her dead husband. Her body melts into his.*

Scene Seven

Bains' *living area. All the characters are onstage as if they are forming a congregation in a Gurdwara. They sit on the floor, their heads covered. They start singing a traditional Punjabi mourning song.*

Scene Eight

Hours later. **Mrs Bains** *quietly says a prayer as the characters move the furniture back. An empty space where* **Mr Bains** *used to sit.* **Surinder** *and* **Kamaljit** *tidy up.* **Tanvir** *sweeps the floor.* **Dhanda** *approaches the empty space.*

Dhanda   A man like him. A titan of a man. How can he be gone like this? (*A beat.*) He never fell before. Not once.

Tanvir   He never had a stroke before.

Dhanda   He must have heard the rallying call of the demonstration, yes . . . this Punjabi lion was trying to get to his people. (*A beat.*) At least there was no suffering. (*To* **Mrs Bains**.) Tell me again that he did not suffer.

Mrs Bains   The doctor said it would have been quick.

Dhanda   Lucky! Quick is the best way.

Kamaljit   How can there be a best way?

Dhanda   One day you will understand, Kamaljit beta [*dear*]. When you are old and broken. Your daddy's soul is free now. Blending with the divine, like a river rippling into the sea.

Kamaljit *starts to cry.* **Dhanda** *turns to her.*

Dhanda   Be strong beta. It is hard to bear. Yes. For me, especially. He was my father too. My father first. What that man lived. What that man saw in his years on this earth. The pain of Partition. You know he came from West Punjab, in a Muslim majority district. As a child he walked out of his house and saw his schoolmates hanging from neem trees. He dipped his hands into their wounds, wiping blood over his face so the attackers would leave him for dead. The family cut his hair short, Muslim style, and sent him alone on the back of a truck to escape to Delhi. My Birji would have joined us on the march that day. And he would be proud that our protest convinced the transport committee to change their minds. You know, I never wanted to buy a shop. It was he who encouraged me. Forced me. 'Go and make your mark, Palwant,' he said. He was mine and I was his. And now my soul is shattered into tiny pieces.

He holds back tears. **Kamaljit** *remains upset.*

Kamaljit   There can't be a God, Mum, there just can't.

Mrs Bains   No more crying! You think your daddy did crying? . . . My husband was a young man and this England made him old. He gave his life to this des [*country*] and it swallowed him, took him . . . from me . . . before he could become everything he was going to be . . . And he was close, so close . . .

Surinder *tentatively approaches her mother.*

Surinder   I'll be good now, Mum. For Daddy.

Mrs Bains   Your daddy is gone.

Surinder   I'll do anything you say.

Mrs Bains   There is nothing.

Kamaljit   The shop won't ever be the same.

Mrs Bains   The shop is the shop.

Dhanda   It is a pity he didn't see his daughters married.

Tanvir   Uncle, now is not the time to talk of weddings.

Dhanda   That time will come. Sooner than you think, Tanvir.

Mrs Bains   Kurreeyoh, go and change your clothes.

Surinder *and* **Kamaljit** *head out.*

Mrs Bains   Tanvir, check the shop front.

Tanvir   Why?

Mrs Bains   People should know we are open for business.

Tanvir   Today?

Mrs Bains   Today and every day.

He leaves. **Dhanda** *sits.*

Dhanda   Back home, it is tradition for a mourner to feed the bereaved family after the funeral. I should make your roti.

Mrs Bains   Our stomachs do not need to be full, at this moment.

They sit for a moment in silence.

Dhanda   You can be satisfied that you were a devoted wife. You have brought up two girls. Two good, simple girls.

Mrs Bains   I did my duty.

Dhanda   This shop is alive because of you, plus your bhindi [*okra*] is the tastiest in the whole of the West Midlands.

Mrs Bains   That is a matter of opinion.

Dhanda   If I had a wife like you, my life would be easier. Roti on the table every night, pressed shirt on the hanger, not too much talking at night-time.

Mrs Bains   Sarjit Bhanji will be back from India soon.

Dhanda   She is not coming back.

Mrs Bains   Why?

Dhanda   Sarjit is old. She does not feel like my wife any more.

Mrs Bains   Does she know this?

Dhanda   She is happy to stay in the pind. The cold weather and closed walls of Wolverhampton never suited her. There is something I want to suggest to you, Bhanji.

Mrs Bains   Er . . . I am very tired, Prahji, it has been a difficult day.

Dhanda   Of course. It is the start of many difficult days. A life with no man in the house is no life.

Mrs Bains   Tanvir is here.

Dhanda (*amused*)   Tanvir . . . Bhanji, there may be a way that I can alleviate some of your difficulties.

Mrs Bains   What way?

Dhanda   You have sweated blood in this country. You deserve peace. Relaxation. If you were to sell the shop, you could pay for the girls' weddings and still afford to retire respectably in India.

Mrs Bains   You want to buy the shop?

Dhanda   I am simply encouraging you to consider the future. A man works hard so that his mother, wife and daughters can be looked after. A shop is not something a woman can manage on her own.

Mrs Bains   Every single nook and cranny of this place is stained with my husband's toil and sweat. My girls and I will run it in his name, in his honour and we will make a better job of it than any man.

Dhanda   I understand. (*A beat.*) But how long will the girls be here to help? They can't be passing time with you and Tanvir forever.

Mrs Bains   No.

Dhanda   Have you started to look for boys?

Mrs Bains   We have just cremated your Birji.

Dhanda   Surinder is the one.

Mrs Bains   What do you mean?

Dhanda   That girl is your greatest asset.

Mrs Bains   She is my daughter.

Dhanda   Perhaps there will not be the need to search too far. If you are looking for a Jat, with a shop, someone with a British passport, of excellent character and someone who Birji would have approved of, your man may be closer than you think.

Mrs Bains   What . . . what do you mean?

Dhanda   The age gap between dearest Birji, God bless his soul, and yourself was not so different from the age gap between, say . . . Surinder and . . . me.

Mrs Bains   But . . . you have a wife.

Dhanda   Our marriage was never registered. So I am a free man.

Mrs Bains *takes this in.*

Dhanda   You know I would treat any wife of mine with the utmost kindness. My shop is thriving so you can be sure your daughter's future will be secure.

Mrs Bains   My daughter is young. Beautiful. She is still . . . like a child.

Silence.

Prahji, I am very tired. I need to rest now.

Dhanda   Of course, Bhanji. You give me your answer when you are ready.

He leaves. Shaken, **Mrs Bains** *watches him go.*

She stands alone, almost crumbles. Then gathers herself together.

Walks towards the telephone. Picks it up.

Scene Nine

Days later. The shop. **Mrs Bains** *and* **Surinder** *are stacking the shelves with goods.* **Tanvir** *brings in a cardboard box of Wagon Wheels.*

Tanvir   Who ordered Wagon Wheels?

Surinder   I didn't.

Tanvir   Stephen Burton and that lot keep asking for them. But Uncle said we shouldn't get any more because the rep tried to diddle him.

Mrs Bains   Those reps are all the same.

Surinder   Not all of them.

Tanvir   Should I put them out?

Mrs Bains   What?

Tanvir   It feels wrong. I mean . . . he didn't want them in the shop.

Mrs Bains   Stephen Burton wants them, stupid! Put them out and order more.

Tanvir *puts them out.* **Kamaljit** *enters.*

Kamaljit (*to* **Mrs Bains**)   Masi's [*Auntie*] on the phone. She says the pips are about to go.

Mrs Bains *hurries out.*

Surinder   Why isn't she phoning from the house?

Kamaljit   Maybe Masur's disconnected it again.

Tanvir   What's he do that for?

Kamaljit   He doesn't like her talking in case she tells people he has Bacardi and coke for breakfast.

Surinder   She only phones to make Mum cry. (*Mimics.*) Oh, your kismet is so bad. Two daughters, no son. And now your husband is dead and you are a widow. People will say you are a husband killer. And they will call me names because I am your sister. Hai hai my head hurts and I have a too weak bladder!

She feigns loud crying when suddenly **Jim** *stumbles into the shop.*

Kamaljit   Shop's not open.

Jim *flails around.*

Tanvir   We're doing a stock take!

Jim *moves towards him.*

Jim   You don't understand!

Tanvir *grabs a nearby mop and whacks* **Jim** *over the head with it.* **Jim** *falls to the floor.*

Surinder   Why did you do that?

Tanvir   I know his type. Hooligan!

Jim   I'm the chocolate fellah. Ask Sue . . .

Kamaljit   Sue?

Jim   I saw a gang of lads breaking into your van. I told them to get lost and one of them socked me in the face.

Tanvir *glances towards the window. He turns to* **Jim** *apologetically.*

Tanvir   Er . . . sorry about that, mate.

Jim   I don't reckon there's any damage but you might want to give it the once over.

Tanvir   Kamaljit, you should ask Mister . . .

Jim   Jim.

Tanvir   If he wants chah.

Kamaljit   But he's a gora.

Surinder   Kamaljit!

Kamaljit   What'll Mum say?

Surinder   Just go and make it!

Mop in hand, **Tanvir** *heads outside as* **Kamaljit** *goes to the kitchen.* **Jim** *contemplates* **Surinder***.*

Jim   How have you been?

Surinder   The day you came . . .

Jim   Yeah?

Surinder   My dad died.

Jim   Sue, I'm so sorry . . .

Surinder   Happened when I was talking to you.

Jim   Oh, that's a lot . . . you poor thing . . .

Surinder   I keep thinking I'm getting used to it, but then I hear him shouting to put new labels in the price guns.

Jim   It's not your fault. People . . . die. We will all die. Cancer, road traffic accidents, some of us might even be murdered.

Surinder   Yeah.

Jim *begins to recite Dylan Thomas's poem,* Do Not Go Gentle Into That Dark Night.

Surinder   You like Dylan Thomas?

Jim   He's the master. I've sent him some of my work.

Surinder   Really?

Jim   He hasn't written back yet. (*A beat.*) I did walk by a couple of times but you must have been at school. Your brother was putting the bins out.

Surinder   Tanvir's not my brother. He's our helper, he lives in the cellar.

Jim   Thing is, Sue . . . you've become my inspiration.

Surinder   Me?

Jim   Since we met, words flow out of me. (*Clears his throat.*) My queen's hair is black. Her eyes as deep as a midnight lake . . .

Surinder   Carry on.

Jim   That's as far as I've got. I was wondering . . . if . . . I might be able to take you to the Golden Egg for a knickerbocker glory.

Surinder   I'm not allowed.

Jim   What?

Surinder   Out.

Jim   Where?

Surinder   Anywhere.

Jim   That's disappointing. I won't be in these parts much longer. I'm gonna try and make it big. London's calling me . . .

Like Dick Whittington . . . only, I'm gonna find the gold paved streets . . .

Tanvir *bustles in, triumphant.*

Tanvir   One look at my mop and they legged it.

Jim *can't tear his eyes away from* **Surinder**.

Tanvir   Got many uses, does a mop. Clean floor. Scare the mice away from the bread. Poke shoplifters. Play a tune when you're on your own behind the counter . . .

Tanvir *starts drumming a tune on the floor with the mop.* **Kamaljit** *comes in with a tray of tea and biscuits.*

Jim *starts to go.*

Kamaljit   Wait, I've opened a packet of Orange Viscounts!

Jim   Better get to the motor in case those louts return. (*Low to* **Surinder**.) I'm usually down the Golden Egg on a Friday lunchtime for a gammon grill.

Bye, Sue.

Surinder   Bye.

He leaves. **Kamaljit** *fixes on the tea and biscuits.*

Surinder   Just eat them, Kamaljit!

Kamaljit *delves in.* **Surinder** *starts dancing to the mop beat.*

Kamaljit   How come he called you Sue?

Surinder   He brought the chocolates that day.

Kamaljit   You told him your name?

Surinder   He asked. And then he couldn't pronounce it.

Surinder   Don't tell Mum.

Kamaljit   What?

Surinder   I dunno . . . anything!

She grabs her sister and they dance together.

Kamaljit   I won't, I never would.

Surinder *breaks off and dances energetically.*

Kamaljit (*joking*)   You've got no sharam!

Surinder   Let's none of us have any sharam today, Kamaljit. Just for today!

She takes her sister and they dance into the next scene . . .

Scene Ten

Bains'*living area.* **Surinder** *sits in front of an open folder.* **Tanvir** *holds one of* **Surinder**'*s text books.* **Kamaljit** *is on her haunches, kneading dough on the floor.*

Tanvir   What happened after the Wall Street Crash in 1929?

Mrs Bains *enters carrying clothes, she sits and starts to sew a kameez.*

Surinder   The loans given to Germany were recalled and the economy collapsed. Unemployment rocketed.

Tanvir   Affirmative.

Surinder *notices what* **Mrs Bains** *is doing.*

Surinder   That kameez doesn't fit me any more, Mum.

Mrs Bains   Why do you think I am taking apart the seam? This is good material, it shouldn't go to waste. (*A beat.*) You will need clothes.

Tanvir   And . . . what did the Enabling Act mean?

Surinder   That there was no political opposition to stop Hitler passing any laws.

Kamaljit (*to* **Surinder**)   You should be sewing your own kameez.

Tanvir   What year did Hindenberg die?

Kamaljit   I know this, 1936.

Surinder   Thirty-four.

Tanvir   Correct.

Kamaljit *gets up, having finished the dough.*

Mrs Bains   Kamaljit, choog [*check*] the dhal.

Kamaljit   I only just finished the atta. Why can't Surinder do it?

Surinder   I'm focusing on the Weimar Republic.

Kamaljit   Everything's easier for you.

Surinder   Tell Mum, not me.

Kamaljit   Mum!

Mrs Bains   Okay, Surinder, you go.

Surinder   Later.

Kamaljit   Now!

Surinder   I haven't got to Hitler yet.

Kamaljit   You just said he died!

Surinder   That was Hindenburg! If you'd stayed on at school you'd know the difference.

Kamaljit   I had to help in the shop and look after you.

Surinder   You didn't want to study, I like it.

Kamaljit (*low*)   More than you like hanging round the Golden Egg?

Surinder *throws her a concerned look.*

Mrs Bains   Surinder, fetch the dhal.

Surinder   This is my last paper, I need to finish World War Two by Friday.

Mrs Bains   You're going to your Masi's on Friday.

Kamaljit   Oh no . . .

Surinder   I can't afford to give up a weekend to go to Southall. They won't let me take history A-level if I don't pass this exam!

Mrs Bains (*interrupts*)   You're not doing any more stupid exams!

Surinder   What?

Mrs Bains   You're staying in Southall until Masi finds you a husband.

Shocked silence.

Mrs Bains   Both of you . . . Tanvir and I will manage the shop. After you are engaged, you will return here to get ready for your weddings. I've spoilt you. (*To* **Kamaljit**.) Letting you wither away behind the counter. (*To* **Surinder**.) Letting your mind go mad by reading books.

Surinder   You promised I could stay on.

Mrs Bains   There are men coming into this shop, looking at you in ways they should not be looking.

Surinder   That's not my fault.

Mrs Bains   I've decided.

Kamaljit   No . . .

Tanvir   Auntie, this is . . . this seems very fast. Perhaps take time to consider.

Mrs Bains   Nothing to consider. Your Masi and Masur will meet you at the train station on Friday.

Kamaljit   But . . . Mum . . .

Mrs Bains   But Mum what?

Kamaljit   What about what we want . . .

Mrs Bains   You, always you.

Kamaljit   You should have told us before, Mum.

Surinder   What's changed?

Mrs Bains   I've seen sense that's what. All this Tess and Tom and Hardy and Latin and biology and being so clever Miss Flan Flan nonsense. It's foolish thinking. Not for us. No. No, Sir . . . Daddy knew . . . when he was alive, he could look after you . . . I should have got you married back then . . . because a married woman is a safe woman . . . Daddy knew . . . we are who we are and that's that.

Tanvir   Auntie . . .

Mrs Bains   And I don't need to hear any words from your big mouth. (*To* **Surinder**.) Go and get the tetchee cases from on top of the wardrobe.

Surinder *leaves.*

Kamaljit   Surinder, wait!

Kamaljit *and* **Tanvir** *appear frozen in shock.*

Agitated **Mrs Bains** *can't find something in her sewing box. She scuttles into the kitchen area.*

Tanvir *rushes up to* **Kamaljit**, *takes her hand.*

Tanvir   Kamaljit . . . I . . .

Kamaljit   Don't, Tanvir . . .

Tanvir   I can't let you . . .

Kamaljit *takes her hand away.*

Kamaljit   You have to forget . . .

Tanvir   Not while my feet are walking this earth. I'll find a way . . .

Mrs Bains *returns.*

Mrs Bains   Go through your clothes and pack the most simple suits. Don't choose nothing fancy.

Kamaljit *blankly heads off.*

Mrs Bains   Fill the stock for the morning.

Tanvir   Please, Auntie . . .

Mrs Bains   Fill the stock, Tanvir.

He leaves. **Mrs Bains** *puts the sewing down. Fights back tears.*

Scene Eleven

Bains' *living area. Two suitcases are on the stage.* **Kamaljit** *enters, wearing her coat. She contemplates the room.* **Surinder** *enters, picks up her coat, puts it on.*

Kamaljit   I don't want to go.

Surinder   You haven't got a choice.

Kamaljit   Aren't you bothered?

Surinder *takes an envelope out of her bag. Puts it on the side.*

Surinder   I can't say what I want . . . So I wrote Mum a letter. I put all my feelings in it. My real feelings, you know.

Tanvir *enters.*

Tanvir   Taxi's coming.

Kamaljit   I . . . don't feel well.

Tanvir   Would you like a glass of water, Kamaljit?

Kamaljit (*shakes head*)   Just need to sit for a minute.

He sits down next to her as **Mrs Bains** *bustles in.*

Mrs Bains   When they collect you, make sure you offer to pay for the petrol in your Masur's car. If they refuse the money, leave it on the mantelpiece. Always cover your head when your Masur is in the room. Remember, they are more traditional than us. You will not be able to flounce around like you do at home. Address everyone as Ji. If they ever have visitors, be sure to give up your bed and offer to sleep on the floor. Do not address your uncle unless he speaks first. Keep your head covered in his presence, do not laugh loudly, don't run anywhere and don't start eating until your Masur has finished.

Silence. **Mrs Bains** *starts to cry.*

Surinder   It's alright, Mum. We'll be alright.

Mrs Bains (*a beat*)   Go and wait for the taxi. And take your case.

Surinder *picks up her case, heads out.*

Mrs Bains   Tanvir, bring the other one. Kamaljit, check the shop is locked.

Kamaljit *goes.* **Tanvir** *picks up the other case, starts to head out and stops. He turns to* **Mrs Bains**.

Tanvir   I want to marry Kamaljit.

Mrs Bains   What did you say?

Tanvir   I want to marry Kamaljit.

Silence.

Tanvir   I know you think we are not well suited.

Mrs Bains   Of course you are not well suited.

Tanvir   I believe we are.

Mrs Bains   Hah, you are a stupid and she is a stupid.

Tanvir   Kamaljit and I have been reading the Granth Sahib and there are no words in there objecting to us getting married. I care for your daughter deeply. I respect you and Uncle, God rest his soul, too much to run away behind your back. And if you do not allow our union, I will obey your decision, leave the shop this very evening and spend the rest of my life alone and . . . celibate.

Mrs Bains   You are a lunatic.

Tanvir   If I am, so what? You know me, Auntie. I am honest and my hands are strong and I work all the hours God sends and if you allow it, I will treat Kamaljit like a precious diamond and I will be her servant until the day my heart stops beating.

Flustered, **Kamaljit** *hurries in.*

Mrs Bains   Wait with your sister.

Kamaljit   She's gone. Taken her case and everything.

She finds the note **Surinder** *left.*

Kamaljit   She . . . said she . . . wrote you a letter.

Mrs Bains   Read it. (*A beat.*) Read it!

Kamaljit (*opens letter*)   Dear Mum, I will not be going to Southall. I am not staying in Wolverhampton. Jim Wilson, the chocolate salesman has become a friend and is going to help me . . . I am sorry for the hurt this will cause. Please do not look for me, or try to contact me, and do not worry about me. I have taken my wedding jewellery. Your daughter, Surinder Kaur Bains.

Scene Twelve

Surinder *and* **Jim** *are in a London restaurant. They sit opposite one another at a table.* **Jim** *drinks a glass of red wine.*

Jim   I've paid for the bottle so don't be shy.

Surinder   Oh, I'm fine.

Surinder *ties up her hair.*

Jim   Such beautiful hair you've got . . . (*Clears throat.*) Her black mane gave him strength . . . She became his Samson . . . this brave lioness . . .

Surinder   Thank you. (*A beat.*) I've never cut my hair. It's against my religion.

Jim   Why?

Surinder   I can't say exactly . . .

Waitress brings two plates of steak and chips. Puts them in front of **Surinder** *and* **Jim**.

Jim   Is this your first meal in a restaurant?

Surinder *nods.*

Surinder   What is it?

Jim   Steak.

Surinder   Beef?

Jim   Yeah.

Surinder   I haven't eaten beef before.

Jim   This is going to be a fine moment then.

Surinder   I'm not even that hungry.

Jim   I've ordered it now.

Surinder *nervously picks up her knife and fork, cuts off a bit of the steak, puts it in her mouth.* **Jim** *pours her some red wine, hands it to her.*

Jim   Wash it down with this.

She drinks it. Sits back. Breathes hard.

Jim   He found the damsel, scooped her up from the inferno, placed her in paradise. (*A beat. Indicates steak.*) What do you think?

Surinder   It's a . . . foreign flavour . . .

Jim   Because it's Français. (*A beat.*) Means a lot to me, you know. That you believe so deeply.

Surinder   What?

Jim   In my writing.

Surinder   Oh.

Jim   Now my muse is by my side, I shall write every day. And with a decent body of work, I'll have a better chance of being published. You've made your dream happen, Sue, and it's given me hope that I can do the same.

Surinder   My dream?

Jim   Coming to London. With me.

Surinder   You know . . . I . . . er . . . had a kind teacher at school, she taught me about books . . . made me love learning.

Jim   How nice.

Surinder   I think my true dream would be to pass that love on. Become a teacher like her.

Jim   For now, I've got you a job in a wireless factory and you'll be looking after the bedsit. Once I'm on the ascent, it'll be your turn to fly.

Surinder   When might that be?

Jim   Give me a chance. When you get home from work, you can read my poems, help me decide which are the best ones to send.

Surinder   Actually, Jim, I . . . really do want to study.

Jim   Right.

Surinder   I could sell some of my jewellery, use it to pay for a college course.

Jim   Your jewellery?

Surinder *nods.*

Jim   I've already sold it.

Surinder   What?

Jim   I had to put a deposit down on the bedsit. I couldn't have you living in some dive. I want you to be comfortable.

Surinder   All of it? You sold all my gold?

Jim (*nods*)   Everything's about us now, Sue. You and me finding light in this dark world. Plus, this city's not cheap. One of us has to be responsible.

Shocked **Surinder** *plays with her food.*

Jim   Don't you want your steak?

Surinder   It just tastes so . . . strange.

An echo of the movement section which showed **Mr Bains'** *decline. This time,* **Mrs Bains** *ends up lying on the makeshift bed.*

Scene Thirteen

Years later. The **Bains'** *living area has been spruced up.* **Dhanda** *and* **Tanvir** *sit, drinking tea.* **Tanvir** *now wears glasses. Both men and* **Kamaljit** *have aged well. An infirm* **Mrs Bains** *lies in the space previously occupied by her husband.*

On another part of the stage, dishevelled **Jim** *sits on a bed in a bare bedsit space.* **Surinder** *is cleaning the floor. She appears world weary, older than her still tender years.*

Dhanda   Did I mention I am buying next door?

Mrs Bains   Shut up, stupid, fucking bastard, kutha, haramjada!

Tanvir   Curly the greengrocers?

Dhanda   The man is an alcoholic who is making a loss. I'm giving him a fair price and he is moving to the Costa del Sol. I will extend the stock room and sell garam masala, green chillis and coriander.

Tanvir   Who will buy those? People want hamburger, pizza, fish fingers.

Dhanda   We shall see.

He takes out some sheets of paper. **Tanvir** *reads.*

Dhanda   Sign and I'll be on my way. Seeto is cooking lamb kofte and jalebi. She starts to sulk if I eat her food cold. Plus little Ranjit misses his daddy if I am gone too long.

Tanvir (*reads*)   You want our children to be learning Punjabi and Sikhi in schools?

Dhanda   Their mother tongue. And their religion.

Kamaljit (*offstage*)   It's here!

Kamaljit *wheels in a trolley containing the entire Encyclopaedia Britannica.*

Dhanda   What is this?

Kamaljit   Encyclopaedia Britannica. He's been saving up for ages.

Jim *starts to pace around.*

Tanvir *takes a tome and starts flicking through.*

Jim   I don't have no luck. Not ever.

Surinder   Maybe look for a sales job again.

Jim   That's not me any more. Not me, at all. (*A beat.*) I need to lend some money.

Surinder   You mean borrow. You need to borrow some money.

Jim   We could sell something.

Surinder   There's nothing. (*A beat.*) The landlord asked if I might be able to help with his accounts.

Jim   What?

Surinder   I've said yes.

Jim   He asked because he fancies you.

Surinder   No. Because I can read and write and because I've got half a brain.

Stressed **Jim** *goes to look for something.*

Tanvir *indicates the encyclopaedia to* **Dhanda**.

Tanvir   Kamaljit and I will read a few pages each day. Knowledge will free us.

Dhanda   In this country, money is the path to freedom. They tore us down. Now we have risen and we run things.

He indicates the papers.

Sign, please. We must make sure our children learn to behave nicely, according to our rules.

Tanvir   Uncle . . . Sikhi, true Sikhi comes from love, not control. You want us to live in a little Punjab when we are in Wolverhampton.

Dhanda   Punjab is a state of mind Tanvir. Nobody owns land. On this earth, a person has a right to move from one location to another. We maintain our identity so we can be ourselves.

Tanvir   We can be us here. With the goreh.

Dhanda   Then we will be inviting chaos.

Tanvir   You sound like Enoch.

Dhanda   No . . .

Tanvir   Filled with foreboding; like the Roman, I see the River Tiber foaming with much blood.

Dhanda   Kamaljit's father, my dear Birji, would have signed without reading a single word, because he trusted me. We lived something. We lived something. Together. You remember how the goreh used to look at us, how they shamed us. If we start to mix up with them, then who do we become? Because they take from you Tanvir, they take and they take and they take! (*Gets up.*) When you are ready to sign, let me know.

Tanvir (*a beat*)   I will not be signing, Uncle. Not this or any other petition you bring.

Awkward silence. **Dhanda** *starts to exit.*

Dhanda   My ears are ringing, little Ranjit must be crying for me. I pray one day you experience the love only a son can give.

Kamaljit   We both pray.

Dhanda   Did I mention I am extending the shop?

Tanvir   You did.

Dhanda   It will be double the size. I want my boy to witness his father's ambition. (*A beat.*) You should consider updating your stock, Tanvir. Shop front is looking too old-fashioned. (*To* **Mrs Bains**.) Sat Siri Akal, Bhanji.

Mrs Bains   Shut up stupid, fucking bastard, kutha, haramjada!

He leaves. **Tanvir** *continues to read.*

Jim *is getting increasingly frustrated.*

Jim   Where's my book? I shall compose a brand new poem. And then maybe a short story . . . yes, that's it. Fiction will be my new path . . .

Surinder   Will you please stop!

Jim   What?

Surinder   Has a single sentence, no . . . has a single word ever made you a penny?

Jim   Not yet . . . but . . .

Surinder   Not yet, not ever. Never. Ever. Can't you see . . .

Jim   This is typical of you.

Surinder   We don't have any money!

Jim   You look so beautiful. If only you could act how you look.

Surinder   I can't do this any more . . . Jim . . . .

Jim   You really don't love me. You actually don't . . .

Surinder   I left my family for you. I let myself become a story that gets passed round people's lips . . .

Jim   You left because you didn't want to marry some stranger. (*A beat.*) You don't care. And now, you won't even deny it.

Kamaljit *faces* **Tanvir**.

Kamaljit   Uncle does care about us.

Tanvir   He cares about driving a Mercedes Benz.

Kamaljit   I would like my child to grow up knowing the history of the Gurus and to read the Granth Sahib. And to love their culture.

Tanvir   I would like my child to go to the finest schools, to cheer for England in the World Cup and eat Yorkshire pudding on a Sunday.

Kamaljit   Maybe our child can do both.

Tanvir *picks up another volume.*

Kamaljit   Tanvir!

She takes his hand, places it on her tummy.

Kamaljit   I said, maybe our child can do both.

Overjoyed, he picks her up, spins her around.

Tanvir   This is the best day. The very best day.

Slowly, **Kamaljit** *turns to her mum.*

Kamaljit   A new beginning's coming, Mum.

Mrs Bains *stares at her.*

Kamaljit   Everything that's passed . . . we won't have to think about it any more.

Surinder   I wish I could cut pieces of my body off and send them back home.

Jim   What are you saying?

Surinder   At least then I'd be there. (*A beat.*) I miss my mum slapping me round the face. So much. Do you miss your mum?

Jim   Stop talking nonsense . . . I love you so much. I love you and it barely registers . . .

Surinder   You love a story, Jim. That's not me. It was never me.

Jim   You're supposed to be my rock, my Samson . . .

Suddenly **Surinder** *gets up, frantically starts looking for something.*

Jim   What are you doing?

She finds some scissors, faces **Jim**. *We don't know what she's going to do. She starts cutting her hair.*

Jim   Stop . . . stop . . . please . . .

Surinder   One of us has to walk into the real world. Make money.

Jim   Not your hair . . .

Surinder   It's mine, Jim. It's the one thing that's still . . .

Clumps of her black tresses fall to the floor.

Jim   Who's going to want that now?

Surinder   Somebody will, Jim. (*A beat.*) Somebody.

Interval.

Act Two

Scene One

Present day. The **Bains***' living area retains a couple of bits of furniture/ photos from the years before. But it has been brought up to date in a blank DFS way. Condolence cards are dotted around.* **Ranjit** *sits, manspreading enthusiastically whilst checking his phone. There's a carrier bag on the floor.* **Arjan** *brings in two mugs of tea, hands one to* **Ranjit***.*

They drink their tea. **Ranjit** *eyes the contents of* **Arjan***'s mug.*

Ranjit   What the hell's that?

Arjan   Camomile.

Ranjit   Stick some milk in it, you pindoo [*villager*].

Arjan   It's herbal.

Ranjit *takes this in.*

Ranjit   Have you gone gay?

Arjan   Yeah.

He looms over **Ranjit** *and pretends to try to kiss him. They tussle.*

Ranjit   Get off! (*A beat.*) Anyway, I like gays.

Arjan   Eh?

Ranjit   They're all down the gym, aren't they? One of them's gonna buy my Peloton.

Arjan   You said the touchscreen broke.

Ranjit   He only wants it for Pilates and shit.

He indicates **Arjan***'s tea.*

Ranjit   Don't you drink chah no more?

Arjan   Camomile's soothing.

Ranjit   If you want soothing, I'll sort you out. I'm buying you a lap dance later.

Arjan   No thanks.

Ranjit   We'll go up the Red Lion then. Have a few glassies.

Arjan   I'm looking after my mum.

Ranjit   What do you think the old ladies are for? (*A beat.*) Come on, I've missed you, chitterface [*bumface*].

Arjan   Another time, Ranjit.

Ranjit   Nobody calls me that anymore. It's Jay, yeah?

Ranjit *indicates the carrier bag.*

Ranjit   Show us then.

Arjan *takes it out. Holds up a smart blue suit.*

Arjan   He liked blue. He looked good in blue.

Ranjit *feels the material.*

Ranjit   Oh yeah. This is quality, man. Quality. Will he be wearing this when they stick him in the furnace?

Arjan   Yes.

Ranjit   Shame he won't get to wear it again. (*A beat.*) How much was it?

Arjan   Three.

Ranjit   Quid?

Arjan   Hundred!

Ranjit   Are you mad? I could have got you this shit for forty, fifty pound.

Arjan   I can afford it, Ranjit.

Ranjit   Jay! (*A beat.*) You still doing that gora job?

Arjan   I'm a creative director. You know I'm a creative director.

Ranjit   Didn't you study painting and decorating?

Arjan   Fine art.

Ranjit   I know, I'm only messing. You wanna get a property.

Arjan   I've got a property.

Ranjit   Use the equity to get another one. And then another one. Then you can be like me.

Arjan   I enjoy my job.

Ranjit   Is your goree coming?

Arjan   Her name's Claire.

Ranjit   I like her. She looks . . . clean. Tell her to cover her legs and sit with the women.

Arjan   She knows.

Kamaljit *and* **Dhanda** *enter. Both have aged.* **Ranjit** *springs up.*

Ranjit   Sat siri akal, Auntie.

Kamaljit   Sat siri akal, beta.

She busies herself tidying.

Ranjit   Sit down.

Kamaljit   I'm better standing up.

Ranjit   Dad.

Ranjit *offers his seat to* **Dhanda** *who sits. He gets emotional.*

Dhanda (*to* **Arjan**)   Your daddy was like my own skin and bones. My first son. When he and your mummy were married, in the absence of his father, I did the Milni. You remember, Kamaljit?

Kamaljit   Yes, Uncle.

Dhanda   We exchanged blankets. Big fat woollen ones. (*To* **Kamaljit**.) Do you still have those blankets?

Kamaljit   Er . . . somewhere.

Dhanda   Tanvir was a better man than other men. He had a big heart. So his heart attack must also have been very big.

Arjan *shows his mum the suit.*

Arjan   What do you think?

Kamaljit   It's blue.

Arjan   Yes.

Kamaljit   Blue reminds me of toilet cleaner.

Ranjit   I know what you mean, Auntie.

Arjan   I can change it, if you like.

Kamaljit   Don't be stupid. Your dad won't mind.

Ranjit   Course he won't.

Dhanda   I was his elder. I should have gone first.

Ranjit   Stop that talk, Dad.

Dhanda   You don't worry, Kamaljit. I will be by Arjan's side. Show him the ropes.

Kamaljit   Thank you, Uncle.

Dhanda (*to* **Arjan**)   This thing we are about to do is no easy thing. When you next see your daddy, you will smell a smell you have never smelt before. And you will see his face and it will be another face. You know a dead man's lips are purple. Like a child who has spent all the day sucking an ice lolly. There will be the usual fluids that ooze from a live body.

Ranjit   Like when a baby's born. That ain't no Yummy Mummies on Insta. Shit and piss all the way, brother.

Dhanda   Once we have washed the body, he will be a king, ready to return to his kingdom. You don't be scared, Arjan.

Arjan   I'll manage.

Dhanda   Would Tanvir like one of his Encyclopaedia in the coffin?

Kamaljit   I don't think he'll be able to read it.

Dhanda   I will instruct the Gurdwara Committee to alert their top Giani for the funeral.

Arjan   I've already called them, Uncle. Thanks for your guidance with the washing, but everything else, well it's up to me now . . .

Ranjit   Dad's trying to help, brother.

Dhanda   It's okay, Arjan, it's okay . . .

He puts a kind arm around **Arjan**.

Dhanda   Ranjit will drive us.

Arjan   I'll meet you there.

Dhanda *goes.* **Ranjit** *follows.* **Kamaljit** *picks up the cups.*

Kamaljit   Uncle's missing your daddy. Try and talk nicely to him.

Arjan   He's here every single day. And Ranjit.

Kamaljit   You two used to play Lego.

Arjan   When I was five. Ranjit's . . . an actual moron.

Kamaljit   And you're not an actual moron? Uncle looked after us when my daddy died and after Mum . . . He did things for us that you can't understand. People aren't the way you'd like them to be, that's how it is.

Arjan (*a beat*)   I'm not sure Dad would have wanted this.

Kamaljit   What?

Arjan   Washing his body. The prayers. Planning to take his ashes to a village he never visited. He might have preferred it if we scattered him on the pavement outside the shop, then he could stay close to us.

Kamaljit   It's not about what he wanted.

Arjan   What is it then?

Kamaljit   Your dad doesn't have to go to the Gurdwara any more. I do.

Arjan   You don't have to go.

Kamaljit   What else am I supposed to do? When I walk in and the ladies' eyes pierce me with their pity, I plan to hold my head up high. Say I did all the proper, traditional things for my husband. Then, and only then, can I start chopping onions with the rest of them.

She picks up a glasses case. Takes out **Tanvir***'s glasses, beholds them.*

Arjan   Shall we put those on him?

Kamaljit *puts the glasses on.*

Arjan   Mum, what are you doing?

Kamaljit   Keeping him close.

Arjan   You'll mess your eyes up!

She starts walking around but she can barely see.

Kamaljit   I don't care.

She wanders aimlessly and bumps into a chair.

He said when we got old we'd go to the cinema every Tuesday.

Arjan   That's nice.

Kamaljit   Twenty per cent off on a Tuesday.

Arjan   I remember when I was little, he'd bring a family pack of popcorn from the shop and empty it out into three cartons.

Kamaljit (*fondly*)   He was so cheap.

Arjan   You and me, we could go to the cinema.

Kamaljit   I don't want to go to the cinema with you.

Arjan   If you like you can come and stay with me in London.

Kamaljit   London smells of wee.

Arjan   Move outside Wolverhampton then. Buy a cottage in the countryside.

Kamaljit   Why?

Arjan   More space, you can potter around in the garden.

Kamaljit   What's the point of that?

Arjan   Just an idea.

Kamaljit   Who'll run the shop?

Arjan   You can't keep the shop, Mum, not without Dad.

Kamaljit   Your father might be gone but he's still my husband. And this . . . here . . . is what we do. What we've always done.

Arjan   You can't even drive. How will you get to the cash and carry?

Kamaljit   There are buses . . .

Arjan   What can I do?

Kamaljit   Have I ever asked you for anything?

Arjan   No.

Kamaljit   You have your flat. Your office. That girl.

Arjan   I need to know you're gonna be okay.

Kamaljit   Let me do what I want, and you do what you want.

Arjan (*a beat*)   I want Dad not to be gone.

Kamaljit *takes off the glasses.*

Kamaljit   You always had your head high up in the clouds . . .

She puts the glasses on **Arjan**.

Kamaljit   . . . just like him.

Scene Two

Bains'*living area.* **Arjan** *is with* **Claire**. *She signals towards the kitchen.*

Claire   I should give your mum a hand.

Arjan   I wouldn't . . .

Claire   I found a YouTube video about how to make rotis.

Arjan   It's fine . . .

Claire   Isn't the daughter-in-law supposed to make rotis?

Arjan   Not necessarily . . . Mum can be quite . . . particular in the kitchen.

Claire   Particular?

Arjan   My dad watched a show about Mussolini once and decided to make a lasagne. He used the wrong pan for the meat and put atta . . . chappati flour in the white sauce . . . when Mum saw the state of the worktop . . . she threatened to kill him and screamed so loud that a customer called the police.

Claire   I'll leave her to it.

They share a warm laugh.

Arjan   I mean obviously she didn't . . . kill him, because he's just died.

Arjan's *about to break,* **Claire** *holds him.*

Arjan   The whole world feels different, Claire.

Claire   Bound to. He's not in it any more.

She takes his hand, strokes it tenderly.

What you said at the crematorium was . . . perfect and true.

Arjan   I meant it. All of it.

Claire   I learned a lot from him reading the encyclopaedias out loud. The confidence when he recited the periodic table that time . . .

Arjan   Knew all the halogens . . .

Claire   And the noble gases.

Arjan   He said once you understand something, deeply understand it, your mind's free to learn the next thing and the next. You know, if he'd had an education, my dad would have done some stuff. Big stuff . . .

Claire   Your dad did plenty. (*A beat.*) I don't think it's really hit your mum.

Arjan (*a beat*)   She wants to keep the shop.

Claire   Thought you said she'd be selling.

Arjan   Not yet. I'm going to help her out for a bit, you know.

Claire   No question.

Arjan   Yeah.

Claire   When are work expecting you back?

Arjan   They said when I'm ready.

Claire   Good.

Arjan   This won't affect the wedding.

Claire   I'm not thinking about the wedding. (*A beat.*) Arj, I'm here for you. Even when I'm not here.

They kiss. **Bill** *enters.*

Bill   Toilet won't flush.

Claire (*embarrassed*)   Dad.

Bill   I tried everything. Brute force, quick-fire motion, a deft flick of the wrist. But . . . nothing.

Arjan   Don't worry. I'll sort it.

Bill   Where's Cameljeet?

Claire   Kitchen.

Bill   Excellent. (*A beat.*) You don't think she'll want to relieve herself soon, do you? Just because . . . er . . . I don't want her to go in there and er . . . I'd rather not cause any distress . . . not on a day like today . . . do you know what I mean?

Arjan   It's fine, Bill.

Bill   I hope she hasn't gone to too much trouble.

Arjan   It's no trouble.

Silence.

Bill   Would you mind sorting the flush out? Only it's going to play on my mind.

Arjan *heads out.* **Bill** *and* **Claire** *stand in silence.*

Bill   I couldn't help . . .

Claire   Don't, just don't . . .

Bill   There's obviously a plumbing issue . . .

Claire   Will you stop going on about it?

Bill   Is it beef they don't eat?

Claire   Yes.

Bill   But pork's alright? Bacon, ham, sweet and sour . . .

Claire   Yes!

Bill   I'm only checking. I don't want to say the wrong thing.

Claire   Then please stop talking.

Arjan *comes back.*

Arjan   Sorted.

Bill   Thank God.

Awkward silence.

Such a nice man, your dad.

Arjan   He was.

Bill   I wish I'd got to know him better. Do you have any other family round here?

Arjan   No, my mum had a sister but she died.

Bill   Oh dear and now your mum has to cope with this.

Arjan   Her sister died a long time ago, when she was sixteen. Car crash.

Bill   Was she wearing a seatbelt?

Arjan   Er . . . I'm not aware . . .

Claire   He wasn't alive, Dad.

Bill   My old optician used to say that before the seatbelt law came in, people's faces used to regularly smash through the windscreen. Into smithereens! The doctors in A and E spent most Saturday evenings stitching noses and lips back together. Once the law was passed, the bodies stopped piling in. Practically overnight, he said. That's good, isn't it?

Silence.

Is it beef you Sikhs don't eat?

Arjan   It's more of a cultural choice.

Bill   But why beef?

Arjan   I don't actually know.

Claire   It doesn't matter.

Kamaljit *comes in, she holds a cloth and cleans around the place.*

Kamaljit   Food is almost ready.

Bill   Can you enlighten me, Cameljeet? As to why Sikhs don't eat beef.

Kamaljit   We don't eat beef.

Bill   Why though?

Kamaljit   We just don't.

Bill   Got it.

Claire *gets up to offer* **Kamaljit** *her chair.*

Kamaljit   It's okay.

Claire   Please.

Kamaljit *continues cleaning.*

Arjan   Sit down for a minute, Mum!

Kamaljit *stops. She cleans the seat where* **Claire** *has been sitting and sits down.*

Claire   Arjan says you're holding onto the shop.

Bill   Are you?

Kamaljit   Yes.

Claire   I suppose you'd miss the customers.

Kamaljit   I don't like the customers. And they don't like me.

Arjan   That's not true, Mum.

Kamaljit   They always asked for him.

Arjan   Amy Burton likes you.

Kamaljit   You know she has eleven children. And they say us Asians have big families. The latest boyfriend is a tattoo artist. He practises on the kids. No shortage of space there.

Bill   Everyone's always stuffing their faces these days.

Kamaljit   They are.

Bill   And it's on the telly all the time, isn't it? Food.

Arjan   The programmes are cheap to make.

Bill   But they're in Tuscany or Sri Lanka every week! I couldn't afford Tuscany or Sri Lanka.

Claire   It's still relatively cheap.

Bill   You've got no idea about money.

Claire   I did maths A-level.

Bill   You don't even know if you're getting married in a few months. I mean, what if you lose your deposit for the venue?

Claire   I don't care about the deposit.

Bill   See, you can't manage your own life.

Claire   I can and I do!

Awkward silence. **Kamaljit** *gets up to go.*

Kamaljit   Better check the sabji.

Arjan   Bill, why don't you help Mum with the plates?

Bill   Certainly.

Bill *follows* **Kamaljit** *out.*

Claire   He's so fucking embarrassing.

Arjan   Forget it.

Claire   It's like he's got . . . no love in him.

Arjan   Don't say that.

Claire   Him and my mum . . . it wasn't like with your parents.

Arjan   He must have some love. He made you.

Claire   Did your mum really meet your dad when she was fifteen?

Arjan (*nods*)   They both said it was love at first sight. And after all these years, my dad told me he still felt like the luckiest man in Wolverhampton.

Claire (*a beat*)   She's going to be lonely, isn't she? When you come back to London.

Arjan   Yeah.

Claire   If she wants to move in with us after the wedding, I'm completely open to living as part of a multi-generational, extended family . . .

Arjan   She doesn't want to move in.

Claire   We could look into supported accommodation. So she's got company.

Arjan   Company?

Claire   And so she's safe.

Arjan   You mean like an old people's home?

Claire   I didn't say that . . .

Arjan   My mum is not old.

Claire   I'm talking about . . . housing, with somebody nearby, like a warden . . .

Arjan   This place is all she's ever known.

Claire   You're misinterpreting my words . . .

Arjan   Claire, I'm staying here. And I don't know how long for, okay.

Claire   Of course.

Arjan   While she needs me, I'm staying.

Scene Three

The shop. **Arjan** *is organising shelves in the shop. A drunk white guy,* **Tommy**, *enters. Flails around.*

Tommy   Alright, Arj . . .

Arjan   Tommy.

Tommy   Where's Tanvir?

Arjan   He's dead, remember.

Tommy   Oh . . . yeah . . . fuck . . . yeah . . . I miss the bones of that man. Your dad . . . he was a fucking giant . . . I loved that geezer . . . I would have even gone to his funeral if I had the right date . . . bet you did all the rituals and singing and that, didn't you?

Arjan   Yeah.

Tommy   I knew it! You lot are kings of that shit . . . that culture shit . . . We've lost it . . . lost our souls . . . our people don't know what to do when pain strikes . . . fuck . . . I loved that man . . . like he was my dad . . .

Arjan   Sure . . .

Tommy   Me and him used to discuss things, you know . . . important things. Life things. I miss those days . . .

Arjan   Yeah.

Tommy   I was telling him, Arj . . . the AI's coming for us. It's gonna like . . . be injected into the bloodstream . . . and next they're gonna put chips in our brains . . . and . . . my brother already lost his job at the Council . . . you know he had a decent job . . . in a office . . . and they got rid of him . . . you know . . . just like that . . . and now he's staring at his phone, day and night . . . he sits there.

Arjan   That's a shame, mate.

Tommy   Your dad used to say people are always moving. You can't stop them moving . . . exploring new lands . . . but I told him . . . there aren't enough . . . doctors' surgeries or schools or KFCs, do you know what I mean? He said it was down to resources and the government hasn't invested and all that and . . . I mean why can't people just stay put . . . in France or some other shithole . . . They're letting the whole world onto our shores. The whole fucking world . . . and my brother hasn't even got his job any more . . .

He picks up a load of goods, almost falls over as he puts them on the counter.

Arjan   I can't serve you, Tommy.

Tommy   Why?

Arjan   You owe us almost fifty quid.

Tommy   Your dad won't mind. He knows I always pay up . . .

Arjan   And you've had too much to drink.

Tommy   Don't go social services on me, Arj . . . come on . . .

Arjan   No.

Tommy   Your dad would have served me . . .

Arjan   No he wouldn't. Go home.

Tommy   Home?

Arjan   Yeah.

Tommy   You've made a mistake there . . .

Arjan   How's that?

Tommy   Because this is my home. Everywhere you see is my house. Not yours.

Arjan   Get out . . .

Tommy   You think because you've got all these fags and tins of beans and packets of sugar . . . that you're better than me . . . who was on the land this shop's built on, first?

Arjan   I said leave!

Tommy   Plus . . . I don't have you lot as mates! Not shit-stained Pakis from Pakistani land.

Arjan   Fuck off.

Tommy   You are in my country! My white country.

Tommy *squares up to* **Arjan** *who aggressively stares into his face. Suddenly* **Tommy** *does a Nazi salute.*

Arjan (*shouts*)   Get the fuck out.

Tommy *staggers and crashes into a stack of tins. They roll onto the floor.* **Tommy** *stumbles and takes a swing at* **Arjan** *who deftly catches him and harshly chucks him out.*

Arjan *eyes the mess. Kicks the tins in fury.*

Scene Four

Ranjit'*s shed. Assorted junk.* **Ranjit** *devours a chicken leg from a box. Offers the box to* **Arjan** *who shakes his head.*

Arjan   I'm not hungry.

Ranjit   Man needs bare protein if he wanna get hench.

Arjan   I don't wanna get hench.

Ranjit   What if that piece of shit comes back and fucks with you?

Arjan   I could have had him, easy.

Ranjit   But you didn't, did you? He got away.

Arjan   He was drunk. I think he's got mental health issues.

Ranjit   You ain't in London now, brother. We have to take care of ourselves in these endz. What you gonna do next time your drunk mentally ill friend passes round? With his mates? What if your mum's behind the counter on her own? You gonna show him how to do reiki or mindfulness or some shit?

Ranjit *finds a huge suitcase. Opens it.*

Ranjit   Take a look at these babies, chitterface [*bumface*].

Arjan   What the fuck?

Ranjit   Pretty, aren't they?

Arjan   Is this . . . even legal?

Ranjit   Man don't business with the feds.

Arjan *takes out an assortment of weapons.*

Ranjit   Those are an exact replica of the nunchucks Bruce Lee had in Enter the Dragon. And that is a katana. Careful brother, this shit could cut your hand off.

Arjan   What the hell are you doing with all this?

Ranjit   When you're a kid helping in the shop and you watch your dad being shat on day in day out, you make yourself a man. And man needs protection. Do you fancy a samurai sword?

Arjan   No!

Ranjit   Take something, you bhenjot [*sisterfucker*]!

Arjan *eyes a stick, balanced against a wall.*

Arjan   What's that?

Ranjit   My mum's mop.

Arjan *picks it up.* **Ranjit** *starts to build a spliff.*

Ranjit   It's good you're home, brother. Back where you belong. What do you do in London anyway?

Arjan   Work. See friends.

Ranjit   You can do that in Wolverhampton. How big's your house down there?

Arjan   It's a flat.

Ranjit   You seen my house, innit?

Arjan   Yeah.

Ranjit   Five bedrooms. Me and my missus have our own dressing rooms. You know how many buy-to-lets I've got now?

Arjan   Four?

Ranjit   Nineteen.

He lights the spliff. Takes a long drag. Hands it to **Arjan**.

Ranjit   Shop's hard graft, innit?

Arjan   Yeah. I mean . . . it's just me and Mum.

Ranjit   Pressure, brother.

Arjan   Yeah.

Ranjit   Pure pressure. On your head and your heart . . . the females of the species don't understand what us lot have to bear.

Arjan   I just wanna be able to walk up the road feeling free, you know . . . just walk up the road and breathe.

Ranjit (*a beat*)   I get you, brother. Me and Dad are here for you. We're family. You know that?

Arjan   Appreciate it. (*A beat.*) You've got masis and bhuas and chachas and cousins . . . blood and biology everywhere you look. You're lucky.

Ranjit   I don't fuckin' know . . .

Arjan   You are.

Ranjit   When you're a son in the middle of the bed, you get spoilt with Xbox and PlayStation and shit. And one day there's half a million in your account, but everything costs, brother.

Arjan   How?

Ranjit   You're the future, the hope of the whole Khandan [*family*]. They gotta believe you're gonna take care of all the shit. Cos if you fuck it up, then the bad looks and the chat from out there's gonna land. And suddenly the whole family goes down. And it's on you. (*A beat.*) You got away, Arj.

Arjan   Now I'm back, I wanna do the right thing, you know.

Ranjit   The right thing, brother. That's why I keep my chin up. Face out front. New buy to let and motor every two years. When they see that, they can have faith. (*A beat.*) You don't have this shit in London.

Arjan   There's different shit.

Ranjit   Maybe I'll come and visit one day.

Arjan   Yeah.

Ranjit   You'll have to take me on the Eye and up the Shard and all that. (*A beat.*) Will you take me?

Arjan   Sure. (*A beat.*) You ever thought about making a different choice?

Ranjit (*a beat*)   What would I wanna do that for?

He gets up, picks up a weapon and brandishes it around.

Ranjit   Gotta keep myself fit and strong, brother. So I can show up for the likes of you. (*A beat.*) I mean it's not like you can ask your Masi to help out.

Arjan   What?

Ranjit   Your mum's sister.

Arjan   Of course not, she died, Ranjit.

Ranjit   My dad was talking about her the other night.

Arjan   Did he tell you she was killed in a car crash?

Ranjit   Probably been better if she had.

Arjan   What do you mean?

Ranjit   He said she ran off with a gora.

Arjan   Eh?

Ranjit *takes the spliff back.*

Ranjit   Big scandal, brother.

Arjan   Are you saying . . . my Surinder Masi . . . is alive?

Ranjit   Yeah.

Arjan   Where is she?

Ranjit   Dunno.

Arjan   Are you being fucking serious?

Ranjit   Why would I lie?

Arjan   But everyone told me she was dead.

Ranjit   She's not in Wolverhampton any more, so in a manner of speaking . . . she is dead.

Arjan   Does my mum know?

Ranjit   They have to bury this kind of shit. You know how it goes.

Arjan   I'll ask her.

Ranjit   Nah, don't do that, brother.

Arjan   Why not?

Ranjit *starts to laugh.*

Ranjit   You are stupid, bhenjot.

Arjan *gets up.*

Arjan   This could . . . she could be the missing piece, Ranjit, for my mum and me.

Ranjit   Nah, man . . . let a sleeping tiger rest.

Arjan   So, she's really out there, somewhere?

Ranjit   Yeah . . .

Arjan   Shit.

Ranjit   Yeah . . .

Arjan   This is a good day, Ranjit. A good day . . .

They both laugh, high from the weed.

Scene Five

Arjan *and* **Ranjit** *loiter outside the door of a non-descript council house.*

Arjan   Definitely this one?

Ranjit   Waze don't let a man down, chitterface [*bumface*].

Arjan   I didn't imagine her on a council estate.

Ranjit   She ended up with a no-good gora, ennit? Plenty of them living round here.

Ranjit *takes out a spliff. Lights it.*

Arjan   They might have bought the place. Your dad was positive about his name?

Ranjit (*consults phone*)   Jim Wilson.

Arjan   What if it's the wrong one?

Ranjit   Let's hope so. I mean look at this shithole.

Arjan (*checks phone*)   If he's kept up his subscription to the West Midlands Sales Reps Association, he must be . . . alright.

Ranjit *passes* **Arjan** *the spliff. He shakes his head.*

Ranjit   Have it, you pindoo!

Arjan *takes it. Inhales. Almost falls over.*

Arjan   What the hell is in that?

Ranjit   The real bad man shit. (*A beat.*) You know . . . if the shop gets too much for you lot, we can help.

Arjan   Thanks.

Ranjit   Could even take it off your hands.

Arjan   What?

Ranjit   When you sell it. If it makes things easier. I mean you lot can't manage the place forever.

Arjan *is really high now. He starts laughing uncontrollably.*

Ranjit   Calm down, chitterface [*bumface*].

The door opens. **Jim** *emerges. Life has not been kind to him. The three men stare at one another for a few moments.*

Jim   What do you want?

Ranjit   We're from His Majesty's Revenue and Customs.

Jim   Eh?

Arjan   We'd like to talk to your wife, Mrs Surinder Wilson.

Jim   Are you joking me?

Arjan   Sorry if we've got the wrong person.

Jim   Right person. Wrong decade. I haven't heard that name since . . . since a long time.

Arjan   But you were married? To Surinder Bains?

Jim   Sue? Tried putting a ring on her finger but . . . no . . . Any money she owes, that's down to her.

Arjan   When was the last time you saw her?

Jim   Like I said, a long time . . . Sue . . . my dark lady . . . my valiant Sue . . . I was never . . . enough for her.

Ranjit   You got any idea where she is?

Jim (*shakes head*)   If you find her, tell her . . . tell her, it's okay. I'm okay. And that I'm sorry . . . and I owe her a couple of packets of Benson and Hedges.

He shuts the door. Silence.

Arjan   Fuck.

Ranjit   Shit.

Arjan   Fuck.

Ranjit   I know . . . she smokes!

Arjan   What do we do now?

Ranjit   Only one thing to do.

Scene Six

Loud, raucous musical montage of **Arjan** *and* **Ranjit** *doing drugs. Dancing in a club. Having drinks with two young women.*

Ending up in a flat with the women.

Ranjit *is passed out in a corner. One of the young women is playing on a PlayStation.*

The other woman and **Arjan** *start to kiss.*

Scene Seven

Arjan *and* **Claire** *sit at a table with a couple of drinks.*

Claire   How much stuff?

Arjan   About two hundred quid's worth. I chased them down the road, but these kids are used to running. So they're fast.

Claire   Sounds like youngsters being stupid.

Arjan   Even if they don't steal anything, there's an edge in the air. As if we've taken something that doesn't belong to us, because we're not from here.

Claire   You are from here.

Arjan   It's like they believe we've got more than we deserve. I get up at 4.30 every morning!

Claire   Most of those kids are likely to be living in poverty.

Arjan   I know that. And I get that all this . . . fucking skullduggery isn't fair.

Claire   Fucking skullduggery?

Arjan   Yeah.

Claire   Have you turned . . . gangster now?

Arjan   This isn't London, living cheek by jowl with refugees and billionaires. Here, everyone's in their tribes. I have to face the shit on a daily basis. And I'm sick of being a target. The police said they'd come and take a statement. They didn't show up for ten days. (*A beat.*) I don't mean to go on, I'm a bit . . .

Claire   Forget it.

Arjan   I've got something to say.

Claire   I've got something to tell you too.

Arjan   Can I go first? Please.

Claire   Okay.

Arjan   This is hard. Might be time . . . for us to take a break.

Claire (*a beat*)   I thought you wanted to get married.

Arjan   I did. I do . . . but I can't.

Claire   Why?

Arjan   Because . . . of everything.

Claire   Spell it out.

Arjan   We fell in love when I was a metropolitan creative director, but now I'm a provincial shopkeeper. (*A beat.*) You know my dad grew up in India. Not like my mum . . .

Claire   Yes . . .

Arjan   So when he spoke Punjabi, it was proper, desi. When he said 'Kiddha Putth', he made these sounds that she can't make. That I can't make. And now he's gone, it feels like those sounds, my dad's sounds are lost. I'll never hear them again.

Claire   This is grief, Arj. Normal grief.

He shakes his head.

Arjan   You don't know what 'Kiddha' means. I used to think Asian men who dated white women and then went on to marry Asian women were cowards who caved under emotional pressure, but now I think they give in because it's . . . impossible. Because you can't understand how responsible I feel for my family . . . my mum . . . more responsible than I am for my own life . . . The problem is, ultimately, you're white. And I'm brown.

Claire   Is that how you see me . . . as someone who's just . . . white?

Arjan   No . . . I dunno . . .

Claire   Do you honestly believe what you've said?

Arjan   I had to speak it out loud.

Claire   Whatever you're feeling . . .

Arjan (*interrupts*)   I had sex with someone. I was drunk. I barely remember.

Claire   No . . .

Arjan   Yes.

Stunned **Claire** *gets up from the table.*

Arjan   I'm sorry. About everything.

Silence.

What . . . what did you want to tell me?

Claire (*a beat*)   I found your aunt.

Arjan *is speechless.*

Claire   You kept looking for Surinder Bains but you said Jim Wilson called her Sue so I looked for Sue Bains. She runs a hotel. I'll send you her details.

She starts to go.

Arjan   Don't go.

Claire   You can't expect me to stay.

Arjan   Say something.

Claire *comes back to the table, picks up her drink and chucks it in his face.*

Scene Eight

Arjan *sits in a lobby.* **Surinder** *enters. She is older, weathered but chic.*

Surinder   Hello, I'm Sue.

Arjan   Hi.

Surinder   You've seen the brochure?

Arjan   Yes.

Surinder   I can show you around the space and we can go through some options.

He stares at her.

Is that alright?

Arjan   We were getting married. But now . . . it's complicated.

Surinder   Well . . . are you still planning to book your reception?

Arjan   My name's Arjan Banga. I'm the son of Tanvir Singh Banga and Kamaljit Kaur Bains.

Long silence.

Surinder   Why have you come here?

Arjan   I wanted to see you.

Surinder   So . . . Kamaljit and Tanvir got together?

Arjan   Yeah.

Surinder   What about my mum?

Arjan   Oh . . . er . . . Bibi died years ago.

Surinder   How?

Arjan   I was only a kid. Cancer, I'm pretty sure it was . . . cancer.

Surinder *takes this in.*

Surinder   Was she in hospital?

Arjan   No, she was at home. Mum and Dad looked after her.

Surinder   That's good. I'm glad.

Arjan   She had dementia towards the end.

Surinder   My mum?

Arjan *nods.*

Surinder   But she was sharp, quick . . . she could add up a basket of shopping in her head in five seconds . . . my mum . . . she kept us all alive . . .

Arjan   I realise this is a lot to take in . . .

Surinder   Yeah.

Arjan   At least you . . . followed your heart.

Surinder   How do you know what I did? (*A beat.*) Sorry, it's . . . I never imagined a moment like this . . .

Arjan   I went to see Jim Wilson.

Surinder   Who told you about Jim?

Arjan Uncle. Mr Dhanda.

Surinder Still going strong, is he?

Arjan Practically runs the town. (*A beat.*) Jim said to say he's okay and that he owes you some cigarettes.

Surinder *half laughs.*

Arjan Do you have a family? Kids?

Surinder No. (*A beat.*) Does Kamaljit know you're here?

Arjan She doesn't. But she'll be delighted. I'm sure she will.

Surinder And . . . how's your dad?

Arjan (*a beat*) There's a lot to catch up on.

Scene Nine

Bains' *living area.* **Kamaljit** *is tidying up, she clatters around loudly.* **Arjan** *tries to help.*

Kamaljit Get out of my way.

Arjan You've already dusted the place to death.

Kamaljit If she runs a hotel, she's used to inspecting rooms.

Arjan I think she just wants to see you.

Kamaljit How do you know?

She stops. Takes a breath.

Kamaljit The dhal and the lamb's cooked. The samoseh are on the side. Did you get the imli chutney?

Arjan Yes.

Kamaljit What if she doesn't eat Indian food anymore?

Arjan She must do.

Kamaljit She's been around goreh for years.

Arjan They eat more Indian food than Indians.

He checks his phone.

Kamaljit You should call that Claire.

Arjan   She's blocked me.

Kamaljit   So block her back.

Arjan   It doesn't work like that . . . I mean she won't know . . . doesn't matter . . .

Kamaljit   Maybe it's better in the long run.

Arjan   I still love her, Mum.

Kamaljit   Love doesn't last. Look at your Masi and that chocolate salesman.

Arjan   You loved Dad.

Kamaljit   No I didn't.

Arjan   You had a love marriage!

Kamaljit   Yes, but after a few years he started getting on my nerves. (*A beat.*) I liked him. And I respected him, but you only love someone at the start. Did you put the ketchup out?

Arjan   What?

Kamaljit   In case she doesn't want chutney.

Arjan   I'll get some from the stock room.

Kamaljit   I told you to do it before.

Arjan   Don't you want her here?

Kamaljit   You should have asked me.

Arjan   I thought it'd make you happy.

Kamaljit   Since the day I was born everyone thinks they know what's best for me.

Arjan   I can tell her not to come.

Kamaljit   Her train must be here by now.

Arjan   I'll text her, we can meet for a coffee instead.

Kamaljit   I've made the dhal and the lamb now! And who's going to eat the fifty rotis I've made?

Arjan   Why did you make so many?

Kamaljit   I don't know!

She sits down.

Go and find the ketchup. And check the chah.

Arjan *leaves.* **Kamaljit** *breathes deeply. Takes out a small book, covers her head. Puts her hands together, quietly says a prayer in Punjabi. As she is praying,* **Surinder** *enters. She stares at her sister.* **Kamaljit** *senses eyes on her, she notices* **Surinder**, *closes the book, takes her chooni off, stands.*

Surinder   Arjan said to come through.

Silence. **Surinder** *indicates the prayer book.*

Are you . . . religious?

Kamaljit   Yeah . . . no . . . I mean I don't know . . . I made samoseh.

Surinder   Oh.

Kamaljit   You still eat them?

Surinder (*nods*)   I'm sorry about Tanvir.

Kamaljit   Yeah . . . well . . . one day he was alive and now . . . he's not.

Surinder   You look the same.

Kamaljit   No, I don't. You don't. When did you cut your hair?

Surinder   Years ago.

Kamaljit   Sit down.

Surinder   I'm fine.

Kamaljit   Sit!

Surinder *sits.*

Kamaljit   So you got the train?

Surinder   Yeah.

Kamaljit   Haven't you got a car?

Surinder   Yes, but it was easier.

Kamaljit   Is there a toilet on the train?

Surinder   What?

Kamaljit   It's a long journey, isn't it?

Surinder   Yeah, but I didn't use it.

Kamaljit   Do you need the toilet now?

Surinder   No.

Kamaljit   You should go.

Surinder   I'm okay.

Kamaljit   You don't want your bladder to burst.

Arjan *comes in.*

Arjan   Everything alright?

Kamaljit   Yes.

Surinder   Yes.

Kamaljit   Get the samoseh. Don't forget the imli. And the ketchup and the chah.

He exits.

He had a girlfriend.

Surinder   Right.

Kamaljit   She was okay. White girl.

Surinder   Right.

Kamaljit   You've probably got a lot in common.

Arjan *comes back in with a tray.*

Kamaljit   She blocked him.

Surinder   Who?

Kamaljit   Claire.

Arjan   We split up.

Kamaljit   Her decision.

Surinder   That's a shame.

Kamaljit   And we sent him to private school. We couldn't afford it, but we sent him.

Arjan   I didn't want to go.

Kamaljit   Tanvir said he was destined for medicine. He wasn't.

Arjan   I hated science. You know I hated science.

Kamaljit   He used to steal cigarettes from the shop and sell them at break time. They phoned us and we had to go and sit in front of the headmaster. In his actual office!

Surinder   Oh . . .

Arjan   I paid all the money back.

Kamaljit   Eventually.

Arjan   I was only twelve.

Kamaljit   Imagine if we'd done that.

Surinder   We'd get battered.

Kamaljit   We'd be dead. (*A beat.*) And I couldn't have any more kids after him because my uterus was upside down. Or back to front. Or something.

Arjan   It's called a retroverted uterus, Mum.

Kamaljit   Now, he's a doctor! (*A beat. To* **Surinder**.) Have a samosa.

Surinder *picks one up. Takes a bite. Eats. Puts the samosa down.*

Kamaljit   Too much chilli for you?

Surinder   No. It just . . .

Kamaljit   What?

Surinder   Tastes like Mum's.

She gets emotional. **Kamaljit** *turns to* **Arjan**.

Kamaljit   Tissues.

He leaves. **Surinder** *composes herself.*

Surinder   Are you angry with me?

Kamaljit   When the internet came out . . . have you got the internet?

Surinder   Yeah.

Kamaljit   I thought you might send an email . . . but you didn't.

Surinder   I couldn't find a way . . . to start . . . of saying what I wanted. (*A beat.*) Was Mum alright?

Kamaljit   No. (*A beat.*) But we were here so after a bit, she managed.

Surinder   Tell me . . . things.

Kamaljit   Things?

Surinder   About her. Your wedding. When Arjan was little . . .

Kamaljit *gets up.*

Kamaljit   I can't . . . colour it all in, not just like that . . .

Surinder   No.

Kamaljit   No.

Surinder   Why did you tell Arjan I died in a car crash?

Kamaljit   Because it was . . . it felt like . . . you did.

Surinder   You knew I was out there.

Kamaljit   At the beginning, we used to get called names, laughed at . . . a hundred stares fixing on us at the Gurdwara. And we took it. Mum and me, we had to tolerate the sky caving in on us . . . I didn't want them to make my son feel shame.

Surinder   You shouldn't have lied.

Kamaljit   You left me! Do you think it was easy to watch our mum turn into a raving bag of bones? Sitting there . . . rattling. She turned old so fast. (*A beat.*) And I didn't even know if you were still breathing. No sister by my side on my wedding day. No Daddy. No Daddy. (*A beat.*) I made up a story so I could miss you and . . . cry. (*A beat.*) But you know what, Surinder . . . I never once stopped praying . . .

Surinder   Did Mum talk about me?

Kamaljit (*a beat*)   Me and Tanvir used to.

Surinder   I asked about Mum.

Kamaljit   She never spoke your name.

Surinder   Not even to curse me?

Silence. **Surinder** *tries to cover her upset.*

Daddy shouldn't have brought us here.

Kamaljit   You can't blame Daddy.

Surinder   I'm trying to understand how they expected us to live . . .

Kamaljit   Daddy got called a Paki every single day of his life. But when he rested his head on his pillow at night, he did it smiling because he knew he was building something. Him and Mum might have got most of it wrong, but they tried. You can't say they didn't try.

Surinder   Yeah.

Kamaljit   You were his boy. His good boy. (*A beat.*) The years that have gone are gone.

Surinder   Some bits have been ugly, Kamaljit, really ugly.

Arjan *brings the tissues.*

Surinder   I'm sorry for . . .

Kamaljit   Shut up! What did you do wrong? Nothing! You're my baby sister.

She starts to sing the chorus from the theme from The Monkees. She points to a box on the side.

Kamaljit (*to* **Arjan**)   Give me that.

He hands it to her. She opens it, gives it to **Surinder** *who takes out an envelope.*

Kamaljit   Open it.

Surinder *opens it, takes out a slip. Reads.*

Surinder   Biology A, Chemistry A, English Language A, English Literature A, French A, History B, Latin A, Mathematics A, Physics A . . .

Arjan *picks up the slip.*

Arjan   You were brilliant.

Kamaljit   Never mind about the B.

Arjan   Why didn't you go to university?

Arjan *gets a text. Leaves.*

Kamaljit   How did you get rich?

Surinder   Me?

Kamaljit   You're not poor. You don't look poor.

Surinder   I worked for a landlord. Learned the property business. Bought a place and then another and then another . . .

Arjan *leads* **Dhanda** *and* **Ranjit** *in.*

Dhanda   Oh my God. Oh my God. It is you.

Surinder   Sat siri akal.

Dhanda   Surinder Kaur. Welcome home.

He holds out his arms. She doesn't move.

Dhanda   She is the exact image of her mum. (*A beat. To* **Surinder**.) You remember your mum?

Surinder   Yes.

Dhanda   Bhanji was a great lady!

Surinder   She was.

Kamaljit   Have a samosa, Uncle.

Dhanda   No, no, no. We are merely passing.

He nudges **Ranjit** *who is holding a box of Indian sweets.*

Ranjit   Bought you some barfi.

Surinder   Thanks.

Dhanda   This is a blessed day. Your mum would be happy to see her daughters reunited. No need to worry about your sister. We are here.

Ranjit   Course we are.

Kamaljit   Uncle's been very kind.

Dhanda   Kamaljit and Tanvir were left alone you see. They needed support.

Surinder   Right.

Dhanda   You should come and see my shop. Buy Express! I have a butcher's counter and a Slush Puppie machine. (*A beat.*) Plus I sell chips, hot from the microwave.

Kamaljit   That's nice isn't it, Surinder?

Surinder   Yeah.

Dhanda   You look like you have had a good life, Surinder Kaur. That is what is important. To have a good life. No matter what has passed, we do not break from each other. Even when we don't see each other's faces. You are our girl. No matter what.

Ranjit (*to* **Arjan**)   You coming out later, chitterface [*bumface*]?

Arjan   I'll message you.

Dhanda   We will leave you in peace.

Kamaljit   See you at the Gurdwara, Uncle.

Dhanda *and* **Ranjit** *head out.*

Surinder   How do you manage the shop on your own?

Kamaljit   Arjan's here. When he leaves, I'll sell the place.

Arjan   What?

Kamaljit   You told me to live in a cottage and potter in the garden.

Arjan   You said you'd never sell.

Kamaljit   Uncle thinks it might be a sensible idea.

Surinder   Uncle.

Arjan   You're not selling the shop, Mum.

Kamaljit   Are you going to stack toilet rolls for the rest of your life?

Arjan   If I have to.

Kamaljit *gets up.*

Kamaljit   I'll check the lamb.

She leaves.

Arjan   Must be strange . . . to be here, I mean.

Surinder (*a beat*)   This place was always . . . full of people . . . every day there was some . . . tamasha . . . And your dad, your dad was the best person . . .

She half laughs.

Surinder   She must be lost without him.

Arjan   We both have been.

Surinder   Perhaps . . . if you like . . . I could help out, now and again . . . if that's useful.

Arjan   You've got your own life.

Surinder   I'm okay. I enjoy myself.

Arjan   What happened to you?

Surinder   Doesn't matter . . .

Surinder *gets up walks around the space, looks around, soaking it all in. Half laughs to herself, almost in disbelief.*

Scene Ten

Bains *'living area.* **Ranjit** *is checking a light fitting, he holds a screwdriver. There is a cup of tea on the side and a plate of biscuits.* **Ranjit** *stands back, admires his handiwork. Picks up the tea.* **Kamaljit** *enters, sets up an ironing board.*

Ranjit   Done. You won't get any more flickering now.

Kamaljit   You didn't have to, beta.

Ranjit   That light'll give you headaches. Can't have you ending up down the doctor's, Auntie.

Kamaljit   You are a sweet boy. How are your little ones?

Ranjit   Pair of wrestlers. Always trying to bite each other's ears off and kick the other's private parts. Nina usually breaks it up.

Kamaljit   You are lucky to have Nina.

Ranjit   Arjan still hasn't found his Juliet?

Kamaljit   I thought he had but . . .

Ranjit   He wants to hurry up. You must be desperate for grandkids.

Kamaljit   I'm okay.

Ranjit   My two keep my mum and dad alive. They know there's a new generation rising up to take their name. Show the world what that name means. You've worked hard all these years, Auntie, time to put your feet up.

Kamaljit   Your daddy keeps busy.

Ranjit   He can't stop work. Jat blood running through his veins.

Kamaljit   Yes.

Ranjit   Although, he's been . . . under the weather recently. Mum reckons he should go to the GP.

Kamaljit   He does eat a lot of sugar.

Ranjit   It's not his sugar.

Kamaljit   What is it then?

Ranjit   It's you.

He takes a biscuit, eats it.

Kamaljit   Me?

Ranjit   These are tasty. Really very tasty.

Kamaljit   What do you mean about your dad?

Ranjit   He's worried about you. (*A beat.*) Your sister's been down the shop a few times, asking questions.

Kamaljit   Surinder's been helping out . . .

Ranjit   Helping?

Kamaljit   She's here most weekends, getting the place into shape. Your dad's very successful, she's probably looking for inspiration.

Ranjit   Did you know she's applied for an alcohol licence?

Kamaljit   Yes, she said if I want to sell, I'll get a better price.

Ranjit   Are you selling?

Kamaljit   I still haven't decided.

Ranjit   So if you keep hold of the shop, you'll stock alcohol?

Kamaljit   Is that a problem?

Ranjit   If you live on Whittington Road and you fancy a bottle of cider, you walk up Bridge Street onto Victoria Road, into our shop. But if you lot are selling that same bottle of cider, you might as well turn off Whittington, go left on Garwood Avenue, through the alley and there's you lot.

Kamaljit   We're much smaller than you.

Ranjit   My dad's a decent man.

Kamaljit   Yes.

Ranjit   This whole thing, the way she's gone about it . . . it's . . . hurt his feelings.

Kamaljit   We don't want to do that.

Ranjit (*a beat*)   How much do you know about her?

Kamaljit   She's . . . my sister.

Ranjit   You know me. And my dad. He's like your dad. We've got your interests at heart. You understand, don't you?

Kamaljit *nods.*

Ranjit   You came to the hospital the day I was born.

Kamaljit   Ranjit . . .

Ranjit   It's not about money. This is not about money. I'd give my life for you, Auntie. And this is what you're doing.

Kamaljit   I'm not doing anything.

Ranjit   I get it, it's her. She's not one of us. We've got on fine all these years. Where was she?

Kamaljit   It's complicated . . .

Ranjit   You don't know, do you?

Silence.

Ranjit   Do you trust her? Trust her in your bones?

Surinder *and* **Arjan** *bustle in, laughing. They see* **Ranjit**. *Take off their jackets.*

Surinder   Hello.

Ranjit   Alright.

Arjan   What are you doing here?

Ranjit *indicates the light.*

Ranjit   Loose wire.

Surinder   I could have fixed that.

Ranjit   Should be down to Arj. You wanna look after your mum, chitterface.

Arjan   I do.

Ranjit   Only messing. We going Red Lion tonight?

Arjan   I don't think so.

Surinder   We're getting a takeaway if you'd like to join us.

Ranjit   Nah, man, can't be eating outside food. Nina'll have my roti ready. Come for one.

Arjan   Not tonight, thanks.

Surinder   I'll order. What do you want, Kamaljit?

Ranjit (*to* **Arjan**)   You're coming!

Kamaljit   Dhal and roti.

Surinder   You have that every day.

Kamaljit   Because I like it.

Ranjit *gets* **Arjan***'s jacket.*

Ranjit   Put this on.

Surinder   I'm having masala fish and a pizza.

Arjan   Ranjit . . .

Kamaljit   That doesn't go.

Surinder   It's what I fancy.

Ranjit   Hurry up . . .

Arjan   No.

Ranjit   Arj!

Surinder   He said no.

Arjan   I can speak for myself, Masi.

Ranjit   You sure about that brother? Looks like this one's running things round here.

Surinder   This one?

Ranjit   You know what I mean. Arj knows.

Arjan   I'll see you another time, Ranjit.

Ranjit   You chucking me out?

Arjan   Thanks for fixing the light.

Ranjit   I'm your brother . . .

Arjan   No, you're not.

Ranjit   Who was looking after your mum and dad when you were drinking soya lattes in London with your goree?

Kamaljit   Ranjit . . .

Ranjit   This woman you haven't seen for years, turns up and takes over. She's not even married.

Arjan   Shut your mouth.

Ranjit   She wants the shop for herself.

Surinder   Not that it's any of your business but I'm here for my sister. I've got my own money.

Ranjit   You want more. I know a dirty gold digger when I see one. Behsharam [*Shameless*].

Suddenly **Arjan** *punches* **Ranjit** *in the face. Loud music plays and there ensues a massive, messy, ungainly fight. The men part and* **Ranjit** *is about to go for* **Arjan** *again when suddenly* **Kamaljit** *slaps* **Ranjit** *round the face. Music stops.*

Kamaljit   Go home. Tell your father, we're waiting for the licence to come through. And then I'm ordering a hundred boxes of lager, vodka and Aperol Spritz.

Ranjit   My dad'll make sure everyone in the Gurdwara knows about this.

Kamaljit   Tell him not to bother, I'll WhatsApp the ladies myself.

Ranjit *starts to leave.*

Kamaljit   This was my daddy's shop when your father was a penniless pindoo off the boat. And now it's mine. And my sister's. And we'll do whatever we like with it.

Ranjit *leaves.* **Kamaljit** *turns to the others.*

Kamaljit   What are you having?

Surinder   What?

Kamaljit   To eat!

Surinder   I already said . . . pizza and fish . . .

Kamaljit   Arjan?

Arjan   Er . . . pizza.

Kamaljit   Right. (*A beat.*) I'm going to have butter chicken. A large portion.

Surinder   Eh?

Kamaljit   With the dhal.

Scene Eleven

The shop. The place has been transformed. Eye-catching displays and a flashy newspaper rack. **Surinder** *unpacks boxes of crisps.* **Claire** *stands nearby, awkwardly sipping a cup of tea. There are a couple of bin bags in front of the counter.* **Claire** *looks around in admiration.*

Claire   You've got a real talent for décor. Your sister must be pleased she found you.

Surinder   Thanks to you. I'd like to take her to Paris or New York for a weekend but she reckons she can see abroad on the telly. (*A beat.*) How come you're still wearing your engagement ring?

Claire   Think I'm just . . . used to it.

Surinder   I had wedding jewellery . . . from my parents. It was meant to give me a decent start.

Claire   Where is it?

Surinder   Lost. (*A beat.*) Do you still like him?

Claire   No.

Surinder   I know that feeling. Once the hate stops . . . make sure you get on with it.

Claire   What?

Surinder   Whatever it is you want.

Arjan *brings in a couple of boxes.*

Arjan   I didn't realise I had so much stuff at your flat.

Claire   Not any more.

Arjan   You kept my old art. I'd forgotten about some of these pictures.

Claire   I almost gave them to the Scouts.

Arjan   The Scouts?

Claire   They were building one of their bonfires . . . but . . . well . . . they are yours.

Arjan   Thank you.

Claire *takes a sheet of paper from her bag. Gives it to him.*

Arjan   I remember when we found the venue. We were so excited . . .

Surinder   Are you getting the deposit back?

Claire   No. (*A beat.*) I need to make a move.

He signs the paper.

Arjan   That's it then.

Surinder *picks up the empty crisp boxes. Exits.*

Claire   Bye, Arj.

Arjan   Claire . . . wait . . .

Claire (*interrupts*)   I slept with my ex-boyfriend.

Arjan   What?

Claire   Ben.

Arjan   That solicitor fuck?

Claire   Actually, he's a barrister now. (*A beat.*) I didn't intend to. But . . .

Arjan   Revenge?

Claire   Perhaps. I don't know . . .

She heads out just as **Surinder** *comes back in with another box of goods. She starts unpacking.*

Surinder   Why did you split up?

Arjan   Because she's . . . English.

Surinder   Are you serious?

Arjan   I thought life would be simpler. I mean . . . Ranjit . . .

Surinder *makes a face.*

Arjan   . . . might be a moron, but he knows who he is.

Surinder   He stinks of skunk. And you know why he smokes so much? Because he needs it to get through the day.

Arjan   I suppose I . . . feel guilty about wanting what I want.

Surinder   Guilt is about the person who's feeling it. If you enjoy wallowing, go ahead. But get your order in with Ranjit for an eighth of weed and be ready for the Red Lion every Saturday night.

Arjan   What about all the things they don't understand about us?

Surinder   What about all the things we don't understand about us?

Arjan   My mum's got so little left. She always dreamed of me being with an Indian girl. Bride in a red lehenga. Me riding up on a white horse . . .

Surinder   Kamaljit married her soulmate. Had you. Still eats fish and chips on a Friday. She's lived the life of a Rani. (*A beat.*) Your mum's gonna hate whoever you bring home. But give her a chance and she might start to love her.

Arjan   Thing is, Masi, the truth is . . . I don't want her to die . . .

Surinder   And you pissing on your own life is gonna stop that? (*A beat.*) Kamaljit and Tanvir always had this . . . something, like my mum and dad. Me and Jim never did. You know when you've got it. And if you and Claire do . . . well . . . it's up to you. (*A beat.*) Why do you think they sent you to that fancy school?

Arjan   So I could be a doctor.

Surinder   So you get a choice. My dad came here because he needed to breathe. Because he had an imagination. Thanks to him and your mum and dad, the sun and the moon and the stars are at your fingertips, and if you're not brave enough to fight for what you want . . . that would really disappoint your mother.

Arjan   What I want most is for her to be happy.

Surinder   Making people happy's the easy way.

Arjan   What's the hard way?

Surinder   Being who you are.

She continues to unpack. From one of the boxes he brought in, **Arjan** *takes out a painting, beholds it.*

Movement/music sequence indicating **Arjan** *coming into his own.*

Scene Twelve

A park. **Arjan** *stands opposite* **Claire**. *He takes a breath.*

Arjan   So . . . what do you say?

Claire   How can I trust you? Properly trust you.

Arjan   Because I've never told you a lie.

Claire   Why should I believe this could work?

Arjan   I think . . . we've got . . . something . . . if you don't agree, I understand . . . but I know I've got it, for you.

He approaches her.

Claire   Is she keeping the shop?

Arjan   Yeah. They're gonna run it together. Mum's introducing a new selection of chocolate bars and Masi's planning to open a deli counter . . . oh, and she wants to sell fresh bread.

Claire   Always a winner.

Arjan   She says a loaf wrapped in brown paper and tied with string always looks fresh. Extremely fresh!

Claire   Okay.

Arjan   It's what she wants.

Claire   What do you want?

Arjan   I'd like to come home.

Claire   Yeah.

They move closer to each other.

Epilogue

Wedding Hall. Punjabi folk music plays over the following sequence which encapsulates a Sikh wedding, it should have the quality of an emotional but uplifting dance –

Milni [meeting] – **Kamaljit** *and* **Surinder** *exchange gifts – blankets and flowers – with* **Bill**.

Post ceremony – **Arjan** *and* **Claire** *sit on the floor in Indian wedding attire.* **Bill, Ranjit, Dhanda, Kamaljit** *and* **Surinder** *throw petals at them. Then put money in their laps. Pose for photographs.*

Music fuses into a bhangra tune. **Arjan, Claire, Bill, Ranjit, Dhanda** *and* **Mrs Bains** *all dance energetically.*

They are joined by **Kamaljit** *and* **Surinder** *as young girls, dancing with carefree joy, as if they have their whole lives ahead of them.*

THE END

Choir

The world premiere performance of *Choir* took place at Chichester Festival Theatre's Minerva Theatre on 2 August 2025 with the following cast (in order of speaking):

Morgan	**Laura Checkley**
Ken	**Timothy Speyer**
Anna	**Danusia Samal**
Joy	**Alison Fitzjohn**
Esther	**Danielle Henry**
Paul	**James Gillan**
Sheila	**Annie Wensak**
Freddie	**Keenan Munn-Francis**
TV Runners	**Hannah Dickinson, Maya Williams, Ruby Woodhead**

Writer	Gurpreet Kaur Bhatti
Director	Hannah Joss
Designer	Anisha Fields
Music & Sound Designer	Alexandra Faye Braithwaite
Lighting Designer	Jai Morjaria
Movement Director	Annie-Lunnette Deakin-Foster
Music Arranger	Rich Forbes
Musical Director & additional arrangements	Michael Henry
Casting Director	Jacob Sparrow
Voice & Dialect Coach	Simon Money
Assistant Director	Nathanael Campbell
Production Manager	Jacqui Leigh
Costume Supervisor	Megan Rarity
Props Supervisors	Lisa Buckley
	Tegan Cutts
Company Stage Manager	Alison Rankin
Deputy Stage Manager	Gareth Newcombe
Assistant Stage Manager	Rebecca Natalini

Characters

Morgan
Esther
Joy
Ken
Anna
Paul
Sheila
Freddie

Location

The back room of a suburban pub.

Note

The songs are only suggestions, they can be changed as required.

Scene One – Monday

Curtain/darkness. A stunning solo male voice singing the first line of Queen's 'Somebody to Love'.

Lights up to reveal it's **Paul**.

Morgan *manages the music on a laptop. It blares out via a couple of huge speakers.*

The room comprises a vast floor space with a small stage and signs for the Exit and the Toilets. A few chairs are arranged in sections of twos. This is where the choir sit.

There is a large canvas placed to the side, whatever is on it remains unseen by the audience.

Morgan *conducts the singers (everyone except* **Sheila** *and* **Freddie)** *as they join in the rest of the song with* **Paul**.

Using song sheets, the choir are disengaged and lacklustre. **Morgan** *stops the music.*

Morgan   Getting there. Really . . . almost . . . getting there. Perhaps invest a bit more . . . from your souls . . .

She sings a line from the song.

Morgan   Imagine being utterly desperate to find another human body to offer affection to.

The group eye one another uneasily.

Morgan   And pour that desperation into the words.

Ken   What words?

Morgan   The ones you're singing. Let yourselves be taken over by the music.

Anna   As if we're possessed?

Joy   By Satan?

Morgan   Just give it . . . whatever you've got.

Esther   Sure.

Joy   Okay.

Ken   I'll do my best.

She turns to **Joy** *and* **Esther**.

Morgan   Altos, think of your second line as a . . . a . . . plea to God.

Esther   God. Right, yeah . . . God.

Joy   You mean . . . God from church.

Morgan   Well . . .

Joy   I don't like churches. Strange things happen in churches.

Morgan   Doesn't have to be religious.

Anna   It does say Lord.

Paul   That's just a word.

Joy   Lord Jesus, the Lord is my shepherd, Lord of the Rings . . .

Morgan   Lord in this context represents anything on a higher plane. It could be . . . the sun or the moon.

Joy   Nah, I don't do all that.

Esther   I sort of see what you're getting at.

Morgan   Excellent, Esther. (*To* **Joy**.) How about nature?

Joy   Like trees?

Morgan   Exactly!

Joy (*nods*)   Trees. Trees . . . Trees.

Morgan   Anna . . . that was a beautiful flourish over the top of the bridge. But it does need more lift!

Anna   Lift?

Morgan   Yeah.

Anna   Sort of . . .

She sings with more verve.

Morgan   Er . . .

She sings again with too much vigour.

Morgan   Bring it down a tad.

Anna   I'll find the level when Sheila's here.

Morgan   Where is Sheila?

Esther   She was going to the shops to buy cutlery.

Joy   I didn't know Sheila needed new cutlery.

Anna   Neither did I.

Ken   She's a dark horse.

Morgan   Remember why we're doing this performance. It really really matters. Try and connect with that simple thought. And let's insert big feelings into those lyrics. Massive feelings . . .

She plays the music again. They start to sing. Strangely, **Ken** *falls to his feet as though he's praying/talking in tongues.*

Confused, **Morgan** *stops the music.*

Morgan   Ken, what . . . what?

Ken   I'm showing the torment from my desperation.

Morgan   Our goal is to entertain. Not cause trauma. I think everyone's getting slightly . . .

Anna   Slightly?

Morgan   Overwhelmed. I appreciate this is your first show in front of an audience . . .

Paul   It is not my first show.

Morgan   I mean everyone else. Honestly, you're all capable of sounding . . . as good as . . . any other members of society.

Suddenly **Sheila** *flies in on roller skates. She can't control herself and launches straight into the choir, knocking a couple of them over.*

Sheila *skids all over the place, bumping into things.*

Sheila   I tied the laces too tight, I can't get them off.

Esther   Come here.

She helps her sit down and starts undoing the laces.

Morgan   You're very late, Sheila.

Sheila   Sorry.

Anna   I didn't know you could roller skate.

Sheila   I can't, I found them in the park.

Paul   What park?

Sheila (*thinking quickly*)   Oh actually, no . . . it wasn't the park . . . it was . . . they were in Morrisons by the Free From section . . . I took them to the till but they said they don't sell roller skates. So I asked where the Lost Property was but they don't have Lost Property in Morrisons . . . I waited ages and then the rageful people who work nights came . . . and threatened me with legal action unless I left the premises . . . So I decided to bring them home and then I thought you could use them for your charity, Anna.

Anna   We protect otters.

Sheila   They might not fit.

Esther *manages to take them off.*

Esther   Give them to a school or something.

Sheila *shakes her head.*

Sheila   The teachers'll start asking for my passport and my library card. And I can't think where that is. I'll just have to hold onto them for a while.

The others start to mess about with the roller skates.

Paul   Did you get your cutlery?

Sheila (*shakes her head*)   They were selling them in fours. I only wanted a teaspoon.

Esther   One teaspoon?

Morgan (*loud*)   No more lateness this week! You might not be professionals but you can choose to approach your work with professionalism.

The others are doing a silly trick on the skates. Someone's doing a handstand. They are laughing and not listening to **Morgan***.*

Morgan   One more time, please!

They gather, she conducts and they sing 'Somebody to Love'. It's not bad.

Morgan   Better. Marginally better. Take a break and don't forget Freddie's joining us shortly, he's not naturally front-footed so let's make him feel welcome. After he arrives, I've got a special announcement.

Ken   What's that then?

Morgan   Patience, Ken.

Esther   Are you pregnant?

Morgan   No.

Joy   She's too old to be pregnant. Anyway, she hasn't got anyone to get pregnant by.

Esther   She might have gone on Tinder and had a one-night stand.

Joy   Or that *Guardian* Blind Date. They give you a free dinner. And it's not a shit dinner either.

Esther   Sounds alright, having a nice dinner and getting pregnant. Well done you!

Morgan   I'm not pregnant.

Ken   I'll get the drinks.

Morgan   Go easy.

Anna   I sound much better when I'm tipsy.

Morgan   I'm not sure that's true.

Sheila   I'd like to be tipsy.

Paul   What's stopping you?

Sheila   Alcohol makes me urinate. A lot.

Anna   I thought *water* made you urinate.

Sheila   I wish it did. My bladder's a bit wrong. And my sphincter.

Ken (*to* **Sheila**)   What about lager?

Sheila   That's the worst.

Ken   Gin?

Morgan (*interrupts*)   She said alcohol, Ken. Means it's all alcohol.

Ken *exits. The others check their songsheets/phones or stretch out.* **Esther** *and* **Joy** *start painting the canvas.*

Paul *approaches* **Morgan** *in a space where they can't be heard by the others.*

Paul   What's going on?

Morgan   I should tell everyone together.

Paul   I . . . saw James last night. He's coming on Saturday.

Morgan   Oh . . . so it's all . . .

Paul   Yeah.

Morgan   Is he actually going to . . .

Paul   That's what he's saying.

Morgan   As long as he doesn't mess you about again.

Paul   He doesn't mess me about.

Morgan   You said he blocked you the other week.

Paul   Because I threw my flat white in his face . . .

Morgan   Because he asked the barista for his number.

Paul   Only because they used to do Tae Kwondo together.

Morgan   Tae Kwondo?

Paul   I know! He unblocked me . . . after I turned up at his office with a knife.

Morgan   What?

Paul   It was only a butter knife. After I held it to my throat, he explained everything.

Morgan   Can't wait to meet him.

Paul   Don't say anything.

Morgan   About what?

Paul   Anything I've said that . . . you know . . . involves him. When you see him, make it seem like the first time you've heard me mention his name.

Morgan   He's all you ever talk about.

Paul   Are you my best friend or do you want me to die, Morgan?

Morgan   Paul . . .

Paul   I want it to look like . . . I don't care about anybody or anything.

Morgan   I will be perfect. Don't worry, Saturday's going to be amazing.

Paul   I'm not worried.

Morgan   Good.

Paul   Are you worried?

Morgan   Do I look worried?

Paul   Yes.

Anna *is watching* **Esther** *and* **Joy** *painting.*

Anna   Morgan, this is really taking shape.

Morgan *approaches.* **Anna** *points to something.*

Anna   Is that a river?

Joy   No. (*A beat.*) It's a moustache.

Esther   I told her it should be black or at least brown.

Joy   When I think of him, I see him with a blue moustache.

Esther   That doesn't make sense.

Morgan   Freddie hasn't actually got a moustache.

Joy   Won't matter if it's blue then, will it?

Ken (*off*)   Help me, please! Help!

Paul *goes out to* **Ken**. **Sheila** *takes out a Greggs carrier bag.*

Sheila   Anyone fancy a vegan sausage roll?

They gravitate towards **Sheila** *and take a sausage roll.*

Sheila   I made them in front of *Bake Off.*

Esther   Did they do vegan sausage rolls on *Bake Off*?

Sheila   No.

They eat the sausage rolls.

Anna   What's inside?

Sheila (*a beat*)   Vegan.

Esther   These are good, Sheila.

Sheila   How good are they?

Ken *and* **Paul** *bring in drinks and hand them out.*

Esther   Delicious.

Sheila   Are they the best you've ever eaten?

Esther   Er, I'm not sure.

Sheila   Don't worry, I'll never make them again.

Esther   Sheila, they're nice, I just don't think about sausage rolls being the best.

Sheila   What do you think about then?

Paul *and* **Ken** *take sausage rolls.*

Esther   I don't know.

Sheila   There's nowt so queer as folk.

Anna *shows* **Morgan** *a sheet of paper.* **Paul** *peers over her shoulder.*

Anna   And this is definitely the final set list?

Morgan   Yes.

Paul   No Whitney?

Morgan   Stop it.

Joy   I love that woman more than a crack baby loves a rock.

Anna   I think I love her more than my children.

Esther   Please, let us!

Morgan   This choir does not sing Whitney. Not while I'm of sound mind.

Morgan *goes to her laptop, starts organising the music.*

Esther   Oh God, I just got a . . . funny quiver going through my body.

Ken   I'm having those all the time, when I'm at the bus stop, when I'm putting my pants on the radiators, when I'm picking off bits of skin from the back of my heel . . .

Morgan   Nerves are part of the process.

Joy   What if I shit myself?

Morgan   You won't.

Joy   But what if I do?

Paul   Keep going. Smile and make sure they can hear you at the back. I was sick three times AND I had a seizure before my first show.

Anna   How many were in the audience again?

Morgan (*low*)   Over a thousand.

Paul   Over a thousand.

Ken   Wowee, I can't fathom . . .

Esther   Do you remember much about it?

Paul   Hardly. But when we came out for the curtain call there were all these bodies on their feet, clapping and screaming. You're faced with this wave of elation, and it swamps you . . . and the first one. The very first one, was the greatest feeling of my whole life.

Sheila   Like an organism?

Paul   Better, Sheila.

Joy *offers* **Paul** *a wipe.*

Joy   Have a wipe.

Paul   No thanks.

Joy   They're lemon-scented.

Morgan   If you fully commit to choir this week, that feeling Paul described is something we can all experience on Saturday.

Ken   Got it.

Morgan   I've also asked Freddie to sing at the gig, so he'll be rehearsing with us.

Anna   Exciting!

Paul   Does he know the arrangements?

Morgan   I've been teaching them during his lessons.

Joy   Is this Freddie allowed to sing on Saturday?

Morgan   Freddie's the young person we're helping and it's simply a way of showcasing his talent.

Paul   I hope introducing another tenor won't overpower the sound.

Morgan   Let me worry about the balance. You all enjoy the spotlight, show off! There are still a few tickets left so tell everyone you know, we want this place to be overflowing with ecstasy.

Sheila   Drug dealers?

Morgan   No.

Esther   I've got my tickets.

Joy   Let's hope the kids behave.

Esther   They do behave.

Joy   Jack took his willy out in Pizza Express.

Esther   That was years ago.

Anna   Ed and the kids can't make it unfortunately. Saturday's a busy day. Activities.

Morgan   Can't he bring the kids in the evening?

Anna   He's very busy. There are lots of activities. Every Saturday. And every evening. And on Sunday.

Sheila   I'm not bothering with other people.

Ken   Me neither.

Joy   I don't know any people.

Esther   If you made an effort to talk to the neighbours . . .

Joy   I talk to that Nigel.

Esther   You accused him of dumping garden waste in your green bin.

Joy   Well he did.

Esther   You didn't have to stick it on the WhatsApp.

Joy   He smeared fox shit on the lid.

Esther   You can't be certain, Joy.

Morgan   Everyone, Paul's boyfriend is coming.

Communal gasp of astonishment.

Sheila   What about his wife and four kids and the guinea pigs . . .?

Paul (*interrupts*)   They're splitting up.

Anna   Fantastic!

Esther   You deserve happiness.

Paul   Nobody talk to him please, he's painfully shy, so when you see him . . . ignore him.

Sheila   I hope he knows how lucky he is, having sex with you.

Ken   Imagine it, me performing with a West End star.

Paul   I wasn't exactly a star.

Anna *coughs.* **Joy** *takes out her wipes, offers* **Anna**.

Esther   'Course you were.

Paul   Remember, don't speak to him!

Joy   Have a wipe.

Anna   Oh, I'm fine.

Joy   They're very fresh.

Esther   She doesn't want one.

Their voices get louder.

Joy   Nobody's asking you.

Morgan   Please, you two . . .

Esther   She said no!

Freddie *tentatively enters. He's dressed in old-fashioned, badly-fitting jeans and top.*

Joy (*fierce*)   Don't you shitting well start on me, Esther!

Morgan   Freddie, Freddie . . . come in!

He gently waves at everyone.

Morgan   Welcome! This is the choir.

Paul   At last, the famous Freddie.

Freddie   Oh, I'm not anyone.

Anna   Not yet!

Morgan   Wait till you hear this boy's pipes! Come on, choir . . . er . . . introduce yourselves!

Esther   Esther.

Joy   Joy.

Esther *points at* **Joy**.

Esther   We're best friends.

Freddie   Hello.

Morgan   This is Sheila.

Sheila *gives him a hug. She doesn't let go.* **Morgan** *intervenes and gently prises* **Freddie** *away.*

Anna   Anna.

Esther   The concert was Anna's idea.

Ken   She's a charity person.

Sheila   For otters.

Freddie   It's my dream to go to music college, thank you . . . thank you so much.

Anna   I haven't done anything.

Morgan   She's too modest! Stop being so modest. It's weird.

Ken   I'm Ken.

Freddie   Hi there.

Ken   My wife left me.

Awkward pause.

Morgan   Come and sit down, Freddie.

Ken   She's not coming back. But I'm fine.

Morgan   Thanks, Ken.

Ken   Absolutely fine.

Paul   Paul.

Esther   He used to be in the West End.

Joy   Lionel Richie came to see him in his dressing room.

Paul   Not just me.

Joy   He touched him.

Paul   We shook hands.

Ken   He said you blew his mind.

Paul   It was a while ago.

Joy   Do you want a wipe?

Freddie   Er, no thanks.

Joy   You've come from outside. There's dirt outside.

Esther   Leave him alone, Joy.

Anna *moves towards the canvas, beckons* **Freddie**.

Anna   Take a look at this.

Freddie *joins her, his face contorts with discomfort.*

Freddie   What is it?

Esther   You.

Freddie   Er . . . okay, how did you know what I looked like?

Joy   I imagined you. In my brain.

Morgan   Joy's . . . artistic.

Joy   I speak French.

Esther   She's learning.

Morgan   It's going to be the backdrop to the gig. We felt we needed something that made a statement!

Awkward silence as they all stare at him.

Ken   Are you alright, Freddie?

Freddie   Yeah.

Morgan   Of course he's alright. Sorry if we're bombarding you . . . can we not bombard him, please?

Paul   Now your young man's here you can tell us your news, Morgan.

Morgan   Right . . . everyone gather round.

They form a circle round **Morgan**.

Morgan   As you all know we are doing this gig on Saturday to raise funds for this hugely talented singer to train so he can get started in the crazy business we call show. And . . . well . . . you're not going to believe it, but a production company approached me a few days ago, they're interested in Freddie's story and what we're doing to support him.

Esther   And?

Morgan   They want to shoot the gig, we're going to be on a television programme!

Silence.

Sheila   Oh God.

Esther   Oh my God.

Joy   Oh God.

Ken   You're not playing a sick joke on us, are you Morgan?

Morgan   It's not a joke . . . a camera crew and production team are coming here on Saturday.

Anna   Oh!

Sheila   Oh God.

Esther   Oh my God, oh my God, oh my God . . .

Sheila   Oh God.

Esther   God, God, God . . .

Sheila   Oh my God, oh my God!

Morgan   I know!

Esther   Oh God!

Freddie   Wow.

Joy   Fuck, fuck, fuck. Fuck!

Anna   Oh . . .

Sheila   God.

Esther   God.

Joy   Fuck.

Morgan   I realise it's a lot to take in . . .

Ken   Us on the telly?

Morgan   It's a segment for *The One Show.*

Joy   Jesus Christ, I love that programme. Fuck!

Morgan   It's a piece on the power of singing together. They're covering three choirs and we are one of them. They've asked for a photo of each of you and some background, which I'll send . . .

Anna   Such fantastic publicity.

Morgan   It means we can hopefully do more gigs, help more young people, possibly expand the choir. And it's all because of you, Freddie.

Freddie   This is a lot to take in, it's . . . much . . . bigger than I thought.

Paul   You're lucky, having all this effort put into you.

Freddie   I'll try not to let you down.

Paul   Don't you dare!

Morgan *moves to her laptop.*

Morgan   Of course he won't.

Esther   Look at him . . . he's clearly reliable.

Freddie   Usually.

Paul   How do you mean usually?

Freddie   I don't generally let people down.

Sheila   Yay!

Freddie   Apart from when . . . I dropped my sister's baby.

Awkward mumbles as they take this in.

Freddie   I was so scared of holding it, my hands were shaking and it sort of flopped out of my arms and . . . it didn't break anything . . . too bad. Just its index finger.

Morgan   Right.

Freddie   And its femur.

Anna   Was the baby okay?

Freddie   Oh, yeah.

Morgan   No harm done then.

Freddie   My mum says she'll never forgive me.

Esther   Give her time.

Freddie   My nephew's five now. Mum says I'm descended from the devil.

Morgan   We're all imperfect, complicated beings, aren't we?

Joy   Speak for yourself.

Anna   Everyone makes mistakes.

Sheila   I call them happy accidents. You dropping the baby and breaking its bones was a happy accident!

Uneasy pause.

Freddie   So there'll be cameras and everything on Saturday?

Morgan   Absolutely.

Freddie   Real cameras?

Morgan   We've got a lot to do, so let's carry on . . . Freddie, do join in.

Lizzo's 'Juice' starts to play.

The choir sing with their song sheets. After a verse or so, **Morgan** *pulls the music.*

Morgan   We're going to have to lose the sheets.

Ken   What?

Morgan   They make you look like amateurs.

Anna   We are amateurs.

Morgan   We don't have to shout about it.

Sheila   How will we know the words?

Morgan   You know them, Sheila.

Ken   I don't.

Esther   Me neither.

Morgan   You think you don't, but you do. Paul and I did loads of gigs when we were younger. It was nerve-racking but we never forgot our words because great song lyrics enter your bloodstream and become part of your muscle memory. Sheets down!

They put the pages down. **Morgan** *starts the music again.*

They all sway along but it's clear they don't know the words and they start to la and ooh and aah. **Morgan** *pulls the music.*

Morgan   Make sure you know the words to every song by the next rehearsal.

Joy   But there are fucking loads.

Morgan   We are going to be on BBC1! Alongside other choirs who have dance moves, children with missing teeth, matching T-shirts.

Esther   Can we have matching T-shirts?

Morgan   My choir would NEVER sink that low!

Ken   I'm worried I don't have time to practise.

Morgan   Ken, you haven't got a job.

Ken   Somehow . . . I'm always . . . stretched.

Morgan *takes the sheets from everyone, tears them up. They watch, aghast.*

Morgan   We are going to make this happen by leaning on each other and working together. It's going to be an intense few days but if you trust me, I promise, spectacular things are on their way.

Anna   Is there a dress code?

Morgan   Smart casual please. We want to look normal, so people can relate to us, but different enough so that they can also aspire to be us.

Ken   Are trousers and a shirt okay?

Morgan   Perfect. I appreciate you're all probably out of your comfort zones but that's how we improve performance.

Ken   So smart-casual trousers and a smart-casual shirt?

Morgan (*nods*)   Can I have sopranos and altos to go over the chorus for Coldplay?

Ken   Any trousers and any shirt?

Morgan   Yes!

The women go and sit by **Morgan**. *They go over a few lines and sing. Sounds of 'Fix You' under the following section.*

Ken *is learning his words on the other side.* **Paul** *finds* **Freddie**.

Paul   I hear you're going to be a star.

Freddie   I dunno.

Paul   Morgan thinks so. You'll need an agent.

Freddie   Really?

Paul   As soon as you get your agent, the best thing to do is pretend they've died. Imagine they fell down a man-hole or choked on a fish bone.

Freddie   Why?

Paul   Because they never call. They say they're going to call but . . .

Freddie   What?

Paul   You can send Krispy Kremes, orchids, stick a Russian Blue kitten in a box and courier it over. Tell them you've kidnapped their grandma. And nothing! (*A beat.*) Have you ever been tortured by a psychopath, Freddie?

Freddie   Eh?

Paul   You know, had pins stuck into your buttocks or wee poured on your head while you're tied to a chair.

Freddie *shakes his head.*

Paul   Pity. It's fantastic preparation for the business. (*A beat.*) Anyway, it's a delight to have you.

Freddie   I'd like to be like you. One day.

Paul   Me?

Freddie   They said you're big.

Paul   I was poised, ready to launch, but I'd go up for auditions and come second and then my career went up my nose . . . I do voice work now. Mainly local radio. If you hear an advert for a bargain basement car showroom with two stars on Trustpilot, that'll be me.

Freddie   Incredible.

Paul   I make my money. I just replaced my sash windows. Hardwood. Triple glazing.

Freddie   And you and Morgan used to sing together?

Paul   Centuries ago. You'll find that the people who run the business are interested in right now, in what's fresh and young. They believe that a new take will help us to understand old things.

Freddie   That's deep.

Paul   I talk facts not philosophy. What matters is, all that really matters is . . . that I've got a sweet boyfriend who adores me. Do you want to see a picture?

Paul *takes out his phone. The women come back to the group.* **Morgan** *is on the laptop.*

Ken   I reckon this news about the telly warrants a new outfit. I'd like to be fresh, you know, clean.

Esther   Aren't you normally clean?

Ken   Depends if there's soap left. Sometimes the bar dissolves in my hand.

Sheila   Same!

Ken   Anyway, this is an opportunity for me to feel brand new. Shirt, trousers, belt, shoes, socks. And a vest and pants.

Joy   Do they still do Y fronts?

Freddie   Y fronts?

Joy   You don't hear people mention them any more.

Anna   No, you really don't.

Joy   Quel dommage.

Sheila   They do do them. (*A beat.*) The men's section is my favourite. Sometimes I open packets of fancy socks and put my hand in and touch them. I know it's illegal, but I feel them anyway!

Ken   Wish I had your courage, Sheila.

Sheila   Share mine, Ken. You need some in this life. Otherwise you get trampled on.

Ken   I'm not sure how to go about buying everything. My wife . . . used to . . . er . . .

Morgan   You find a shop and pick stuff and buy it.

Ken   Which shop?

Esther   One that sells men's clothes.

Ken   What do I choose?

Anna   Whatever you like.

Ken   But how do I know what I like?

Morgan   You just do.

Ken   I don't. I really don't.

Anna   Get everything online.

Ken   I'm no good at that.

Esther   We'll sort something out.

Morgan   Quiet please! First two verses and chorus.

Mash up between 'Seven Nation Army' and Eurythmics' 'Sweet Dreams' plays. **Morgan** *conducts as the choir sing along.* **Freddie** *is phenomenal.*

When the music stops, **Paul** *pointedly gathers his stuff – coat, bag, etc. And noisily moves his chair. He starts to walk out.*

Morgan   Paul, what are you doing?

Paul   You clearly don't . . . need me any more.

Esther   Of course we do!

Sheila   Nobody can do what you do.

Joy   Lionel Richie knows.

Freddie   Was I singing too loud?

Paul   No. I mean, you were a bit.

Ken   As a fellow tenor, I don't feel whole without you, Paul.

Anna   Come back! Please, Paul . . .

Esther   We can't sing without you.

Paul   You can.

Joy   Morgan, make him stay!

Morgan (*to* **Paul**)   You are part of this choir!

Paul   I fear I've become the bottom end of a straggly, overgrown fringe . . .

Morgan   None of this works without you, Paul.

Paul   Are you sure?

Morgan   Yes.

Paul (*a beat*)   Well . . . perhaps I'll stay for a bit.

He loudly puts his stuff down and returns to the group. **Anna** *gets a message on her phone.*

Freddie   How many cameras do you think there'll be on Saturday?

Morgan   I don't know.

Freddie   More than one though?

Morgan   Forget about the cameras.

Esther   Joy, we don't sing the first line of the second verse and you sang the first line of the second verse.

Joy   I didn't.

Esther   I heard you.

Joy   Might be time to get the wax removed from your ears again.

Esther   And we've got the melody, not the harmony. You're sounding a bit soprano.

Joy   I am not.

Anna *gets up, starts moving around with her phone.*

Morgan   Esther, it's not for you to judge what Joy's . . .

Esther (*interrupts*)   It's *The One Show*! It has to be right.

Joy *walks off and positions herself on the other side of the room.*

Morgan   I need the altos together.

Joy   She's putting me off.

Anna *continues to wander around.*

Morgan   We won't get the right sound for the gig.

Joy   I'll sit here for the rehearsal then.

Freddie *turns to* **Anna**.

Freddie   Are you okay?

Anna   I'm looking for a signal.

Morgan   You don't need a signal at the moment.

Esther *points to the back chair.*

Esther   You normally get one there, don't you?

Anna   Not tonight.

Freddie   She doesn't look okay.

Morgan   Anna, can you stop moving . . .

Anna   No, I can't . . . I really can't . . .

Sheila *starts playing with the roller skates.*

Ken   It's been raining. Water droplets absorb a certain radio frequency and partially block the access to the router.

Freddie   How do you know that?

Morgan   Anna!

Ken   Often when I'm listening to the radio or watching my dinner rotate in the microwave, a thought or a question occurs to me and I'll look it up on the internet. Sometimes even write down the answer in my notebook.

He takes his notebook out, shows **Freddie**.

Ken   Before I got made redundant, I was in charge of installing sprinkler systems in motorway service stations. I can show you some diagrams if you like.

He flicks through the notebook. **Sheila** *wheels herself around on one skate.*

Freddie (*to* **Morgan**)   Will the cameras be on me?

Morgan   Yeah!

Paul   A performer has to fall in lust with the camera, isn't that right, Morgan?

Anna *is still moving.* **Sheila** *starts to whizz herself around the space.*

Ken   We bring our best selves to choir, Freddie. And choir seems to bring out the best in us. We have our ups and downs, but generally you'll find we're a happy bunch.

Sheila *knocks into* **Morgan**, *who stumbles.*

Morgan (*shouts*)   Will you please all just fucking well do what I say?

They all stare at her, bemused.

Morgan   I mean . . . can we focus on the music?

Joy   Yeah.

Esther   Definitely.

Anna   Sure.

Sheila   Not a problem.

Paul   It's only about the music.

Ken   Don't you worry, Morgan, everything's going to be marvellous.

Morgan   Of course . . . it's all . . . going to be marvellous.

Scene change as they all sing 'Sweet Dreams'.

Scene Two – Wednesday

Sheila, **Ken**, **Anna** *and* **Freddie** *are sitting together.* **Ken** *is apprehensively looking over a song sheet.*

Sheila   Are you ready?

Ken   Give me a minute.

Anna   Ken . . .

Ken   Please . . .

Anna   Be confident!

She takes the sheet away.

Ken   There are so many words, they're jumbling up in my mouth.

Freddie   You almost did it . . .

Ken   Only because you lot helped. Morgan won't allow that on the night. Needing help isn't professional.

Sheila   Go over it a few times now and you'll get there for Saturday.

Ken   I don't want to disappoint her.

Anna   Sheila's right, let's continue.

Freddie   I'll count you in . . .

Sheila   Nice deep breath, Ken.

They all stand and face each other.

Freddie   One, two, three.

Anna *plays music on her phone.*

Ken *braces himself and starts singing the first verse of Beyoncé's 'Crazy in Love'. As he sings, the others pointedly mime a few key words, e.g. eyes/touch/kiss to help him remember.*

They all join in with the chorus and continue to mime the key actions.

Morgan *enters, slightly agitated.*

They all finish the song and cheer. **Anna** *stops the music.*

Morgan   How come you're so early?

Sheila   We're practising for the television people.

Morgan   I'm impressed. I'd usually be here by now, but my bike's gone awol.

Anna   Oh no.

Morgan *takes off her coat, starts setting up her music equipment.*

Anna   What happened?

Morgan   It was outside Morrisons, thought I'd locked it but . . . oh, it doesn't matter. It's a piece of junk. Then I had to wait ages for the bus . . . the 261 is like an elusive lover.

Ken   I never touch the 261. It's a heinous route.

Morgan   So how do you get here?

Ken   I take the 48, then the 391 and the 7 or the 83.

Morgan   But that means you do zig-zags through town, must take hours.

Morgan *'s phone beeps. She checks it.*

Ken   Oh, it does. But you get to see the drunks relieving themselves at the back of the old church and those huge 4 by 4s driving into the shopping centre, and up the hill there's a splendid view of the sheep sculptures on the new estate.

Morgan   Who wants to see that?

She replies to the message.

Ken   They're lives being lived, Morgan. All of us with our wins and losses and we're together on this planet, breathing the same air. It's a . . . a comfort.

Anna   You should write a memoir, Ken. You're so . . . alive.

Morgan *'s phone beeps again. She is getting increasingly stressed.*

Sheila   You might get invited to the Hay Festival. What do you reckon, Morgan?

Morgan *replies to the message.*

Morgan   Possibly.

Freddie   And, he's practically word perfect.

Morgan   Well done!

Ken   I'm not.

Anna   When he sings the verse it's like listening to Beyoncé's identical twin.

Freddie   Everyone here's really nice.

Morgan *gets another message.*

Morgan   Everyone's nice when you first meet them. When you get to know someone, that's when the darkness appears.

Sheila   I'm horrible.

Morgan   No, you're not . . .

Sheila   But I am slowly improving.

Morgan   I was joking, Sheila.

Esther *and* **Joy** *come in, they're holding hands.*

Esther   Hello.

Joy   Hello.

Phone goes again. **Morgan** *reads the message.*

Esther   We've decided to start afresh. Because we're best friends.

Joy   Neighbours actually.

Esther   Neighbours who are best friends. And when we're on television we're going to look happy, aren't we?

Joy   I'm always happy.

Morgan *replies to the message, tries to mask her stress.*

Esther   Not always, Joy.

Joy   I'm always happy inside, Esther. You can't see my insides.

Morgan   Okay, there've been a few emails flying around with the production company. I'm going to make some minor, well tiny but significant . . . adjustments to the show . . .

She checks her computer. **Esther** *hands* **Ken** *a large bag.*

Esther   Got you a selection of Dave's bits and pieces.

Ken   I'm a lucky, lucky man.

Esther   Try a few bits on and see how you go.

Joy *picks up a paint brush, starts painting on the canvas.*

Sheila *and* **Ken** *rummage through the bag.* **Paul** *saunters in wearing a trendy and flamboyant jacket.*

Ken *finds some clothes and starts taking his own clothes off.*

Anna (*to* **Paul**)   Gorgeous!

Paul   James watched the last episode of *Strictly* with his wife, so I threw a Le Creuset at him. We broke up.

Esther   That's awful.

Paul   Not really . . . because while he was on the trolley in A and E, we made up. (*Indicates jacket.*) He bought me this old thing from McQueen. And we had Five Guys in bed.

Sheila   Yum.

Paul   And he sent me a slice of luxury cheese made from donkey milk. And he's taking me to a rooftop restaurant the night before the gig. I've checked the menu and I'm having soufflé de fromage, longe de veau followed by tarte de citron avec crème anglaise!

The others notice that **Ken** *is almost naked, down to his pants.*

Morgan (*shocked*)   Ken, what are you doing?

Ken   Esther told me to get changed.

Esther   Not here!

Paul   Who cares? I don't.

Paul *grabs him and sings 'I Feel Pretty' as they dance across the space together.* **Paul** *twirls* **Ken** *and he spins off on his own and* **Esther** *immediately tries to cover him up.*

Ken   Sorry, I forget about other people.

Ken *takes the clothes and puts them on.*

Ken   I'm only around human bodies when I come here.

Morgan   It's okay.

Sheila   I never remember to lock public toilets.

Ken *shows off his clothes. They are ill-fitting and badly mismatched. He tries to be enthusiastic.*

Ken   Smart casual enough?

Anna   You don't look very comfortable.

Ken   I'll get used to it.

Anna *helps* **Ken** *find some better clothes.*

Morgan   So, the television people have suggested we do a duet.

Joy *and* **Anna** *start to sing Elton John's 'Don't Go Breaking My Heart'.*

Esther *walks around to look at the canvas.*

Morgan   No, it's the wrong tone . . .

Esther   What is that?

Joy   What?

Esther   On his head, that . . .

Joy   Isn't it obvious?

The others gather round, mystified.

Joy   It's a Frida Kahlo headdress.

Esther   Why?

Joy   Symbolises his artistic expression. Plus it makes him interesting. No offence, Freddie, but you're not interesting.

Esther   Looks . . . odd.

Joy   Morgan asked *me* to do this painting.

Esther (*to* **Morgan**)   You said I could help.

Morgan   Well . . .

Joy   Assist. She said you could be my assistant. Because *you* didn't get a B in your Art GCSE, did you, Esther?

Esther   I didn't do Art GCSE.

Joy   Exactement!

Esther   It's making me feel . . . uncomfortable.

Joy   Do you want a wipe?

Esther   No thanks.

Freddie   I don't mind a headdress.

Morgan   Let's leave it.

Esther   Okay.

Ken   How about . . . (*Sings.*) My love, there's only you in my life. The only thing that's right . . .

Morgan   Too obvious. There's actually an arrangement I've been wanting to share but it's . . . difficult . . .

Paul   What's the song?

Morgan   You're all I need to get by. Marvin Gaye and . . .

Esther   Tammi!

Paul   We used to do that, years ago.

Anna (*to* **Freddie**)   Morgan and Paul had a band.

Freddie   An actual band?

Paul   We did weddings.

Morgan   Not at the beginning. We got together at college. I wrote the songs. Paul was the frontman. We had things to say about homelessness, war, poverty.

Joy   Sounds fun.

Morgan   Remember . . . (*sings in a punk fashion*) I am broken in my heart, ravaged in my soul, dead in my bones, I am dead . . . dead . . .

Paul   Oh yes.

Morgan   They were vibrant songs. Radical songs that . . . were about . . . humanity!

Paul   People didn't really go for them though.

Morgan   We had a following!

Paul   Until we started doing cover versions at weddings. Not nice weddings. Ones where the bride and groom didn't like each other and noses got broken.

Anna   They almost got signed by a record company.

Morgan   I had spiky blue hair and my skin was flawless. We were going to change the world.

Freddie   So what happened?

Morgan   The big break didn't materialise and we went our separate ways, I got my job at the FE college . . . and the years passed and recently I realised how much I missed making music. So I started thinking about setting up a choir, got in touch with Paul and put a few posters up . . .

Ken   There was one in the GP surgery.

Esther   And in Morrisons.

Sheila   And in the police station.

Morgan   And here we are.

Joy   Who came up with the shit name?

Freddie   What is the name?

Ken   The Morgan Jackson People's Choir.

Paul (*indicates* **Morgan**)   She wanted something snappy that rolled off the tongue.

Morgan   I'm not changing it.

Sheila *takes out a Greggs carrier bag.*

Sheila   Vegan sausage roll, anyone?

They each gravitate towards **Sheila** *and take a sausage roll.*

Esther   These look good.

Anna   So good, Sheila.

Sheila   Really?

Anna   Mmmm . . .

Sheila   I made them in front of *Bake Off.*

Freddie *looks at the carrier bag.*

Freddie   But that bag . . .

Sheila   Yes.

Freddie   It's a Greggs bag.

Sheila   I used that because it was in the carrier bag drawer, it was the one at the top.

Awkward silence.

Ken   Perhaps the carrier bag is a red herring.

Freddie   They look like the ones from the shop . . .

Sheila (*interrupts*)   They're from my kitchen!

Freddie   I don't reckon so.

Morgan   Let's say they are.

Anna   They are because they are.

Sheila   Doesn't sound like he believes me.

Morgan   He does, don't you Freddie?

Freddie   Er . . . okay.

Sheila   I won't make them again.

Esther   Please make them again.

Ken   These are nectar from the Gods.

Sheila   Oh, alright then.

Anna   Thank you, Sheila. (*To* **Freddie**.) She adores baking, you see.

Sheila   I hate it. But they love them so much, what can I do?

Morgan   So, 'You're All I Need'!

Paul   I'm not convinced.

Esther   Whitney, Morgan, just this once.

Morgan   Never!

Freddie   Why not Whitney?

Morgan   Too obvious. Too . . . I feel there are certain artists that should remain untouched. Like 'Over the Rainbow'. Nobody else should sing that song.

The choir pointedly start singing a rendition of 'Over the Rainbow'. It's joyful and uplifting. **Morgan** *smiles but signals to them to stop.*

Morgan   This isn't karaoke. We're using our voices as a collective to transport our audience.

Paul   I'm not sure my voice can cope with 'You're All I Need' now.

Morgan   Doesn't matter.

Paul   Morgan, it didn't fly back then, the top notes were always a stretch.

Morgan   That's why I want Freddie to do it.

Silence.

Freddie   Me?

Morgan   Yes.

Freddie   But . . . I don't know it.

Morgan   As a singer, you have to be nimble, get to know a song fast, make it your new best friend.

She turns to the others and presses a button on her phone.

Morgan   I'm sending the other parts now, I realise it's a mammoth task but if we get this right, we're going to achieve something that none of us have ever achieved.

Joy   You must be flushing something down the toilet to make room for Marvin Gaye . . .

Morgan   Primal Scream.

Anna   But that's Paul's song.

Morgan   I have to take into consideration the flow and cadence of the whole night.

Esther   His boyfriend's coming.

Morgan   Paul, I should have said, there's been a lot to do . . . sorry.

Awkward silence.

Ken (*to* **Paul**)   You okay?

Paul   James will be here anyway.

Sheila   I think his feelings are hurt but he's not saying.

Paul   My feelings are not anything.

Morgan   Paul's an old boot. Robust enough to climb Everest.

Freddie   I don't mind not doing it.

Esther   Not your fault, sweetheart. I'm just . . . Morgan, you've always, since day one, given everyone a chance to shine.

Morgan   You are all, always shining. This is a performance. A performance is different. Paul gets it.

Paul   Of course I do.

Morgan *glances at her phone.*

Morgan   I have to reply to this. Begin learning your sections off the Dropbox. Freddie, Anna will be doing the duet with you.

Freddie   I haven't got a smartphone.

Morgan   What?

Esther   Why not?

Freddie   Can't afford one.

Anna   You can share mine.

Morgan *retreats to the side. The others all look at* **Paul**.

Paul   Nobody speak.

Sheila   Paul looks sad . . .

Paul   Nobody!

They go to sit in their sections and using their phones/headphones, they start learning the words. As they do this, they continue to be in the space – going over words, etc.

Esther *paints on the canvas.*

Lines they are singing can cut across the dialogue.

Ken   I'll get the drinks. Freddie, what's your poison?

Freddie   Lemonade.

Ken   And?

Freddie   A glass.

Ken *exits.* **Anna** *sits with* **Freddie**. *They do a section from 'You're All I Need'.*

Freddie   I've upset them.

Anna   No.

Freddie   It's what I do.

Anna   People get upset, we all get upset and then . . . twenty-four hours later, we're okay.

He takes some knitting from a bag, starts to knit. **Anna** *watches.*

Anna   What's that?

Freddie   A balaclava.

Anna   Oh . . .

Freddie   Do you want one?

Anna   No.

Freddie   I can't make anything else. Arguments aren't . . . I don't like them. This helps.

His knitting gets more frenetic and then he stops.

Anna   My son's a worrier. He's wonderful. But quite . . . he feels everything . . . like a wound, you know? They say alpha fathers have beta sons. Have you heard that?

He shakes his head.

Anna   So . . . you love singing?

Freddie   It's the only thing I can do.

Anna   Well you are extremely good at something and that's enough.

Freddie   So are you.

Ken *brings drinks in, hands them out.*

Anna   I'm just very grateful.

Freddie   For?

Anna   Everything. (*Half joking.*) My husband sometimes wishes I was less average but, this is me.

Esther *goes to the canvas, picks up a paintbrush.*

Freddie   Sheila is . . . weird.

Anna   You're making a balaclava.

Freddie   But she's not telling the truth.

Anna   What's the truth?

Freddie   You know what I mean.

Anna   Freddie, you come to choir and watch and listen and your heart can just . . . beat. You can love people here and they don't even know, but they . . . feel something from you. And you feel something back . . .

Anna *'s phone vibrates. She hurriedly answers it.*

Anna   Hello . . . hello sweetheart . . . okay . . . yeah . . . he's busy probably . . . I can read it if you like . . . give me a few minutes . . . go to the toilet and call me back. Love you.

She comes off the phone.

Anna   Have you got a partner?

Freddie *shakes his head.*

Anna   Make sure you wait. For a long time. The longest. And if the singing doesn't work out straight away, I mean it will eventually, how about you get a nice job in Pizza Express? Work your way up to assistant manager. Be part of a clockwork machine serving customers. Fill their stomachs and get them drunk. Make them happy. And at the end of your shift go out dancing with your team and then go home and sleep. And the next morning you get up and do it all over again. It's simple . . . and it's all you do. It starts and it ends, nothing else. I would love that. I'd really love it.

Freddie   People . . . are too much for me.

Anna   Yeah. (*A beat.*) Can I show you something?

Then takes out a ring box, gives it to **Freddie**. *He takes it out.*

Anna   It's an eternity ring.

Freddie   I've never heard of that.

Anna   Represents neverending love. Do you want it?

Freddie   What?

Anna   It's worth thousands. You could sell it. Or save it for your special person.

Freddie   No, thank you.

Anna   Please, have it . . .

Freddie *puts the box down.*

Morgan *goes to the laptop and 'You're All I Need' music starts to play.*

Morgan   Once through together please.

They all sing 'You're All I Need', **Morgan** *conducts with passion but it's really bad.*

Paul   That was a disaster movie where the whole cast perishes.

Joy *heads to the canvas.*

Esther   Sounded like a farm.

Morgan   We'll get there. We will . . .

Joy *regards the canvas. Her face fills with dismay.*

Joy   Bars . . . across his face?

Esther   The idea is that singing lets him out of the prison of society. It . . . releases him.

Joy   You've been listening to a podcast again!

Morgan   Joy . . .

Joy   She's made it literal, obvious! I was trying to create something unique and beautiful.

Esther   By putting dandelions on his head?

Joy   It's figurative! Fucking hell . . .

Morgan *intervenes.*

Morgan   Calm down. The producers are interested in us, in our individual stories and I've told them that you've been best friends since primary school.

Joy   She never talked to me at primary school.

Esther   We were in different schools!

Morgan   The point is you've known each other a long time.

Joy   Everyone stayed away from me back then.

Esther   Because you used to say bizarre things.

Joy   I was imaginative. Mrs Baker said I might become an artist.

Esther   You told everyone you had green skin. Why would you do that?

Morgan   Stop it, both of you! The television people are coming to interview you. Millions are going to be watching and that audience has to believe in you, to even . . . want to be you for a few minutes. They need to hear that you started your periods on the same day and take turns basting the turkey at Christmas and that you delivered Esther's first-born in a Topshop changing room. So please for the sake of a young man's future, start looking like you'd take a bullet for each other!

Joy *and* **Esther** *both smile, reluctantly.*

Paul   They're doing interviews?

Morgan   On the morning of the show.

Sheila   Ken could share one of his poems.

Morgan   They don't do poetry on *The One Show.*

Esther   That Carol Ann Duffy was on the other week!

Sheila   She can't touch Ken, wait till you hear one of his.

Joy   Go on.

Ken   My work's quite . . . personal.

Anna   It's only us.

Paul   Speak, man!

Ken *braces himself.*

Ken   I'm sad, sad, sad I tell ya. I feel so bad it's making me mad. I look in the mirror and all I see is my dad. It's too bad I tell ya, too bad.

Silence.

Sheila   Ask *The One Show,* won't you Morgan, if they can fit him in.

Morgan   I will. Everyone must practise 'You're All I Need' but for now . . . let's try Amy.

Anna *starts moving around, trying to get a signal again.*

Morgan   This is your solo, Anna.

Anna   My son's going to call. He wants me to read him his story.

Morgan   Get Ed to do it.

Anna   Ed's busy.

Morgan   You're needed here!

Anna *'s phone rings.*

Anna   Hi darling, I've got it on my phone . . . yes. *She reads from 'The Tiger Who Came to Tea' by Judith Kerr.*

Anna *moves to the side.*

Anna   Now you read . . .

Fed up, **Morgan** *addresses the others.*

Morgan   Okay, positions for the show!

She takes each person and places them on the small platform at the back. She positions **Ken** *to the far left.*

Morgan   That's it. That's us. There'll be an extra rehearsal on Friday evening.

Ken   Another one?

Morgan   I am not being turned into a meme!

Under pressure, **Morgan** *retreats to her laptop.*

Morgan   They've asked me to finalise the running order. If you head into the bar, I'll call you and we'll go over Amy.

The singers disperse. **Anna** *leaves but remains on her phone.*

Paul *lingers, waits still everyone has left.*

Paul (*shouts*)   'You're All I Fucking Need'!

Morgan   It was one of their suggestions.

Paul   You could have countered with a suggestion of your own.

Morgan   The producers want to showcase Freddie.

Paul   Oh yes, your great young hope.

Morgan   There's a nasty tinge in your voice and there's no need for a nasty tinge.

Paul   You really think he's special.

Morgan   Yes.

Paul *makes a face.*

Morgan   You said you were alright.

Paul   I'm not going to say anything in front of them, am I?

Morgan   Them? Let's not patronise anyone, Paul, they are us and we are them.

Paul   You choosing that song is nostalgic bullshit!

Morgan   If you don't like my choices, you're free to go!

Paul   You asked me to be part of this . . . charade.

Morgan   Leave then! Go on, get lost!

Paul   What's wrong with you?

Morgan   I'm . . . tired.

Paul   Everyone over forty's tired, Morgan.

Morgan   I am tired of looking after everyone, of managing seven different personalities. Each one needs something different. And I can't always . . . . I haven't always got it.

Paul   You love bossing everyone. Controlling, organising, perfecting . . .

Morgan   . . . massaging egos! And some of those egos are big, Paul, quite enormous! I'm sorry about the duet, okay, but a lot of this is . . . it's out of my hands.

Paul   Forget it.

Silence.

Morgan   I'll ask if we can do Primal Scream as the encore.

Paul *shrugs.*

Morgan   It's the least you deserve.

Paul   Nobody deserves anything. You roll the dice and that's that.

Morgan   I'm sorry. It's . . . the pressure . . . Saturday means a lot, we have to pull this off. We have to.

Paul   First concert, first cut. It's the deepest.

Morgan   I sent the information to the producers about everyone. And the photos.

Paul   Did you use my Spotlight picture?

Morgan   I did.

Paul   2005 or 2008?

Morgan   Eight.

Paul   Thank God. (*A beat.*) My agent said when she squinted, I looked like George Clooney.

Morgan   Totally. (*A beat.*) You were so beautiful.

Paul   That was then . . .

He goes to leave.

Morgan   They've asked me to lose Ken.

Paul *stops.*

Paul   What?

Morgan   The producers, they don't want him to sing in the choir.

Paul   Why?

Morgan   They've said he . . . they've said he looks like a serial killer.

Silence.

Paul   Which one?

Morgan   I didn't ask, did I?

Paul   So tell them to fuck off.

Morgan   Obviously.

Paul   Good.

Morgan   I mean . . . I'm going to . . . once I find the right moment.

Paul   What?

Morgan   I've got a lot on, managing all of this, teaching at the college during the day.

Paul   They don't even care what we sound like, do they?

Morgan   Of course they care.

Paul   Fuck this, fucking shit business. I had a lucky escape.

Morgan   You still do your voiceovers.

Paul   I turn up so I can put food on the table. That's all. I give my outsides, not my insides. And this is why, this is the exact reason why.

Silence.

Paul   He's learnt all the words. Every single ooh and ah.

Morgan   I've only just found out. They keep making demands.

Paul   Until there's nothing left of you. Of your thing. Of who you are. I get it. We know it. (*A beat.*) Make sure you tell them.

Morgan   I will.

Paul   We'll still do the gig for Freddie, but without . . . *The One Show* shit. There's no choice here, you know that.

Morgan   Yes.

Paul   Seriously, Morgan. Seriously! You cancel this whole television thing, right?

Morgan   Absolutely.

Paul (*a beat*)   How did the production company know about the gig in the first place?

Morgan   Social media. They find out everything. You know what it's like.

Paul   Yeah.

Paul *heads out.* **Morgan** *is left on her own.*

The choir come back on stage and sing Amy Winehouse's 'Back to Black' over the scene change. **Anna**'s *solo.*

Sheila *picks up the ring box which* **Anna** *has left. She opens it.*

Interval.

Scene Three – Friday

The choir (except **Paul***) are in their performance positions and are singing George Michael's 'Freedom'.* **Freddie** *is doing lead vocals and* **Morgan** *is conducting.*

Sheila *is wearing a prominent pair of mittens.*

Paul *enters and observes. He gets on the stage and joins in. The song comes to an end.*

Morgan   Nice.

Paul *puts his arm around* **Ken** *and points at him.*

Paul   This guy's the real backbone of the tenors.

Ken   Me?

Paul *and* **Ken** *sing the song together.*

Paul   Special, isn't he Morg?

Morgan *checks her laptop.*

Paul   Morgan?

Morgan   Oh . . . yes.

Morgan *regards* **Freddie** *and sings a line.*

Freddie *repeats the line.*

Morgan   Lower at the end.

Morgan   Better. Well done everybody.

The choir relax for a moment. **Morgan** *turns to* **Paul** *as she checks her laptop.*

Morgan   Shouldn't you be eating soufflé and canoodling in a rooftop restaurant?

Paul   I can do that anytime.

Morgan   He hasn't called?

Paul   No.

Morgan   Can you call him?

Paul   No.

Morgan   Sorry he's so shit.

Paul   James will be here for the show.

Morgan   Right.

Paul (*a beat*)   Why did you say 'Right' like that?

Morgan   What?

Paul   You said 'Right'. Not 'Right'. Not 'Right' like you were agreeing. You said 'Right' as if . . . he's not coming . . .

Morgan   Maybe because he's always letting you down . . .

Paul   Not always . . .

Morgan   I don't want you getting lost in someone's fantasy.

Paul   Our relationship is real. James is real. He left a sock in my bedroom.

Morgan   A single sock?

Paul   I'll bring it in.

Morgan *turns to the choir, takes a deep breath. She observes them closely.*

Morgan   Sheila, why the hell are you wearing mittens?

Sheila   My extremities freeze up . . . you see my kidneys get overloaded and the heat leaves my body. Started when I was little and my dad used to forget my name.

Anna   What did he call you?

Sheila   Geoff.

Esther   Okay.

Sheila   After our next-door neighbour. He was round our house a lot . . . I think my dad liked him better than us.

Anna   That's sad.

Sheila   Not really, Geoff died in a car crash.

Morgan   Take them off please.

Ken   What if she catches a cold?

Morgan   Mittens scream community choir.

Anna   We are a community choir.

Morgan   No, we are a choir *for* the community. There's a difference. Off!

Sheila *takes them off. Starts fussing with her hands.* **Morgan** *gets an alert on her phone.*

Morgan   We just sold out!

Esther   Oh God.

Joy   Fuck.

Paul   Shit.

Morgan   This is . . . actually happening.

Joy *and* **Esther** *walk to the picture which is covered with a sheet.*

Joy   The backdrop . . . c'est fini.

They all move towards it. **Joy** *and* **Esther** *stand by the canvas with pride.*

Esther   We decided to compromise.

Joy   Because what's important is we help this young person.

Esther   And because we're best friends.

Joy *removes the sheet. The choir recoil, they are all visibly shocked.*

Freddie   Is that what I look like?

Joy   This isn't you any more. It's its own being.

Anna   Is it human?

Esther/Joy   Yes/No.

Sheila *continues to play with her hands.*

Esther   Maybe we should colour the face in a bit more, make it clearer.

Joy   That'd ruin the contrast between the foreground and the distant horizon.

Esther   They're confused.

Morgan   It's completely fine.

Joy   Thank you!

Morgan *gets another message. Covers her concern.*

Morgan   Joy, can I borrow you to check the alto line with Freddie and Paul?

Joy *moves to the other side where* **Morgan** *conducts as* **Joy** *and the two men do the part from 'Freedom'.*

Meanwhile, **Esther** *surreptitiously takes a paintbrush and makes some strokes on the canvas. She signals to* **Anna***.*

Esther   Now, everybody will understand!

Ken *and* **Sheila** *are at the back.* **Ken** *notes that* **Sheila** *is fiddling with her hands.*

Ken   Itchy hands, Sheila?

Sheila   Slightly.

Ken   I hope it's not hives.

Sheila   What's that?

Ken   Little bumps on your skin that show up when you're not quite right inside.

Sheila   I'll probably get them then.

Ken   I get them seasonally. Seasonal hives. GP gives me an injection, so I can cope.

Sheila   I'm glad you've found a way to cope.

They share a shy smile.

Morgan   Back in your sections, please!

Paul *catches sight of a ring on* **Sheila***'s finger.*

Paul   Those are some rocks, Sheila.

They all look at the ring.

Sheila   Oh, this . . . was my grandmother's.

Ken   Exquisite.

Sheila   She gave it to me on her deathbed. It had been given to her by her grandmother on her deathbed. And she said the same words to me that her grandmother had said to her.

The choir eye her expectantly.

Sheila   She said . . . er . . . she said . . . 'Where you lead, I will follow. Anywhere that you tell me to. If you need, you need me to be with you. I will follow where you lead.'

Silence.

Anna   How . . . beautiful.

Sheila   And then she told me never to take it off. But I forgot she'd said that and I found it the other day . . . next to the Cheerios.

Morgan   That's a lovely story, Sheila.

Esther   Very moving.

Morgan   So, I've had a thought about the start of the show . . .

Freddie   Wait . . .

Morgan   Time to sing, Freddie.

Freddie   That's not her ring!

They all stop.

Freddie   It's Anna's, she showed me the other day.

Anna   I showed you a ring, yes.

Freddie   She must have found it and picked it up.

Sheila *gasps, upset.*

Morgan   If Sheila says it's her ring . . .

Sheila   I said it was my grandmother's.

Esther   That's right, you did.

Sheila   Her name was Pam . . .

Paul   She sounds cute.

Sheila   She was. Dear Pam . . . Pamela . . . Anderson.

Freddie   The words she said on her deathbed are from a song.

Sheila   My Pamela Anderson was poetic.

Freddie   It's not true!

Sheila   I thought people here trusted me.

Morgan   Of course we do.

Sheila   I don't understand what's going on.

Freddie   You're lying.

Ken   The fact is, Freddie, everyone in choir's got different personalities. I'm rather slow off the mark.

Anna   I'm forever making lists.

Joy   I'm too fucking laid back.

Freddie   Admit it!

Sheila   He doesn't believe me.

Morgan   It doesn't matter what anyone thinks.

Sheila *is getting upset.*

Sheila   It does. Because my mum and dad didn't believe me either. Nobody did. I told the truth but none of them listened and that's why they banished me from Hounslow.

Freddie   You steal stuff!

Sheila   I make unwanted things feel wanted.

Silence.

Sheila   Because no matter what people think, they have a right to be in the world.

Morgan   It's okay, Sheila.

Sheila *holds out the ring, gives it to* **Anna***.*

Sheila   I won't do it any more.

Anna *shakes her head.*

Anna   You have it. It's yours.

Freddie   She obviously needs help.

Morgan   Sheila's one of those people who's been through things. We don't need to know what they are. When we are in this room, we do not judge anybody who walks through that door.

Freddie   I'm being honest!

Morgan   You dropped a baby, Freddie!

Freddie   Yeah . . .

Morgan   That was a huge mistake. And you know what, you're going to make more. Bigger ones. Terrible ones that will plague you for years and years. You will hurt people and they will hurt you and sometimes you will want to murder and other times you will want to die and that's just . . . that's the way it is, Freddie. So let's sing. We're here to sing. That's something we can do and at least be better than we are . . . out there. Plus, we're doing it for you. We don't have to do it for you. But we are doing it for you, even though you dropped a baby! Okay?

Freddie *nods awkwardly.*

Morgan   Sheila . . . are you alright to continue?

Sheila *nods.*

Morgan   Let's go through Edge please.

The choir move into their sections. **Morgan** *plays music. Conducts the different sections as they do their parts.*

They carry on. After a few bars, **Morgan** *cuts the music.*

Morgan   What's this song about? Anyone?

Silence.

Freddie   Is it about a white winged dove?

Morgan   No.

Anna   Coming of age?

Morgan *shakes her head.*

Esther   Falling in love for the first time!

Morgan   This masterpiece explores spiritual release.

Ken   Right.

Morgan   Freedom. Death. Sex.

Joy   I knew that already.

Morgan   To make this work, you have to connect with the raw power inside you. Deep, raw power.

Unsure murmurs of agreement.

Morgan *plays the music and they sing 'Edge of Seventeen' once more.*

Halfway through, **Joy** *wanders towards the picture and picks up the paint palette, but when she looks at the painting she makes a wailing animalistic sound while falling to her knees.*

Morgan *cuts the music.*

Morgan   Joy?

Joy *eyes* **Esther.**

Joy   What have you done?

Esther   A few finishing touches. You can hardly see them . . .

But before she can finish, **Joy** *attacks the picture and tears it apart.*

Esther *tries to stop her but cannot. Everyone looks on as* **Esther** *scrambles onto the floor and tries in vain to put the torn-up picture back together. She gives up.*

Esther   I was helping you.

Joy   Morgan asked me, because I like art. Because I used to be . . . because I wanted to do . . . painting. You took over.

Esther   No . . .

Joy   It's what you do. What you've always done. That's why . . . I can't forgive you.

Esther   Forgive me? For what?

Joy   The dog.

Esther   What dog?

Joy   Phoebe, of course. Phoebe dog! (*A beat/to the others.*) Years back, I used to look after my neighbour's dog. Mrs Williams was an old lady and couldn't take Phoebe out for long walks, so I did it.

Anna   That was kind.

Joy   I loved that dog and she loved me. Then one day, Esther got chatting to Mrs Williams. Said the kids wanted a dog and she asked to borrow Phoebe. They walked her every week and started having her overnight. Then Mrs Williams stopped asking me and Phoebe didn't come round any more.

Esther   You could have carried on borrowing her.

Joy   She wouldn't walk to my front door, she used to cry.

Esther   Because you never gave her any treats.

Joy   You gave her so many beefy chews she left a trail of dog sick up the pavement.

Esther   She was old and she liked her food. You starved her!

Joy   But I didn't kill her. Did I, Esther?

Sheila   How did she die?

Joy   Heart attack . . . well, more of an explosion, actually. She was so vast when she went to the vet, they couldn't find her ribs.

Esther   Phoebe wasn't your dog.

Joy   When she was with me, she was mine. One little thing I had, that you didn't.

Esther   I was being nice. I like being nice.

Joy   Well sometimes you have to stop.

Esther   I try hard with you Joy. I try to be considerate.

Joy   Why? Why do you try so hard?

Esther   Because . . . I want you to be okay . . .

Joy   I'm brilliant. I mean fucking look at me!

Esther   I want . . . I want you to like me.

Joy   I do like you.

Esther   You don't show it.

Joy (*a beat*)   I drive us to choir every week, don't I?

Esther   Yeah, you do, Joy.

Joy   There's not a single person around who knows about me. Nobody, except you. You've . . . got my story . . . and I've got yours. So, if I don't like you, who the fucking hell do I like?

Silence.

Ken (*bright*)   I had no idea about any of this. Anyone else?

Morgan   I think we should take a break.

Joy   Nah, let's keep going.

Morgan   Esther?

Esther   Yeah. Okay.

Joy (*to* **Esther**)   Do you want a wipe?

Esther   No . . . thanks.

Joy   Have one! Please . . .

Esther *slowly takes one.*

Anna   What about the backdrop?

Morgan   We'll work something out. Let's get refocussed.

She signals to them all to gather round. They do and she stands before them.

Morgan   In through the nose and out through the mouth.

They breathe collectively.

Morgan   Stretch your arms out, feel the space in the room.

Ken *reaches out and his hand touches* **Sheila**'s.

Ken   Sorry, I didn't mean to . . .

Sheila   I don't mind, Ken.

Ken   Really?

Donna Summer's 'I Feel Love' starts to play. The rest of the choir continue to do their breathing exercises/warm ups while **Ken** *and* **Sheila** *are in a kind of dream sequence.*

They dance sensually together. When they reach a crescendo, the music fades and they both fall back into the scene.

Morgan   Back into the room. Deep breath in and out. And relax. (*A beat.*) Well done everybody.

Anna   What's your thought about the start of the show?

Morgan   I've decided we're opening with something completely different. No parts, we'll sing in unison.

Esther   But we need to learn the words.

Morgan   You know them.

She goes to her laptop and plays the first few bars of the backing track to Whitney Houston's 'I Wanna Dance With Somebody'.

They are all delighted and dance around joyfully while singing along. After the first chorus **Morgan** *turns off the music.*

Morgan   Happy?

All   Yes!

Paul   You said never!

Anna   What made you change your mind?

Morgan   Er . . . the television company asked for it.

Paul *freezes.*

Joy   They know their shit.

Paul   I thought we weren't doing *The One Show.*

Freddie   Really?

Anna   Why wouldn't we?

Paul   Something Morgan said . . .

Morgan   Maybe you misunderstood.

Esther   You always told us Whitney was too obvious.

Morgan   Sometimes obvious is . . . the . . .

Ken   The obvious choice.

Sheila   You nailed that one, Ken.

Paul   But you hate Whitney.

Morgan   I don't hate anybody.

Paul   Sure you're still of sound mind, Morgan?

Morgan   The producers wanted something fun and poppy and I have to admit this is the perfect opening.

Paul   And the whole choir is singing it? All of us?

Morgan   Yeah. We're a team.

Joy   Like Aston Villa.

Ken   I should mention . . . I've been assigned a new role.

They all look at him, agog.

Paul   Which is?

Ken   Creative Producer.

Morgan   We said Executive Creative Producer.

Ken   We did!

Sheila   Wow!

Anna   Congratulations.

Paul   And what does the Executive Creative Producer do?

Ken   I'm making a short documentary film of the backstage proceedings on the day of the show. The story behind the story. Imagine . . . er . . . Tony Benn's Diaries on film.

They regard him, bemused.

Freddie   Who's Tony Benn?

Joy   He sang that duet with Amy Winehouse.

Morgan   That was somebody else.

Esther   Have you ever made a film before?

Ken   No, but there's a 4K video zoom camera integrated into my mobile phone that I'm going to use. I'm calling the film *The Making of A Star* in honour of our Freddie.

Freddie   That's . . . overwhelming.

Paul   Who's it for, this documentary?

Morgan   Us.

Anna   What a brilliant idea.

Paul   You're still singing though?

Ken   We discussed that. Danger is the two roles might split my focus.

Sheila   But we need you.

Morgan (*to* **Paul**)   With you and Freddie, the tenors are probably our strongest section. So . . . I think it'll be fine.

Esther   Course it will.

Morgan   It's important to have this record. For archive purposes. And we know we can trust Ken to make it memorable.

Ken   I'll do my best.

Paul   Don't you want to sing?

Ken   I'm not bothered.

Morgan   He's not bothered.

Paul   I need to talk to you, Morgan.

Morgan   We have got quite a lot to get through.

Paul   It's not a request!

Morgan   Okay. (*A beat.*) Why don't you go over your words in the bar, I'll message you once we're done. Anna, can Freddie use your phone for 'Nothing Compares to You'?

Anna   Absolutely. Here.

She hands **Freddie** *her phone.*

The choir head out, singing Whitney Houston.

Ken *remains and overtly starts videoing* **Morgan** *and* **Paul** *on his phone.*

Morgan   You can leave the filming until tomorrow, Ken.

He heads out. **Morgan** *types on her laptop.*

Morgan   Say what you have to say. And then let's move on.

Paul   Move on?

Morgan   Yes.

Paul   Even my close friend in whom I trusted, who ate my bread, has lifted his heel against me. Psalm 41, verse 9.

Morgan   I don't follow . . .

Paul   Judas Iscariot! He's the reason they put 11 icing balls on a simnel cake. 11 not 12. Because he betrayed the Messiah.

Morgan   Ken is not the Messiah.

Paul   You know he chucked the pieces of silver away and hanged himself. And don't think I'm coming to cut you down.

Morgan   I won't be hanging myself.

Paul   What a shame.

Morgan   Do not think for one second that this hasn't been tough for me.

Paul   Funny how you make it look effortless.

Morgan   I have to think of everyone.

Paul   Ken is everyone.

Morgan   I sent the producers a long message explaining why he's important and what the choir is about, they didn't even open the email. Then I spoke to some researcher who said they had another choir ready to go if we dropped out.

Paul   Fuck it, call their bluff.

Morgan   I can't risk them pulling us Paul. I've weighed it up and the best thing to do is carry on.

Paul   It's wrong!

Morgan   You think I didn't fight for him?

Paul *shrugs.*

Morgan   Why do this lot come to this shitty room? Because . . . they don't have anywhere else and this is the best they can do. This group keeps going because I show up week after week. I lug the equipment back and forth, I do the arrangements that people forget and end up singing the tune to, I make sure there are no images of genitalia on the WhatsApp and I take the calls after midnight when there's a queue for The Samaritans. These are my choir members, and they matter to me. (*A* *beat.*) It would be wrong to pass up this opportunity, after all the work they've done. You've seen them, fizzing with excitement! Plus, Ken doesn't mind.

Paul   You do what you like, I'm no part of this.

Morgan   How come you're suddenly rooting for the underdog? All those times you've complained . . . Ken's boring, Joy's strange, Sheila needs to be sectioned . . .

Paul   That's just nonsense . . . chatter.

Morgan   You've been bitching about them since the beginning. You're so embarrassed you won't even let them speak to James. Why do you even come?

Paul   You asked me.

Morgan   I suppose it can't hurt to be told how fabulous you are. On repeat.

Paul   I might be an arrogant bastard but I would never let them down. Especially not Ken.

Morgan   So you want me to take this away from him? This experience, where he can do something, be part of something. If it doesn't happen, they are all going to be gutted. You know they are.

Paul *takes this in.*

Morgan   One performance to launch us. Once we've had the coverage, a few bookings will start coming in, I'm not imagining a huge triumph, simply a morsel, a taste of better things. And after that, Ken'll be with us again, where he belongs.

Paul   You're not thinking straight.

Morgan   Our best thinking turned us into a wedding band, Paul. I'm learning how to do this, how to be strategic. We thought if we were brilliant and talented we'd make it. But we didn't get chosen. This time we have been. Because I wasn't waiting for someone to find us. I answered an ad and I sold what we do and that's why this is our moment.

Paul   We didn't make it because we weren't good enough.

Morgan   We were. We fucking were.

Paul   We didn't have it. We did not have it.

Morgan   I'm sick of failing, Paul. Of keeping going and making do and being grateful for what I've got. I want it to be my turn to be special.

Paul   Stop . . .

Morgan   Don't you want James to watch you on the television? First time he'll see you singing live, isn't it? Once he hears you, he'll fall head over heels because that is what your voice does to people.

Paul   You think I'm that shallow?

Morgan   Paul, you're not shallow, you're as desperate as the rest of us. (*A beat.*) Don't pretend it doesn't hurt when people not as talented as you start to fly.

Paul   I don't care any more.

Morgan   This way everyone will see us. Hear us.

Paul   It's *The One Show.*

Morgan   Don't you want a glimmer of possibility? Something that isn't this day and tomorrow and every other fucking day that you know is coming. To believe that there's still magic out there for us, some unknown magic . . .

Paul   Not like this.

Morgan   Doesn't matter how it comes. (*A beat.*) I miss it. Don't you miss it? And I'm so lonely. Aren't you so lonely?

Paul (*a beat*)   Yeah.

Silence.

Paul   And what about Freddie?

Morgan   Exactly . . . Freddie is exactly the point . . . we're going to make sure he gets the chances we never had.

Paul   No. This is you, right at the bottom of the barrel.

Morgan *shakes her head.*

Morgan   We are offering something . . . new.

Paul   A new take to help us to understand old things?

Morgan   Yes.

Paul   And what if it's all been said before?

Morgan   It hasn't. Not by us.

Silence.

Paul   You should go back on the dating apps.

Morgan   I'm not interested in . . . I'm not like you.

Paul   At least I'm willing to take a risk.

Morgan   By letting a married man turn you into a lost boy, waiting to be picked for the football team.

Paul   Stop . . .

Morgan   Yeah, let's stop this . . . stupid talking . . . it's basic shit isn't it . . . this . . . we all just want love, don't we . . . fucking love.

Paul   I love you.

Morgan (*a beat*)   It's not the kind that matters.

Silence.

Paul   Do the right thing by Ken, please?

Morgan   I am doing the right thing. (*A beat.*) We could be someone, Paul.

Paul   We are someone.

Paul *starts to head to the door.*

Morgan   This might be my choir but you're everything to them. You'll break their hearts if you walk. (*A beat.*) I'm calling them back in.

She sends a text.

Morgan   So that's it? You're going?

Paul *stops.*

Paul (*a beat*)   Where have I got to go?

He takes off his jacket, hangs it up on a hook on the door. The others return with drinks.

Esther   We thought you could do with these.

She hands them a couple of ostentatious cocktails.

Paul   Thanks.

Anna   Cocktails make everything okay.

Joy   The ones with cream in make my bottom explode.

Esther   There's no cream in these.

Joy   I'm just saying.

Morgan *plays 'Nothing Compares to You'.*

Checking **Anna**'s *phone,* **Freddie** *sings the first lines but then stumbles.*

Morgan *stops the music.*

Morgan   We're on tomorrow. You ought to be ready.

Freddie   I am . . . I get a bit . . . you know, when it's a solo . . .

Morgan   Put that nervous energy into the song. Everyone into position.

They start to move when suddenly **Anna**'s *phone beeps continuously.* **Freddie** *looks down at it, he's about to give it to her but stops as he reads.*

Freddie   The pasta was cold and you forgot to take the bathroom bin out, you are the worst mother on the fucking planet and a disgusting bitch . . .

Silence.

Anna   Can I have my phone back please?

All eyes are on her.

Esther   Who sent you that?

Anna   My phone!

He hands it to her. It continues to beep.

Morgan   Anna . . .

Embarrassed, **Anna** *gathers her stuff and hurries out.* **Esther** *starts to go after her.*

Morgan   Leave her . . .

Esther *pauses.*

Morgan   I'll call her later.

Joy   I fancy some fresh air.

Sheila   And me.

They all head out until it's just **Morgan** *and* **Ken**.

Ken   Poor Anna.

Morgan   Yes.

Ken   Do you know much about her?

Morgan *shakes her head.*

Ken   What can we do?

Morgan   Probably nothing.

Ken   Doesn't seem right.

Morgan   It's not. I guess . . . we should try and concentrate on what we're in control of. Big day tomorrow.

Ken   The biggest.

Morgan *nods.*

Ken   Bet you're glad you're not singing those songs about being dead any more.

Morgan   They weren't so bad.

Ken   Now, you're doing Whitney. You've finally arrived!

Morgan   Yes.

Ken   I am pleased. About being Executive Creative Producer.

Morgan   You should be.

Ken (*a beat*)   But I am hurt.

Morgan *takes this in.* **Ken** *smiles gently before he turns and leaves.* **Morgan** *is left alone.*

The choir sing 'Hotel California' as the lights go down.

Scene Four – The day of the concert

Darkness. The One Show *music. A blaze of lights.*

Various researchers and runners/assistants swarm into the space. They are setting up lights, cameras and a catering table.

Spotlight on **Esther**. *A researcher holds out a microphone in front of her.*

Esther   I've been coming since the beginning . . . I work in a supermarket . . . no, I've never had cancer . . . er, none of my children have had it either . . . is that alright? My son gets a terrible rash if he eats pineapple. Does that help? . . . Oh, the choir's changed my life . . . I don't really know how . . .

She retreats and **Joy** *takes her place.*

Joy   Joy.

She looks around awkwardly. She's overwhelmed and can't speak.

Joy   I need the toilet.

She retreats and **Paul** *takes her place, he moves around trying to give the camera his best side.*

Paul   They describe me as the lead singer but that's a label I refute. I'm much more content as a tiny cog serving the big machine . . . Well of course, I do perform most of the solos . . .

Sheila *comes over, takes his position.*

Sheila   I come to choir every week. No . . . my mother died in an armed robbery, before I was born . . . I did have a husband but then, he went missing . . .

Sheila *and the television crew leave the stage. Lights go up.*

Morgan *anxiously flits around tidying, moving chairs, getting the space ready.*

Paul *and* **Freddie** *are going over dropbox on headphones.*

Ken *is filming randomly.*

Joy *and* **Esther** *are painting another canvas.*

Esther   You don't think it's too . . . sentimental?

Joy   I don't fucking care if it is.

Esther   Should we write his name?

Joy   Won't fit.

Esther   I'll draw a boxing glove.

Joy   Nice.

Esther   Thanks.

Joy   For what?

Esther   I dunno. (*Draws.*)

Joy   It's funny, you do so much for everybody but you're the one who needs the most love.

Esther (*moved*)   Joy . . .

Joy   En silence, mon amie!

They continue painting.

Morgan   Ready everyone?

They all take off their tops to reveal matching T-shirts, emblazoned with 'The Morgan Jackson People's Choir.' **Morgan** *does her best to admire them for a second.*

Morgan   We're lucky the printing company could fit us in last minute. Turn around.

They turn around to reveal their names on the back of the T-shirts. **Ken***'s top says STAG.*

Morgan *joins* **Paul** *and* **Freddie** *who starts 'Nothing Compares'. He quickly falters.*

Morgan   You should know the lyrics by now!

Freddie   I know them!

Morgan   So what's wrong?

Freddie   The words won't come. They won't . . .

Agitated, he finds his knitting. Starts to knit. He turns away from the audience and sings.

Paul   What are you doing?

Freddie   It's a balaclava.

He sings the first verse of the song, all the while knitting. **Morgan** *takes the knitting from him and throws it on the floor.* **Freddie** *stops singing.*

Morgan   You can't knit in front of the audience.

Freddie   Then I can't sing.

Morgan   But you want to be a singer.

Freddie   I know, I'm a disappointment.

Morgan   You were completely fine in your lessons.

Freddie   It was just you and me.

Morgan   People are coming to watch you. We're raising thousands so you can become a singer.

Freddie   That's what I want, more than anything in the universe. But I can only do it as long as I'm allowed to . . .

He picks up the knitting.

Morgan   If you want it more than anything, you have to be prepared to do anything.

Freddie   I'm trying but . . .

He shakes his head.

Morgan   This is not supposed to be happening! We are sold out! For fuck's sake, Freddie, you fucking fuck!

She goes to shake him, **Paul** *gets in the middle and pulls her off.*

Paul   Get off, Morgan!

Esther *puts her arm around* **Morgan***, pulls her away.*

Paul   Give me a minute with him.

Morgan (*to* **Freddie**)   I'm sorry, I shouldn't have said that . . . I didn't mean it.

Freddie   Don't worry. You've done all this for me, and I'm just . . .

Paul *positions himself opposite* **Freddie***.*

Paul   You lot go . . . go!

He shoos the others away. They retreat to the side, leaving **Paul** *and* **Freddie** *together.*

Freddie   I've let everyone down.

Paul   Shut up.

He indicates they should sit down. They do.

Paul   You know how people say stuff about you, like you're a fantastic singer.

Freddie   Yeah.

Paul   People used to say the same about me. Only I wasn't fantastic. I was one of the best. Much much better than you.

Freddie   And?

Paul   And, whatever happens, if you win some crappy talent show or even a Grammy, you will never touch me.

Freddie   Why are you saying that?

Paul   Because it's true. (*A beat.*) Don't like it, do you? (*He laughs.*) So, there is something more to the hollow prince.

Freddie   Leave me alone.

Paul   What are you going to do? Cancel me?

Freddie   What?

Paul   Well you can't. I'm queer and my sister works in Asda. I'm uncancellable.

Freddie   I don't have a problem with you. I don't have a problem with anybody.

Paul   You should have a problem with a bastard like me. You should have a problem with everything and everybody. You should be raging.

Freddie   Against what?

Paul   The whole thing.

Freddie   How is this going to stop me knitting?

Paul   I don't care about that. Nobody cares about that. Your problem is . . . you think you're it.

Freddie   Me?

Paul   You can't stop thinking about how you sound. Is anybody even listening? Do they know I dropped a baby? And while your brain is whirring around, you are not doing your job which is to share every single second with them. (*Points at audience.*) You've abandoned them when you should be feeling their every breath. An audience doesn't care about the past, they want to forget. They come so they can be with you, in this moment, so every single thing that isn't now has to be dead to you. Or do you want to be stuck in an ensuite singing into your mum's deodorant in front of an Ikea mirror?

Freddie *shakes his head.*

Paul   Then, let them have you. And let them make you . . . magnificent.

Freddie   What about the knitting?

Paul   Unless you know any terrorists, start on a jumper. And . . .

He looks **Freddie** *up and down.*

Paul   . . . get some better clothes.

Freddie   Paul . . .

Paul   What?

Freddie   You should sing it. You'd tear it apart.

Paul   Probably.

Freddie   Please, I want you to.

Silence.

Paul   No. (*A beat.*) I reckon it's time for a new take.

Paul *goes to the laptop, plays the music for 'Nothing Compares'.*

Freddie *starts to sing.* **Morgan** *and the others gather. He knits but slowly drops the needles. He sounds amazing and is emotional and heartfelt. Comes to an end.*

Morgan   You are sensational, Freddie. And this . . . today . . . is going to launch you, so high.

Esther   We could turn the balaclava into a story . . .

Morgan   Yes, we could . . .

Ken   What if he makes it during the show and puts it on during the encore!

Joy   No, Ken.

Morgan   We'll work something out. Thank you, Paul. (*Checks watch.*) Some housekeeping for you . . .

Esther   Wait, Sheila's not here.

Freddie   Or Anna.

Morgan   I'll fill them in. The production crew will be back shortly. Music will be playing from my laptop but via their speakers. We'll let the audience in about ten minutes before we start, they'll go into the bar until we're ready. I will give you a signal. (*She shows them.*) Which means it's time to get into position.

Esther   Gonna be quite a thing, this.

Morgan   More than a thing.

Suddenly **Sheila** *rides in on a bike. She circles around the others.*

Ken   Where did you get that from?

Sheila   My neighbour gave it to me.

Sheila *gets off but is attached to the bike with the lock. She tries to take it off but can't. Others try helping her.*

Sheila   Oh dear, I can't get it away from me.

Joy   Use the key to unlock it.

Sheila   I lost the key, I was in such a rush, it fell down a drain.

Esther   Then it has to be cut off.

Paul   How?

Freddie   That needs a special tool.

Paul   There isn't time.

Sheila   What do I do?

Morgan   Hold on. This is . . . this is my bike . . .

Sheila   Er . . . I don't think so . . .

Morgan   You stole my bike!

Sheila   Oh God, oh my God, my neighbour . . . she's . . . she's a twisted human being.

Morgan   Sheila! I don't care what's wrong with you, you shouldn't have . . . you promised not to do this any more.

Sheila   I am trying.

Ken   She is trying.

Freddie   She's traumatised.

Joy   We're all traumatised.

Morgan   No we aren't! Some of us are functional human beings. I don't steal. I don't tell lies! I don't pretend and make up shit!

Slowly, she falters, turns away from the others.

Sheila   I didn't intend to cause any harm.

Ken   Sheila's just doing her best with what she's got.

Sheila   Once it's off, you can have it back.

It's as if **Morgan** *'s in a daze.*

Sheila   If you want me to go to the police station, I will. They know my name already . . .

Morgan   Never mind. It's okay, Sheila. Just . . . let's leave it.

Joy   Only thing is . . . she's going to have to sing with . . .

She indicates the bike.

Morgan   We'll cover it up.

Ken   I'll zoom in, so it won't feature in *The Making Of A Star.*

Esther   Very thoughtful, Ken.

Freddie   Has anyone heard from Anna?

The choir shake their heads.

Morgan   I sent a couple of messages. But nothing.

Freddie   We could go round her house, check on her.

Morgan   Not appropriate. Plus we won't make it back in time.

Paul   It is getting late.

Morgan   I'll do her part.

Sheila   But I always stand next to Anna.

Paul   You've got the bike for company.

Freddie   What about 'You're All I Need'?

Morgan   I can sing it.

Joy   You?

Morgan   Yeah.

Freddie   Doesn't feel right without her.

Morgan   You have to make it feel right.

Freddie   How?

Morgan   Sing as usual. And trust me . . .

Freddie (*interrupts*)   If she's not here, I can't do it.

Morgan   Of course you can.

Freddie   I mean . . . I won't.

Morgan   Don't be ridiculous.

Freddie *moves away from her.*

Joy   You have to admit, it'll feel different.

Esther   For all of us.

Ken   It will.

Morgan   If somebody's not here, we don't fall apart like a game of Mousetrap. This choir is bigger than that.

Paul   What if we're not?

Morgan   We are, Paul. Everyone here knows we are . . .

Esther   Maybe . . . maybe we don't actually have to do the show. I mean we have raised the money.

Morgan   People are expecting a concert, they haven't given us their money for nothing.

Joy   It's not for nothing, it's to help this . . . young man.

Morgan   We are putting on this concert!

Sheila   To be honest, I don't mind not doing it.

Morgan (*a beat*)   What?

Sheila   I don't mind if the show doesn't happen.

Morgan   But this moment we've arrived at, is the whole . . . point.

Esther   That's one way of looking at it.

Morgan   Are you saying you don't want to do the gig?

Sheila *nods tentatively.*

Morgan   After all the work I've done. We've done.

Sheila   Yes.

Silence as **Morgan** *takes this in.*

Morgan   And . . . is there anybody else who . . . doesn't want to perform?

Slowly they all put their hands up. Stupefied, **Morgan** *sits down.*

Morgan   Because of Anna?

Esther   Not only that.

Morgan   Then why?

Sheila   I just like coming.

Ken   Same.

Joy *nods.*

Morgan   Esther, your family are going to be in the audience. The kids . . .

Esther   They'll never sit still.

Morgan   But this is a chance, your chance . . . to be more.

Joy   More what?

Morgan   Just . . . more . . . (*A beat.*) Don't you all want that?

Ken   I think . . . I'm alright as I am.

Silence.

Freddie   Do you know where she lives?

Morgan *nods.*

Paul   Shall we go? Morgan?

Morgan   James is coming to watch you.

Paul   I told him not to.

Morgan   Why?

Paul   I got tired of waiting to be chosen.

They all look to **Morgan**.

Esther   It's Anna. Our Anna.

Morgan   I don't believe this.

Morgan *gets up, they don't know what she's going to do.*

Morgan   Let's go . . .

As they start to hurry out, **Anna** *appears.*

Anna   I just bumped into Alex Jones.

Joy   You're late.

Anna   Sorry.

She takes her coat off, puts bag down.

Freddie   We thought you weren't coming.

Anna   I wouldn't not come. (*A beat.*) I hope this dress isn't too much. I'm nervous, is anyone else feeling nervous?

Morgan   Anna, we can't pretend we don't know . . .

Anna   I'm not asking anyone to pretend.

Morgan   I have to check that you're okay.

Silence.

Anna   The truth is . . . I'm not who you think I am. I know I look okay and I sound okay. I do lots of okay things in the world. And I definitely seem more okay than all of you. But I'm probably the least okay person here. (*A beat.*) Being here . . . is basically the one thing that makes me happy so when I'm here I don't want to talk about texts or anything else. And I'm not so not okay that I'm going to leave anybody. I like my home, I like it when people admire the bi-folds and the summerhouse. It makes me feel like . . . it makes me feel like someone. I don't want to live in a flat. Have my kids for half a week. (*A beat.*) I know what I'm doing and who I am. I really do. And what I'd like, what I need from you is not to ask me. Can you please not ask me . . .?

Morgan   Are you sure?

Anna   I want to sing. Let's get ready to sing.

Morgan (*a beat*)   Everyone . . . are we happy to continue?

They all nod.

Esther *signals to* **Joy**.

Esther   Joy.

Esther *and* **Joy** *go to the canvas. They turn it around. It says ME WE and has the image of a boxing glove under it.*

Sheila (*like a cat*)   Mewe.

Ken   I'm a cat person.

Esther   It says Me We.

Joy   Muhammed Ali said it. It's . . .

Morgan   The shortest poem in the English language.

Freddie   I like it.

Morgan   It's perfect. Thank you, both of you.

Morgan *glances to the door.*

Morgan   The audience are arriving . . .

They start to go. **Paul** *hangs back. The others look him.*

Ken   Paul?

Paul   I'm frightened.

Esther   But you've done this loads of times.

Paul   Not for years.

Freddie   You'll be okay.

Anna   Come on, there's nothing to be frightened of.

The choir take each other's hands, like a chain. And they lead **Paul** *together.*

A couple of crew return to organise the equipment.

The choir get into their positions on stage.

Morgan   Let's show them what we've got.

A researcher puts headphones on **Morgan**.

Stage management turn on lights.

Ken *is at the side filming.*

Morgan *gets ready to conduct.*

Sound of The One Show *music. The* **Director** *(unseen) speaks via headphones to the* **Presenter** *who also remains unseen. Sound of the* **Director**'*s voice should have a different quality, as if they are in a different space.*

Director *(voiceover)*   Okay, Studio, let's do this thing.

Morgan *checks her headphones, she can hear the director. She looks round, smiles uneasily.*

Morgan   Er . . . excuse me . . . (*To* **Researcher**.) I can hear him talking to the studio, is that right?

Researcher *urgently indicates that she should keep going.*

Director (*V/O*)   And welcome the choir . . .

Presenter (*V/O*)   Please welcome the Jackson Morgan Community Choir.

Applause. **Morgan** *is concerned at the error. Tries to get the researcher's attention.*

Director (*V/O*)   These are the ones raising the money . . .

Presenter   This choir is singing to raise money for a young man so he can go to college and study music.

Applause.

Presenter   And here's an interview with that very special young man, Frankie!

Unhappy **Morgan** *looks around, she's not sure what to do.*

They play the recorded interview.

Freddie   The best thing about the choir is . . . er . . . it lets people just . . . be. And the people here . . . they make you feel like . . . they're bothered about you. It's made me realise there are still good people . . .

Morgan *goes to her laptop and 'I Wanna Dance With Somebody' starts.*

Ken *starts filming from the front.*

Director (*V/O*)   I thought we told them to cut this guy . . .

Muffled response.

Director (*V/O*)   He's making me feel uneasy. Is anyone else feeling uneasy?

Ken *is getting in the way of the audience's sightline.*

Director (*V/O*)   What the hell is he doing?

Disturbed, **Morgan** *looks at her choir – no* **Ken**, **Sheila** *attached to a bike. The Me We sign falls down.*

Giggles from the audience.

Director (*V/O*)   Can we get rid of Hannibal Lecter please?

Morgan *pulls out her headphones. Hurls them to the floor.*

Morgan (*shouts*)   Stop!

The choir stop singing. She turns off the music. Bemused silence.

Morgan (*points to* **Ken**)   Ken is one of our tenors. (*Finds* **Freddie**.) And this is Freddie. His name is Freddie.

Unsettled murmurs.

Morgan   And we are The Morgan Jackson People's Choir. We meet every week and we are here because we . . . because we love singing and because . . . we don't sound right without each other.

Morgan *hurriedly takes the iPhone from* **Ken** *and puts him on the stage.*

She goes to the laptop.

Morgan   And this . . . this is who we are.

The Killers 'All These Things That I've Done' starts to play.

She grabs the paint pots that **Joy** *and* **Esther** *were using and chucks paint everywhere. The choir join in and throw paint/use the paintbrushes to paint each other. It's utter joyful chaos as if toddlers had been set free.*

Sheila *puts on a balaclava and dances around the stage.*

Freddie *hurls balaclavas out into the audience.*

All the while, the choir sing the song impeccably.

The song comes to an end. It's a scene of mayhem, they are all covered with paint.

Stage management come on and quickly wheel off the lights and cameras.

Joy *takes out her wipes, holds them up triumphantly.*

Each choir member takes one and they wipe each other clean. Lights dim.

Scene Five – Aftermath

The choir clean up the room.

Joy   That was the greatest day of my life.

Esther   Yeah.

Ken and **Freddie** are stacking chairs. **Sheila** remains chained to the bike.

Ken   I still feel giddy.

Freddie   Me too.

Ken   Would you like to come to the cinema with me, Sheila?

Sheila thinks on this.

Sheila   No thank you.

Ken   Right.

Sheila   We can do sexual intercourse, though.

Freddie   There's only one thing I feel bad about . . .

Anna   What?

Freddie   Paul didn't get his encore.

Paul   Oh fuck that.

Morgan is at her laptop.

Morgan   Who said he didn't?

Music for Primal Scream's 'Movin' on Up' starts to play.

Paul sings a rapturous version. The choir join in. Convivial joy at the end. Happiness and connection. They are as one.

THE END